twenty-six years. He later became the president of Union College in Schenectady, New York, and was instrumental in formulating in 1801 the Plan of Union, which attempted to unite Presbyterian and Congregational missionary efforts on the western frontier.

No doubt Edwards lacked the brilliance of his father. His interpretation of the theology which his father had developed failed to meet the challenges posed by contemporary society and floundered finally in legalism. Nevertheless, the younger Edwards is an important figure in his own right, and the study of his life and thought offers a unique opportunity to view the theological and ecclesiastical problems of early America.

Robert L. Ferm is Professor of Religion at Middlebury College, Middlebury, Vermont. He received his Ph.D. from Yale University and has published *Readings in the History of Christian Thought* and *Issues in American Protestantism: A Documentary History from the Puritans to the Present.*

Jonathan Edwards
the Younger:1745-1801

A COLONIAL PASTOR————————

Jonathan Edwards the Younger:1745-1801

BY

Robert L. Ferm

WILLIAM B. EERDMANS PUBLISHING COMPANY

Copyright © 1976 by Wm. B. Eerdmans Publishing Company
255 Jefferson Ave. SE, Grand Rapids, Mich. 49502

Printed in the United States of America

Library of Congress Cataloging in Publication Data

Ferm, Robert L
    Jonathan Edwards the Younger, 1745–1801.

    Bibliography: p. 184.
    Includes index.
    1. Edwards, Jonathan, 1745–1801. I. Title.
BX7260.E3F4   230'.8'0924 [B]   76-12408
ISBN 0-8028-3485-X

To
Alison and Eric

Acknowledgments

To acknowledge this simply the interest, criticism, and encouragement which many, known and unknown, have given to this study is only a modest token of my gratitude. Librarians and benefactors of libraries cited in this volume have been generous with their time and gifts. My appreciation also is given to the Haynes Foundation for research support and to the administrators of the Middlebury College Faculty Research Fund.

Had not Professor Sydney Ahlstrom's contagious excitement, energy, and perceptive criticism been generously given, this book probably would not be; I hope it will serve in some way as a compliment to him and to Mr. Edwards, my most severe critics.

And to an educator and historian, E. Wilson Lyon, President Emeritus of Pomona College, I express my gratitude for many acts of benevolence.

R.L.F.

August, 1975
Middlebury, Vermont

Contents

Introduction

Reflect, my hearers, on the great things God hath done for the United America, in making us a nation, and bestowing upon us privileges superior to those of any nation on earth. Judging from past events, it may be the design of his providence to elevate us above all nations—to exhibit to the world an instance of a government founded in freedom of election, a government which inseparably unites the interests of the constituted authorities and of their constituents—affords equal protection to the individual states, and secures to every citizen the just fruits of his own talents, industry and virtues.[1]

With these words, James Dana summed up the spirit of the new American nation in the early nineteenth century.

At first hesitantly, then eagerly, the colonists sought to break their ties with England and establish a government of their own. They were disgruntled by what seemed to be unjust and odious restrictions on their sense of accomplishment; fed by enlightenment thought and the desire for self-determination, their new spirit of independence and freedom brought the new nation into existence.

The American church did not escape the effect of the currents of the age. The deism of Ethan Allen and Tom Paine influenced many; seeds of Unitarianism were ripening; Arminianism was widespread, especially in the regions where contact with the Old World was frequent. The American Reformed tradition faced the issues and felt the mood of the day; its concerns were shaped considerably by the humanized frame of mind which emerged in the New World. Calvinists wrestled with several ideas that challenged their order:

---

1. James Dana, *Two Discourses* (New Haven: 1801), 49.

the principle of liberty, the right of men to happiness and self-government, the spirit of hard-won responsibility for their own destiny which nourished the men of the new nation.

Jonathan Edwards the Younger lived in the midst of this age. When he assumed his first pastorate in 1768 colonial rebellion against England was taking shape. By the time of his death in 1801, independence was achieved and the new government formed; the nation had become preoccupied with the West.

Edwards sought to defend Calvinism against new patterns of thought, both indigenous and imported from England and France. Loyalty to the premises of Reformed theology and fear of liberalizing inroads shaped his theological labors. His was a time when the church had to justify its message in the face of searching criticisms of its Calvinistic core.

The senior Jonathan Edwards stands as a giant of American history. Furthermore, he gave rise to distinguished progeny. His grandson, Timothy Dwight, experienced almost equivalent renown for a time. Jonathan Edwards the Younger, his son, has tended to be lost in the long and heavy shadow of his illustrious father, seeming to exist only as a source of confusion to librarians and bibliographers.

Edwards' early years were spent in Northampton and Stockbridge, Massachusetts. The family moved to Princetown, New Jersey, in 1758 when Edwards, Sr. was called to become president of the College of New Jersey, a Presbyterian school, later to become Princeton. Edwards the Younger was graduated from that college in 1765, and after serving there as tutor he became pastor of the White Haven Congregational Church in New Haven where he remained for twenty-six years. He was dismissed from that pastorate in 1795 and for a time thereafter served a small mission church in Colebrook, Connecticut. His last days were spent as President of Union College in Schenectady, New York, where the Dutch Reformed tradition was joined closely with Presbyterian and Congregational activity. During his lifetime he was engaged in the theological controversies current in New England. His interest in the Presbyterian Church was sustained by many contacts preserved from his college days, and in his later years much of his work was directed toward the formation of the "Plan of Union" of 1801 which attempted to unite the missionary work of the Presbyterian and Congregational Churches in the frontier areas of the "western reserve."

Especially because of his association with both Presbyterian and Congregational traditions, traditions which he viewed with equal loyalty, Edwards the Younger offers a unique perspective on the development of the American Reformed tradition during the latter half of the eighteenth century. To understand his context and his contribution, attention must be given to the complex party structure of the New England churches during the post-Edwardsean period.

Our task in the succeeding pages is to uncover the details of his life, to study the early history of the two largest branches of the American Reformed tradition—the Presbyterian and Congregational Churches—and his role in their relations, and to define the early issues of American Reformed theology and his contribution to its development and character. The thought and experience of Jonathan Edwards the Younger casts much light on the vexing theological and ecclesiastical problems of his day.

CHAPTER ONE

The Early Years

Jonathan Edwards the Younger was born on May 26, 1745, in Northampton, Massachusetts, during a time of difficulty for the Edwards family. His father had become pastor of the Northampton Congregational Church in 1729, after serving two years as the assistant to his own grandfather, Solomon Stoddard. In the years following, the senior Edwards won a place of esteem and respect in the churches of New England. When he became pastor it was assumed that he would continue the more liberal policies concerning church membership which had been inaugurated by the beloved Stoddard.

For the first seventeen years of his ministry he did continue those policies, but, although he gave little indication during those years, he was becoming uneasy about practices which he believed had contributed to the breakdown of the Puritan experiment. Thus in 1744, he inaugurated the policy that a person was required to give public testimony of regeneration before he might be admitted to communion. The affectionate relationship between pastor and congregation rapidly disappeared. Once the good feeling between the parties had been lost, other instances of dissension became apparent. During the later years of Edwards' ministry the dissension brought forth new issues of debate; Edwards' position became uncomfortable, then untenable. When a council of ministers was called to deal with the situation, Edwards knew it would be impossible to repair the damage.

In the midst of this strained situation Sarah Pierpont Edwards gave birth to the family's ninth child, the second boy, who was given his father's name.[1] Five years later, in 1750, his father preached a farewell sermon to the Northampton Congregation. A council of ministers had recommended the dissolution of the pastoral relationship, though the senior Edwards had served for twenty-three years and had no new charge to assume. Few churches appealed for his services. It was not until late in 1750 that he received a call from the small mission church in Stockbridge, Massachusetts, and in May of 1751 he accepted that invitation.

The Edwards family did not escape an atmosphere of controversy by moving to Stockbridge. The village had been founded in 1722 by land speculators who bought the site from the Indians for "460 pounds, three barrels of cider, and thirty quarts of rum."[2] In 1743 the mission was established by a group of Massachusetts clergymen, and John Sergeant, a native of New Jersey and a graduate of Yale College, was installed as its minister. Sergeant gave devoted service to the mission until his death in 1749. Tension between the mission, whose policy had been to protect the Indian rights to the land they had long occupied, and the land speculators, who sought personal gain, increased as the demand for land in western Massachusetts grew. Ephraim Williams, a leading citizen of Stockbridge and father-in-law of John Sergeant the previous pastor, had considerable influence over mission policy. With Edwards' arrival this control was threatened; the Williams family had long been at odds with Edwards. In his student days at Yale he had been involved in controversy with his tutor, Elisha Williams; Solomon Williams had vigorously attacked his *Humble Inquiry Concerning Qualification for Communion;* Israel Williams had been one of his severest critics during the Great Awakening. Soon after Edwards' arrival, Elisha Williams was made a member of the governing board of the mission on behalf of the London Society for the Propagation of the Gospel,

---

1. Jonathan and Sarah Edwards had eleven children, three boys and eight girls. Sarah (1728–1805), Jerusha (1730–1747), Esther (1732–1758), Mary (1734–1750), Lucy (1736–1786), Timothy (1738–1813), Susannah (1740–1802), Eunice (1743–1822), Jonathan (May 26, 1745– August 1, 1801), Elizabeth (1747–1762), and Pierrepont (1750–1826).
2. Sarah Cabot Sedgwick and Christina Sedgwick Marquand, *Stockbridge, 1739–1939; A Chronicle* (Great Barrington, Massachusetts: Berkshire Courier, 1939), 9. Also Electa F. Jones, *Stockbridge, Past and Present; or, Records of an Old Mission Station* (Springfield, Mass.: Samuel Bowles and Co., 1854).

the group which provided financial support for Edwards and his missionary work. Edwards was not in an enviable situation.

Jonathan Edwards the Younger spent his early years in Stockbridge. Having Mohegan Indian children for playmates and neighbors did not seem to disturb this six-year-old. Later in life he recalled: "The Indians being the nearest neighbors, I constantly associated with them; their boys were my daily school mates and play fellows. Out of my father's house, I seldom heard any language spoken, beside the Indian." He readily admitted that the Mohegan tongue became more familiar to him than English: "I knew the names of some things in Indian which I did not know in English; even all my thoughts ran in Indian."[3]

His father encouraged these contacts with an eye to preparing young Jonathan for future missionary work. Edwards, Sr. must not have regarded the rigorous weather or isolation of Stockbridge sufficient testing for a future "worker of the Lord," for in 1755 he sent his son to live in an Iroquois settlement, Onohoquaga, some 200 miles southwest of Albany. Young Jonathan's companion in this venture was Gideon Hawley, a close friend of the family who was in his early twenties and had spent some time studying under Edwards. Hawley's duties in this mission, in addition to instructing the Indians in English, were to instill "the principles of Religion, & good manners, & teaching a couple of English boys who are put into the school by the government, to learn the Iroquois language."[4]

The age of ten was not too early a time to be committed to the pursuit of the ways of the Lord, or to dedicate oneself to the work of the ministry. Young Jonathan was continually made aware of the seriousness of this time of his life.

Stockbridge, May 27, 1755

Dear Child:

Though you are a great way off from us, yet you are not out of our minds: I am full of concern for you, often think of you, and often

---

3. Jonathan Edwards the Younger, *Observations on the Language of the Muhhekaneew Indians* (New Haven: Josiah Meigs, 1788), Preface. Edwards states that Mohegan is a "corruption of Muhhekaneew."

4. Ms. letter of March 10, 1752, from Jonathan Edwards, Sr. to Jaspar Manduit of London (Andover-Newton Seminary Library).

pray for you. Though you are at so great a distance from us, & from all your Relations, yet this is a Comfort to us, that the same God that is here, is also at Onohoquaha; and that though you are out of our light & out of our reach, you are alwaies in God's hands, who is infinitely gracious; and we can go to Him, and commit you to his Care and Mercy. Take heed that you don't forget or Neglect Him. Alwaies set God before your Eyes, and live in his Fear, and seek him every Day with all Diligence: for He, and He only can make you happy or miserable, as He pleases; and your Life and Health, and the eternal salvation of your soul and your all in this life and that which is to come depends on his will & Pleasure. The week before last, on Thursday, David died; whom you knew and used to play with, and who used to live at our House. His soul is gone into the eternal world. Whether he was prepared for Death, we don't know. This is a loud call of God to you to prepare for Death. You see that they that are young die, as well as those that are old; David was not very much older than you. Remember what Christ said, that you must be born again, or you never can see the Kingdom of God. Never give your self any Rest, unless you have good evidence that you are converted & become a new Creature. We hope that God will preserve your life & health, and return you to Stockbridge again in safety; but alwaies remember that Life is uncertain; you know not how soon you must die, & therefore had need to be alwaies ready. We have very lately heard from your Brothers and sisters at Northampton & at Newark, that they are well. Your aged Grandfather and grandmother, when I was at Windsor gave their love to you. We here all do the same.

  I am,

    your tender and affectionate father,

      Jonathan Edwards.[5]

Because the "French and Indian War" was taking place in the area to the north and west of Onohoquaga, Jonathan remained with Hawley for only six months. When he returned to Stockbridge late in the winter of 1755, he resumed his training under the guidance of his father. It was at this time that Edwards, Sr. was completing his theological essays on original sin, true virtue, and freedom of the will. Though young Jonathan may not have understood all the intricate arguments woven by his father, he was exposed to the

---

5. Ms. letter of May 27, 1755, from Jonathan Edwards, Sr. to Jonathan Edwards the Younger (Yale University Library). Used by permission. All Yale manuscripts cited in this study are deposited in the Beinecke Rare Book and Manuscript Library.

development of these theological doctrines and to the spirit of his father's mind. Even more significant were the tightening theological and personal bonds between the three theological giants of New England life: Edwards, Joseph Bellamy, and Samuel Hopkins. Constant exchanges of letters and visits among them helped cement young Jonathan's devotion to their theological interests. His later life displayed the strength of the allegiance he developed at this time.

Late in 1757 his father was invited to become President of the College of New Jersey. This was not an unnatural choice. Edwards, Sr. was a highly respected theologian who would give stature to the young college at a time when it was undergoing severe hardship. The free-flowing exchange of ideas between Edwards and his congregational followers, and men of the Presbyterian Church, created strong bonds between the Connecticut-western Massachusetts Congregationalists and the Presbyterians to the south. Many of the senior Edwards' most devoted followers were found among these Presbyterians in the middle colonies. The marriage of his daughter Esther to Aaron Burr, pastor of the important Presbyterian Church in Newark, New Jersey, and himself for a time the college's president, brought a familial tie. That the trustees of the college looked to the north for a leader was no surprise.

Accompanied by his daughter Lucy, Edwards left Stockbridge early in 1758; Mrs. Edwards and the rest of the family waited until spring before they made the long trek to New Jersey.

Once again, Edwards came into a difficult situation. The College of New Jersey had been established at Princetown for only two years. From its founding in 1746, until its permanent settlement in 1756, the school had had two other homes. One of them, during Jonathan Dickinson's tenure as president, was at Elizabethtown, where Dickinson was pastor of the Presbyterian Church. At his death in 1748 the trustees of the college quickly elected Aaron Burr his successor, and the college moved to Newark, New Jersey, where Burr had his church.

Financial, political, and ecclesiastical difficulties plagued the new school. Dickinson, Burr, and other supporters visited throughout New England and the middle colonies seeking donations to help the college. Lotteries to secure financial aid were established by the states of Pennsylvania, New Jersey, and Connecticut; appeals were made to Europe. Samuel Davies and Gilbert Tennent set sail for England in November, 1753, to plead the college's case before clergymen and churches throughout England, Scotland, and Ireland. Though they met with suspicion, generated by disgruntled Presbyterian clergy, they secured considerable financial backing for the college. The friendship between John Erskine of Edinburgh and Jonathan Edwards, Sr., witnessed to in a prolonged exchange of letters, no doubt helped pave the way for the visit of Davies and Tennent to Scotland.[6] This trip made clear to many in Europe and America the desperate need of the new school.

By the early 1750's it was clear that the college needed a permanent home. Elizabethtown, Newark, and New Brunswick all promised land and money if it would be established in their villages. The small community of Princetown was finally chosen "as the most convenient situation; being near the center of the colony, on the public road between New York and Philadelphia, and not inferior in the salubrity of its air, to any village upon the continent."[7] With the new site decided upon, construction was begun on Nassau Hall, the campus' main building.

In the period from 1746 to 1757 the college grew from a faint hope to a center of education which had a physical plant of increasing value, a President and two tutors, and a graduate class of twenty-two students. It had come to be a respected part of American higher education.

Edwards, Sr. was called to lead the school as it was entering a new phase. The stature of this well-known theologian from New England was looked upon as a good omen for the future of the college. Unfortunately, Edwards' life was cut short soon after he arrived at Princetown. In early 1758 the village was in the midst of a severe smallpox epidemic. Since Edwards had not had the disease, he submitted, in late February, to an inoculation. Though he passed through the first stages after the inoculation with normal reactions, he later became severely ill and died on March 23. Mrs. Edwards had

---

6. A major portion of the Erskine-Edwards correspondence can be found in the Andover-Newton Seminary Library.

7. *An Account of the College of New Jersey* (Woodbridge, N.J.: Published for the Trustees of the College of New Jersey by James Parker, 1764), 12.

been summoned from Stockbridge, but she and her family did not reach Princetown in time. To add further tragedy for the children, Mrs. Edwards died only six months later while en route to Newark to visit her daughter, Esther Burr.

With the sudden death of both parents, the Edwards children found themselves living in an unfamiliar town, their ties in Stockbridge and Northampton broken. But Edwards, Sr. had not been without devoted friends in the Princetown area. Provision was made for Jonathan to enter the local preparatory school in October, 1760. The adequacy of his previous training enabled him to master the course of the school; in the following fall he was admitted to the freshman class of the college. The ensuing ten years that Edwards the Younger spent among the Presbyterians were formative ones for his later work. Though the major portion of his work was done within the framework of the Congregational Church, he, perhaps more than any other New England figure, devoted himself to *rapprochement* between the two main branches of the American Reformed tradition, the Presbyterian and Congregational Churches.

Jonathan Edwards was sixteen years of age when he entered the College of New Jersey in 1761. The school, only fifteen years old, was already under the guidance of its fifth President, Samuel Finley, a graduate of Tennent's Log College and an ardent supporter of the revivals. Finley and three tutors constituted its staff.

The course of study Edwards was to follow was clearly laid out. The freshman year at the College of New Jersey was mainly spent in language training. Horace, Cicero's *Orations,* the Greek *New Testament,* Lucian's *Dialogues,* and Xenophon's *Cyropaedia* constituted the basic freshman year's academic diet. In the sophomore year the student was introduced to "the sciences, geography, rhetoric, logic, and mathematics." The third year was devoted to mathematics, moral philosophy, metaphysics, chronology, and physics, and, for the ministerial student, the study of Hebrew. In the senior year, composition, public speaking, and general work in "the most improving parts of the Latin and Greek classics, part of the Hebrew Bible and all the arts and Sciences constituted the program."[8] It is

---

8. *An Account of the College of New Jersey,* 24ff. See also Francis L. Broderick, "Pulpit, Physics, and Politics: The Curriculum of the College of New Jersey; 1746–1794," *William and Mary Quarterly,* Vol. VI (January, 1949), 42–68.

clear that Latin and Greek were the primary disciplines; after mastering these the student could explore the more exciting realms of science and moral philosophy.

Life at the College was not limited to academic pursuits. The interests and calibre of the first five Presidents indicate that the college was regarded as a training center for Christian service. The lectures and preaching of these Presidents must have impressed upon their listeners the need of men for "spiritual regeneration." The college years were regarded as a time of life commitment. Though the fervor of the Great Awakening had cooled by the 1760's there were periodic renewals.[9] In 1763 such a revival affected young Edwards, for, on September 17 of that year, being now eighteen years old, he felt himself able to make the declaration of faith for which his early years had prepared him.

Nassau Hall September 17, 1763

I Jonathan Edwards, Student of the College in N. Jersey on this seventeenth Day of September 1763, being the Day before the first Time I proposed to draw near to the Lord's Table; after much Thought and due consideration, as well as Prayer to almighty God, for his Assistance, resolved in the Grace of God, to enter into an express Act of Self Dedication to the Service of God; as being a thing highly reasonable in its own Nature, and that might be of eminent Service, to keep me steady in my Christian course, to rouse me out off (sic) Sloth, and Indolence, and uphold me in the Day of Temptation.

Eternal and ever-blessed God! I desire with the deepest Humiliation and Abasement of Soul to come, in the Name and for the sake of Jesus Christ, and present myself before thee, sensible of my infinite unworthiness to appear before thee, especially on such an Occasion as this; to enter into a Covenant with thee. But notwithstanding my sins have made such a Separation between thee and my soul, I beseech thee thro' Christ thy Son to vouchsafe thy presence with me, and Acceptance of the best Sacrifice which I can make.

I do O Lord! in Hopes of thy assisting Grace, solemnly make an entire and perpetual Surrender, of all that I am and have unto thee, being determined in thy Strength, to renounce all former Lords who

---

9. Samuel Blair, while still a minister in Virginia, described the power of a revival which passed through the student body of the College of New Jersey in 1757 in his: *Little Children Invited to Jesus Christ, A Sermon preached at Hanover County, Virginia, May 8, 1757* (London: J. Buckland, 1758).

have had Dominion over me, every Lust of the Eye, of the Flesh and of the Mind, and to live entirely devoted to thee, and thy Service. To thee do I consecrate the Powers of my Mind, with whatsoever Improvements thou has already or shalt be pleased hereafter to grant me in the literary way, purposing if it be thy good Pleasure, to pursue my Studies assiduously that I may be better prepared to act in any sphere of Life, in which thou shalt place me.

I do also solemnly dedicate all my Possessions, my Time, my influence over others, to be all used for thy Glory. To thy Direction I resign myself, and all that I have trusting all future Contingencies in thy Hands, and may thy Will in all things, and not mine be done. Use me, O Lord! as an Instrument of thy Service! I beseech the[e] number me among thy People; may I be clothed with the Righteousness of thy Son; ever impart to me thro' him all needful Supplies of thy purifiing and chearing spirit! I beseech thee O Lord! that thou wouldst enable me to live according [to] this my vow constantly avoiding all Sin, and when I shall come to die in that Solemn and awful hour may I remember this my covenant, and do thou O Lord remember it too, and give my departing Spirit an abundant Admittance into the Realm of Bliss! And if when I am laid in the Dust, and surviving Friend should meet with this my memorial [. . .] may it be of Good to him, and do thou admit him, to partake of all the Blessings of thy Covenant of Grace, thru Jesus the great Mediator, to whom, with thee O Father, and thy Holy Spirit, be everlasting Praises ascribed by Saints and Angels![10]

When Edwards "drew near the Lord's table" the next day it was at the Presbyterian Church in Princetown. This church became his first real denominational home, and his membership there the first of his several official connections with the Presbyterian Church. Shortly after making this declaration of faith he began his Junior year at the college. There is no evidence to indicate that the remainder of his course deviated from the prescribed pattern. In 1765 he was granted an A.M. degree.[11]

As was customary for a ministerial candidate, Edwards turned to a clergyman for further theological training. It was natural and

10. Ms. in Yale University Library. At first glance this statement of faith may appear to be a "contract" between Edwards and God. It is more properly understood as a concrete illustration of covenant theology.
11. *Catalogue 1765* of Princeton University.

significant that Joseph Bellamy and Samuel Hopkins, his father's two chief disciples, became his mentors during the years 1765– 1766. Edwards spent the winter months of 1765–1766 studying at Great Barrington, Massachusetts, with Hopkins, whom he no doubt remembered from his father's years in Stockbridge. An early biographer of Hopkins described the visit.

> . . . Not long after the death of Mr. Edwards, his son, bearing his name, Jonathan Edwards, graduated. He had not examined the theological system adopted by his father, but objected strenuously and with much confidence to some of the leading doctrines. Mr. H. from regard to his father, and concern as well as affection for the son invited him to make his house his home for the winter, offering him a room with a fire, and every facility that he could give him in the pursuit of his studies; and as a particular motive mentioned that he had the manuscripts of his father, which he would have opportunity to peruse.
>
> Young Mr. E. without much persuasion, accepted the offer. He was amiable in his temper, but prompt and self opinionated. Mr. H. soon put into his hands a manuscript of his father's, maintaining a doctrine which he had controverted. When he had read it he brought forward objections which he appeared to think conclusive. But Mr. H. attempted to correct his misapprehensions, and to explain and strengthen by additional proof the arguments of his father. Young Mr. E. was not convinced though his zeal was in some measure abated. He retired for reflection and the adjustment of his ideas, expecting to bring new force in the morning. But in the conversation he became more embarrassed, and found that the subject required a deeper investigation than he had ever paid to it. Under a conviction of his conscience, he became docile as a child, and made rapid proficiency in that belief in doctrine for which he could give a reason....[12]

Whether this account of young Edwards questioning his father's writings is accurate, or whether it is the attempt of Hopkins' biographer to build the character of his subject, is, with the evidence at hand, impossible to determine. But it is safe to assume that if young Edwards were having difficulty with Edwardsean doctrine, Hopkins would make every effort to clarify the issues involved.

When Edwards left Great Barrington in the spring of 1766 he

---

12. William Patten, *Reminiscences of the Late Rev. Samuel Hopkins, D.D. of Newport, R. I.* (Providence: I. H. Cady, 1843), 45–47.

went to study with Joseph Bellamy in Bethlehem, Connecticut. Bellamy had studied in the home of the elder Edwards and was perhaps the most respected and demanding teacher in the many "schools for prophets" located throughout New England. Like other students Edwards lived with his teacher's family and received social as well as intellectual guidance. Bellamy's method of instruction was to give to his students lists of questions about a variety of subjects, such as:

> The existence, attributes and moral government of God; our moral agency, and the law under which we are placed; the sinful state and character of mankind; the need of a divine revelation, and the fact that one has been given; the great doctrines of revelation, especially of the gospel; the character, offices and work of Christ; the atonement, and regeneration through the truth, and by the Holy Spirit; justification by faith; the distinguishing nature and fruits of repentance, love and other Christian graces; growth in grace; the perseverance of the saints; death, the resurrection, and final judgment; heaven and hell; the nature of the church; particular churches, their officers and ordinances; the nature, uses and ends of church disciplines, etc.[13]

Bellamy's students were invited to use his library to examine writings by various divines concerning these subjects. His library of 100 titles included the prominent Reformed writers of the day, as well as selected authors who challenged the prevailing orthodoxy.[14] Bellamy's own writings, Hopkins' works, and the manuscripts and publications of Jonathan Edwards, Sr. constituted the major diet of these young theologians. The rigorous, intensive, and individual training that Jonathan Edwards received from Bellamy and Hopkins must certainly have sharpened his awareness of the issues of New England theology in the eighteenth century, and made firm his line of descent in the New Divinity tradition.[15] Edwards was licensed to preach on October 21, 1766, by the Litchfield Association. By

---

13. Joseph Bellamy, *The Works of Joseph Bellamy, D.D.* (Boston: Doctrinal Tract and Book Society, 1853), Vol. I, lvii.

14. Mary L. Gambrell, *Ministerial Training in Eighteenth-Century New England* (New York: Columbia University Press, 1937) contains a survey of the books in Bellamy's library, 108ff.

15. The theological debt that Edwards owes to these men will be analyzed in succeeding chapters. It is emphasized here that Edwards' training was in the New Divinity school of New England theology.

the time he left Bellamy's home in the winter of 1766 he had received excellent theological training; his formal education was now complete.

During the rest of his life Edwards never lost his deep connection with the Presbyterian Church or separated himself from its concerns and conflicts. Though he desired to return to a New England parish, he continued many close friendships with Presbyterian clergymen and later became a participant, as a Presbyterian, in efforts to effect a concrete tie between the two churches.

CHAPTER TWO

The Ecclesiastical Heritage of Jonathan Edwards the Younger

To fully understand Jonathan Edwards the Younger's heritage from both the Congregational and Presbyterian denominations one must first understand the fact that these two churches were closely related in the New World. The most fundamental distinction between them might well have been geographical: the Presbyterian Church was located in the middle colonies, and the Congregational Church in New England.

A discussion of either their separate histories, or their relationship, is complicated by the fact that both were divided into branches. In each case the branches themselves were defined geographically, as well as in terms of church government and theology. Thus, one's attention is directed not only to ecclesiastical history, but also to immigration patterns and the economic development of the New World.

1. American Presbyterianism

In terms of immigration patterns the middle colonies present a striking contrast to New England. In the early decades of the eighteenth century, immigrants from different nations entered the New World through the mid-Atlantic ports; no single group dominated the scene as did the English in New England;[1] nowhere else in

---

1. Thomas J. Wertenbaker, *The Founding of American Civilization; The Middle Colonies* (New York: Charles Scribner's Sons, 1949).

25

the Americas would one find settlers of so many nationalities mixed together: Dutch, Swedes, English, Swiss, Germans, French, and, of course, Scotch-Irish.

In the eighteenth century the Presbyterian Church in America was divided into two main branches. Each had a national and geographical definition, and the two were to differ concerning both church government and matters of theology. The one branch was composed of Scotch-Irish immigrants who settled primarily in Pennsylvania and the area south of Philadelphia. The other, situated in northern New Jersey and in New York, was composed mainly of immigrants from England. Each of these areas of settlement had its commercial center: New York became the center of trade and cultural development for New Jersey, New York state, and Connecticut; Philadelphia became the correspondent center for Pennsylvania and the area to the south and west.

As a national group the Scotch-Irish can be traced to the seventeenth century immigration from Scotland to Ireland.[2] It was not until the 1720's and 1730's that substantial numbers of Scotch-Irish emigrated to the New World; the attraction of untamed land and the promised freedom from secular control overcame whatever hesitation to leave for unknown parts which these pioneers may have felt. Gradually, during the following decades, the Scotch-Irish moved westward, and by the end of the century they were one of the largest national groups in western Pennsylvania. Their road of march was south and west from the two major coastal ports, Philadelphia and New Castle.

The Scotch-Irish branch of American Presbyterianism differed most from its English counterpart regarding church government. From the Scottish Kirk it inherited a polity which emphasized the power of a strong synod composed of member congregations.

The Edwards family and many other prominent New England figures were associated with the other branch of the Presbyterian Church, the English branch. Because the political situation in seven-

---

2. They came mainly from the lowlands of Scotland where the Cameronians had settled after their secession from the Church of Scotland. The similarities between the Cameronians and the Scotch-Irish are clear: concern for doctrinal purity and strict discipline. For a thorough discussion of the national and ethnic make-up of the Scotch-Irish see: James Heron, "The Making of Ulster Scot," in Henry J. Ford, *The Scotch-Irish in America* (Princeton: Princeton University Press, 1915), Appendix C, 555ff.

teenth century England was quite different from that in Scotland, English Presbyterianism practiced a less restrictive polity than that which developed in Scotland. English Presbyterians encouraged local church organization and jurisdiction rather than national control; neither Presbyterian synods nor a national General Assembly was formed until 1647 in England. Thus, the English Presbyterian Church never achieved the solidarity that characterized the Kirk of Scotland.

In the New World, there were enough Presbyterian congregations in 1716 to warrant the formation of the first American Synod. It was composed of the presbyteries of Philadelphia, New Castle, Long Island, and Snow Hill.[3] The nature of the Synod's jurisdiction over the presbyteries was not clearly worked out at that time, but it was similar to the advisory role filled by the consociations of Connecticut Congregationalism.

A series of debates concerning the necessity of subscribing to the Westminster Confession occurred within the Synod of Philadelphia in the 1720's. In 1728 the New Castle (Delaware) Presbytery offered to the Synod an overture calling for subscription to the affirmations of that Confession. Jonathan Dickinson, a transplanted New Englander, the pastor in Elizabethtown, New Jersey, and a recognized leader of the English strain within the church, attacked the overture by insisting that subscription to human formulations of God's word cannot be demanded.[4] The subscription issue came to a head at the Synod meeting of 1729 where the "Adopting Act," one of the most important documents in the history of American Presbyterianism, was written. This Act stated that the ministers of the Synod

> shall declare their agreement in, and approbation of, the Confession of faith, with the Larger and Shorter Catechism of the Assembly of

3. *Records of the Presbyterian Church in the United States of America* (Philadelphia: Presbyterian Board of Publication, 1841), 92. This volume contains the minutes of the early judicatories of the church.

4. Jonathan Dickinson, *Remarks Upon a Discourse Intituled an Overture. Presented to the Reverend Synod of Dissenting Ministers Sitting in Philadelphia, in the Month of September, 1728* (New York: Printed by J. Peter Zenger, 1729). We note in the background an issue which had been discussed previously in Scotland and England. At the Salter's Hall meeting in England in 1719 the Presbyterians were defending the same point against more conservative-minded Congregationalists; while in Scotland, subscription, after proper discussion, had been accepted by the judicatories of the church.

Divines at Westminster, as being in *all the essential and necessary* articles good forms of sound words and systems of Christian doctrine, and do also adopt the said Confession and Catechisms as the confession of our Faith.[5]

It left the Presbyteries to determine exactly which articles were essential and necessary. Within three years, however, the Presbytery of New Castle again required unqualified subscription to the Westminster Confession. Seven years later, in 1736, it was necessary to write an "Explanatory Act" interpreting the decision of 1729. This "Explanatory Act" does not mention "essential and necessary articles" and points out that all members of the 1729 Synod (which composed the "Adopting Act") subscribed fully to the Westminster Confession at that time.[6]

One of the issues underlying the subscription controversy which erupted in the 1729 Synod concerned the qualifications of the clergy. The subscriptionists insisted primarily on doctrinal purity; Dickinson and the non-subscriptionists were more concerned with the piety and religious vigor of the ministry. The Great Awakening brought this difference into sharp focus.

The area around New Brunswick, New Jersey, where the Tennent family carried on much of their work, became a seed-bed for

---

5. *Records,* 92. (Italics are mine.)

6. An examination of the biographies of the ministers of the Presbyterian Church on the roll of the Synod of 1736 substantiates the thesis that the division of the church was at this time largely based on national origin. Of the twenty ministers present at the meeting of the Synod of Philadelphia in 1736, sixteen were directly from Ireland or Scotland, three were from New England, one was from Wales. Two of the three from New England were New Side men; one, Richard Treat, was a member of the New Brunswick Presbytery and a close friend of the Tennents; the other, Ebenezer Gould, was a member of the Long Island Presbytery. The only two clearly New Side men of Scotch-Irish extraction were William Tennent and his son, William, Jr. The remaining fourteen ministers of Irish or Scotch background were members of the Presbyteries of New Castle, Donegal, Philadelphia, Lewes, or Snow Hill—all of which were located around Philadelphia or to the south or south west. Of the twenty ministers on the rolls of the Synod but who were not present at the Synod of Philadelphia in 1736, eleven were of New England origin; six were from Ireland; one from Wales; one from New Jersey; and one from Scotland. Of the six from Ireland, two were Log College men, Gilbert Tennent and Samuel Blair; the remaining four from Ireland were all members of the New Castle Presbytery. The ministers from Scotland and Wales joined the Philadelphia Presbytery. Most of the New England ministers joined either the Long Island, East Jersey, New York, or New Brunswick Presbyteries. Very few of them went to the Presbyteries dominated by the Old Side. This illustrates a geographical division according to national origin which is an important fact for the development of American Presbyterianism. These figures are based on the *Records of the Presbyterian Church,* and Richard Webster, *A History of the Presbyterian Church in America* (Philadelphia: Presbyterian Historical Society, 1858).

revivalistic activity. In the 1730's, William Tennent, of Scotch-Irish background, had established a school at Neshaminy which was dubbed the Log College by its critics; the graduates of the school, particularly Gilbert Tennent, Samuel Blair, John Blair, Samuel Finley, and John Rowland, became a formative influence in Presbyterian history. Though most of these men were from a Scotch-Irish background, their interests and concerns put them in opposition to the dominant Scotch-Irish party. The revivalists emphasized the terror of being in an unconverted state. Subscription to orthodox formulations of doctrine and regular attendance at church were not signs of the converted Christian; men must recognize that they are lost and that it is only through the mercy of God that they have any hope of being saved. There were clear similarities between the Log College and the New England groups within the church; by the middle of the 1730's they were uniting in opposition to the Scotch-Irish.

At the Synod of 1730 the Presbytery of New Brunswick was formed at the insistence of the New Side (English) wing of the church. In many other cases, however, the Old Side (Scotch-Irish) ministers controlled the Synod. A resolution was offered to exclude all ministers who did not have a degree from a European or New England college; those who did not have such a degree were to be examined by a committee of the Synod.[7] The Synod appointed two examination committees: one to the north of Philadelphia and the other to the south of Philadelphia. By this action the Synod clearly acknowledged that it was geographically divided.

The English revivalist George Whitefield arrived in Philadelphia in 1739 and precipitated an open rupture between the opposing parties. Whitefield had not intended to stay in the middle colonies, but at the insistence of William Tennent he conducted a revivalistic campaign in the churches of the Log College men and in Jonathan Dickinson's church at Elizabethtown. Whitefield's criticisms of the unconverted state of the ministry caused the opponents of the revival to collect their forces for a full fight against the inroads of "new measures." The laity in the church, however, welcomed Whitefield's work, and as a result many came to look with greater favor

---

7. *Records,* 139.

upon the Log College party. "But for Whitefield, the opponents of the revival might have stamped it out. After Whitefield's tour the opposition fought on, but theirs was a losing fight."[8] Elsewhere throughout the colonies the Great Awakening was approaching its high point.

Encouraged by Whitefield's reception, Gilbert Tennent criticized the state of religion in the Presbyterian Church. In March of 1740 he preached his famous sermon, "The Danger of an Unconverted Ministry," berating the state of piety among the clergy by charging that too many Presbyterian clergymen had no "call of God." At the Synod meeting in 1729 Dickinson's call for an examination of the piety of the candidates for ordination had gone unheeded. Now, with the revival at its height, the same plea from Gilbert Tennent broke the church in two. Underlying this issue was the question of the jurisdiction of the ruling bodies of the church. Did the judicatories of the church determine the qualifications of the ministry, and was their judgment therefore "to be accepted by all men as the voice and act of God,"[9] or, as the Log College men insisted, was "the call of God to the Office of the Ministry . . . distinguished from . . . the Presbyteries trying and Ordaining a Person to that Office"?[10] There was unrestricted competition for the uncommitted areas of the church. Because of their reliance on itineracy and their revivalistic techniques the New Side was able to spread into areas of the church where the limited Scotch-Irish party was not able to go. In retaliation, the Synod of 1740 decided that those who were ordained by a Presbytery without examination by the Synod, though recognized as "gospel ministers," were not regarded as members of the Synod. The Log College men, therefore, were not fully accepted Presbyterian ministers. Tennent, on the contrary, insisted upon the right of a Presbytery to ordain men to full ministerial status within the church.

When the Synod of 1741 met in May, the church confronted several unsolved issues: differing views concerning the authority of the Synod over the presbyteries, differing estimates of the Great

8. L. J. Trinterud, *The Forming of an American Tradition* (Philadelphia: Westminster Press, 1949), 87.

9. Quoted in Trinterud, *The Forming of an American Tradition,* 91.

10. Samuel Finley, *Clear Light Put Out in Obscure Darkness* (Philadelphia: Printed by B. Franklin, 1743), 59.

Awakening, and differing criteria for the examination of ministers. A group of Old Side ministers offered to the Synod a *Protestation* which called for full subscription to the Westminster symbols, not in light of the "Adopting Act" of 1729, but "according to our last explication of the Adopting Act," that is, the "Explanatory Act" of 1736.[11] It refused to recognize those who had been ordained by a Presbytery but not examined by the Synod's committee. It condemned itineracy and the revivalists' view of the qualifications of the ministry. In short, the *Protestation* demanded that the revival party either surrender to the Old Side or be cut off from the church. It concluded with the judgment that

> a continued union . . . is most absurd and inconsistent, when it is so notorious, that our doctrine and principles of church government, in many points, are not only diverse, but directly opposite. For how can two walk together, except they be agreed?[12]

Though no formal vote was taken on the *Protestation*, the only course left for the New Brunswick group was to withdraw. The views of the opposing parties were so far apart that no compromise was possible.

Soon after the Synod adjourned, the Log College men, assisted by Dickinson and his group, formed the Conjunct Presbyteries of New Brunswick and Londonderry. In 1745 they joined with the New York Presbytery to form the Synod of New York,[13] basing their union upon the "Adopting Act" of 1729.

In the years which followed its formation, the Synod of New York increased in number until, by the middle of the eighteenth century, it was, perhaps, the strongest church in the middle colonies. Several factors contributed to its growth. Of primary importance was the founding of a college which offered the New Side a supply of clergymen. William Tennent had left his pastorate at Neshaminy in 1742, and with his departure the Log College ceased to function. Immediate efforts were made to construct another school. With the consent of Governor Hamilton of New Jersey, and over the protests of the Anglican clergy, the College of New Jersey was given a charter in October of 1746, and Jonathan Dickinson was

---

11. *Records*, 155–158.
12. *Records*, 158.
13. *Records*, 232–233.

chosen its President.[14] The school had no formal connection with the Presbyterian Church, but the Board of Trustees consisted entirely of New Side men who were members of either the New Brunswick or New York Presbyteries.

An additional source of strength for the rapidly expanding New Side group was the increasing interchange of opinions and of men between New England and the middle colonies. Jonathan Edwards, Joseph Bellamy, and Samuel Hopkins were all invited to accept Presbyterian pastorates in the New Side area. Invitations were also extended to Presbyterians to occupy Congregational pulpits. Between the graduates of the College of New Jersey and the increasing number of New Englanders filling Presbyterian churches, the New York Synod was able to carry on missionary work in much of the frontier region and in the south, as well as in many churches throughout the middle colonies.[15]

The Synod of Philadelphia, on the other hand, has rightly been called "The Withered Branch."[16] It had no place to look for reliable ministers to fill its vacant churches. Though it sought to use the College of Philadelphia and an institution established at New London, Pennsylvania, neither proved satisfactory. The resultant deficiency continued to plague the cause of the Old Side. Their insistence on doctrinal subscription, their avoidance of revivalistic techniques, and their efforts to pattern church government after the models of Ireland and Scotland all restricted their contribution to the development of American Presbyterianism. The New Side men were the innovators. They formulated new measures to meet the peculiar needs of the Church; meeting these needs, they grew. The Old Side did not.[17]

With the passing of years the hard feeling caused by the split of 1741 gradually softened, though intransigent Old Side men remained. By 1757 the Synods were ready to entertain serious propo-

---

14. See T. J. Wertenbaker, *Princeton, 1746–1896* (Princeton: Princeton University Press, 1946). Wertenbaker has included the Charter of the College in an appendix, 396ff.

15. For a discussion of the total impact of the New York Synod on American Presbyterianism see R.H. Nichols, "The First Synod of New York, 1745–1758, and its Permanent Effects," *Church History*, Vol. XIV (December, 1945), 239ff.

16. Trinterud, *The Forming of an American Tradition*, 135.

17. In 1741 the Old Side numbered 27 clergymen; in 1758 that total had dropped to 23. In the same period the New Side increased in number from 22 to 73.

sals for reunion. Though the New York Synod took the initiative, the members of the Synod of Philadelphia agreed to bargain concerning a basis for reunion.

In May of 1758 the two Synods met together to discuss a plan of reunion. Gilbert Tennent, who had made many efforts to reunite the church, was chosen moderator. This, in itself, reflected the changed temper of the leaders of both parties. The two groups agreed to regard the Presbyteries as the ordaining courts of the church; candidates for the ministry did not need to submit to Synodical examination. The joint Synods, in their plan of union, included an article which commended the revivals as a definite work of God, but admitted that grievous errors had accompanied them. The omissions of the meeting of 1758 are as noteworthy as its positive accomplishments. There was no formal discussion of the "Adopting Act" of 1729 or of the "Explanatory Act" of 1736. Even the *Protestation* of 1741 escaped examination when the Synod simply stated that it was "the act of those who subscribed it . . . the said Synod declare, that they never judicially adopted the said protestation, nor do account it a Synodical act."[18]

During the few years following the reunion of 1758 there were repeated outbreaks of the old division between New Side and Old Side. Some new Presbyteries were organized. The New Side party, though in control of most of the judicatories of the church, permitted the formation of Presbyteries along the lines of theological affiliation. This policy proved to be a disruptive move, for the parties within Presbyterianism were thus able to continue unchallenged. In the following years, the Presbyterian Church in America, though outwardly united, was divided between a small Old Side group and a large New Side group.

One other factor which influenced the development of the Presbyterian Church in America, particularly the English branch, was its close tie to the Congregational Church. In England, the line of distinction between Presbyterianism and Congregationalism had been thin indeed for some time, and it had become even thinner after the "Heads of Agreement" of 1691. The "Heads of Agreement" was a statement by Congregational and Presbyterian clergy-

---

18. *Records,* 186.

men which urged that the names of the particular denominations be dropped and that the term "United Brethren" be substituted. This so-called "Happy Union" was based on Congregational polity. Though it did not last long, its effect on Presbyterian-Congregational relations, both in England and in America, was strong.

When English Presbyterians left their homeland and immigrated to New England, rather than the middle colonies, many became Congregationalists. The Congregational churches of inland and lower New England, particularly Connecticut and western Massachusetts, also developed a polity structure of denominational control over individual churches which distinguished them from the freer church control practiced by Congregational churches in eastern Massachusetts. The Saybrook Platform of 1708 (a document of Connecticut Congregationalism, discussed in the next section of this chapter) advocated association control over churches—a system not unlike the Presbyterian form of church government—and blurred the line of demarcation between Connecticut Congregationalism and Presbyterianism; a Connecticut Congregationalist had to make very little adjustment to become a member of a Presbyterian church. Many New England clergymen, Jonathan Edwards the Younger among them, regarded their churches as interchangeably Congregational or Presbyterian.

During the early years of the eighteenth century many New Englanders, particularly from the New Haven area, moved into New York and New Jersey. This migration continued the westward movement which had occurred within New England itself, though very few of the settlers penetrated into that portion of the middle colonies which was still frontier country. Rising population and the search for richer farm land, plus the fact that New England offered limited economic opportunities for its inhabitants, contributed to this migration, and the entire northern portion of New Jersey became a replica of New England life.[19] Because so many New Englanders settled in northern New Jersey and in New York, many new churches were formed. Quite naturally, these settlers looked to New England for their ministers; the similarity between the polity

---

19. See Wertenbaker, *The Founding of American Civilization; The Middle Colonies*, Chapter IV, "The Puritan in New Jersey."

of Connecticut Congregationalism and middle colony Presbyterianism made possible an easy interchange of clergy between the two denominations, although during the eighteenth century the New Englanders within the developing Presbyterian Church remained a clearly definable group.

2. American Congregationalism

Between 1620 and 1688 hesitant changes were made in Congregational theology and church polity in order to meet the novel situation which obtained in the New World. The church was influenced by expanding commercial interests in New England and a widening cultural and ideological separation between eastern and western New England. The period from 1688 to 1727 was a time of widespread rebellion against church leaders. In this period definite theological and ecclesiastical parties were formed and clear geographical and social divisions became evident in New England society. A third period began with the arrival of Jonathan Edwards, Sr. at Northampton. Through his work in the Great Awakening and his theological writings, Edwards became a powerful influence.

The New England Puritan enterprise was founded on covenant theology. Within the Reformed tradition there had been uneasiness over the seemingly conflicting doctrines of the total and unfathomable sovereignty of God, and the responsibility of man.[20] Covenant theology, as it developed, sought to unite these affirmations. The covenant of works, made with Adam, put the responsibility for man's destiny on man's own shoulders; his full obedience was required. Man, through Adam's sin, had broken this covenant; it had been abolished. The covenant of grace instituted by Christ was seen as expressing the fact that God in Christ has restored man: that those who are covenanted with God will acknowledge their responsibilities through their actions. The initiative for the covenant comes from God, and man has certain active obligations to Him. Such an understanding of the covenant does not imply a belief in works

---

20. In 1619 the Synod of Dort dealt with this problem as it had arisen in the controversy between Arminians and strict Calvinists; the decision of Dort was in favor of a stringent Calvinism. See Philip Schaff, *The Creeds of Christendom* (New York: Harper and Brothers, 1905).

righteousness. Through the course of time, however, stress was placed on the response of man in such a way that it came to be viewed as the indispensable part of the relationship. In later New England theology, the free action of God was made dependent on the work of man. This offered the believer an assurance of his salvation, but tied to it was the demand for earnest performance of duty.[21]

The test for acceptance of this covenant was a public "testimony of regeneration"; only those who had given it were eligible for church membership. In Congregationalism the church officers and regenerate members took the responsibility for determining the validity and sincerity of the "testimony." This method of determining church membership was satisfactory for the first generation in New England, a closely knit group. But the arrival of new immigrants and the birth of the second and third generation, who frequently lacked the early Puritan's religious convictions and experiences, presented a threat to the "marvellous perfection" of New England Congregationalism. Some were not prepared to claim the definite experience of regeneration which was required.[22]

In 1662 a Synod was called to discuss the problem of church membership for those who had not had a definite "change of heart." After prolonged debate the Synod decided that:

> church members who were admitted in minority, understanding the Doctrine of Faith, and publickly professing their assent thereto; not scandalous in life, and solemnly owning the Covenant before the church, wherein they give up themselves and their children to the

---

21. Covenant is not to be equated with contract. ". . . Contract with God is entered into for the sake of mutual advantages; covenant implies the presence of a cause to which all advantages may need to be sacrificed." H. Richard Niebuhr, "The Idea of Covenant and American Democracy," *Church History*, Vol. XXIII (June, 1954), 134. Despite its brevity this article is one of the most adequate discussions of covenant theology.

22. In this connection see the writings of Perry Miller, *The New England Mind: The Seventeenth Century* (Cambridge: Harvard University Press, 1954), particularly Book IV, "Sociology"; also "The Half Way Covenant," *New England Quarterly*, Vol. VI (1933); "Preparation for Salvation in Seventeenth-Century New England," *Journal of the History of Ideas*, Vol. IV (1943); "The Marrow of Puritan Divinity," *Publication of the Colonial Society of Massachusetts*, Vol. XXXII (1933–1937). Also, *Errand Into the Wilderness* (Cambridge: Harvard University Press, 1956). A rebuttal to Miller's tendency to use "covenant" as meaning "contract" is found in Everett H. Emerson, "Calvin and Covenant Theology," *Church History*, Vol. XXV (June, 1956).

Lord, and subject themselves to the Government of Christ in the Church, their children are to be baptised.[23]

No requirement for a "change of heart" was made, but new provisions did state that such "members" were not to be admitted to the Lord's Supper even though they and their children could be baptized. In this sense they were "half-way members." Here was a parting with the old New England way, the first major break in the unified character of New England Congregationalism. This issue of 1662 was to be raised many times in the century to follow.

An important factor in all of this was that as a steadily growing number of immigrants came to the New World for economic rather than religious reasons a merchant class developed, yet church leaders retained control over many aspects of social as well as religious life. As a result, a conflict of interest between the merchant and the church leader arose. For the merchant to be successful in his commercial activity and yet remain a loyal member of the church involved definite contradictions.

> It meant to extend to the life of business a religious enthusiasm which must be continuously dampened lest it singe the corners of another's life. It meant to accumulate as much wealth as one righteously could, only to dispose of it like a steward, according to the principle *uti non frui*. . . . Above all, it required an amount of self discipline that only great faith could sustain.[24]

The resentment against ecclesiastical authority over commercial practices contributed to the alliance of the growing merchant class with the dissenters within the New England churches, and confirmed a progressively broadening split in New England life.

One obvious result of the new commercial activity was the growth of large centers of population where the merchant class assumed expanding powers.[25] The "cities" became the symbols of a new independent spirit. For their "guiding principles were not social stability, order, and the discipline of the senses, but mobility,

---

23. Williston Walker, *Creeds and Platforms of Congregationalism* (New York: Charles Scribner, 1893), 328. The Synod's justification for this change is found on pps. 328–334.

24. Bernard Bailyn, *The New England Merchants in the Seventeenth Century* (Cambridge: Harvard University Press, 1955), 44.

25. See Carl Bridenbaugh, *Cities in the Wilderness* (New York: Ronald Press, 1938).

growth, and the enjoyment of life."[26] The Puritan community did not always look with favor upon this new spirit which was created by expanding commercial activity in New England. Among other things, it destroyed the isolation which the New England churches had to have to continue their early ways. The rise of the merchant class facilitated wider contacts with England and Europe; the merchants' increasing prestige challenged the authority of the church leaders; the growth of coastal cities helped strengthen social distinctions within the colonies and contributed to the division of New England.[27]

Even the geography of New England was influential. The isolation of New Haven and the villages along the Connecticut river valley became an unconscious uniting bond for that region. On the other hand, Boston, Salem, Newport, and the rest of eastern Massachusetts shared common interests which naturally separated them from the inland area. This economic and geographical bifurcation of New England greatly influenced the developments taking place within New England Congregationalism.

The old pattern of homogeneity was being changed, not only by the growth of seacoast cities, but also by the breakdown of inland village life. It was the custom for the "meeting house" to be the center of the village, and the proximity of home to church contributed to religious solidarity. As the demand for good farm land became great, families built homes far distant from the village and the church. This change in the village pattern of life and the emigration from New England to lands in the "West" further disrupted society. The change in village solidarity contributed considerably to the rapidly changing status of the churches.[28]

Church leaders were aware that changes were taking place. They realized that the zeal of church members had declined, but did not know where to look for the causes which brought the change. The Reforming Synod of 1679 was called to seek an answer to the question: "What are the Evils that have provoked the Lord to bring

---

26. Bailyn, 139.
27. "Intellectually the distance of Boston or Philadelphia from London was less than that between any town and its respective frontiers." Bridenbaugh, *Cities in the Wilderness,* 139.
28. See L.K. Mathews, *The Expansion of New England* (Boston: Houghton Mifflin Company, 1909).

his Judgments on New England?"[29] This concern over the state of New England life stemmed not only from smallpox and shooting stars, but from deeper and more permanent effects of social change. Had the members of the Synod looked more candidly and more deeply into the changing character of New England life they might have seen the birth of a new spirit.

At the end of the seventeenth century the churches were rent by severe divisions. In three different areas, Northampton, Boston, and Connecticut, the church's difficulty adjusting to a changing society became evident. Definite theological and ecclesiastical alliances were developing.

In Northampton a devastating inroad on historic Congregationalism was made by Solomon Stoddard (1645–1729), who left as great a mark on New England Congregationalism as any other figure of the seventeenth century. Stoddard's "heresy" contributed to a spirit of independent thinking which influenced others who defied the ruling order.

With the adoption of the "Half Way Covenant" in 1662, Northampton, and other New England towns, were artificially divided into three groups: professing saints, the half-way members, and those remaining outside the doors of the church. The need for cohesion, particularly in a place threatened by Indian raids and stultifying isolation, must certainly have been felt by many besides Solomon Stoddard. In 1667 Stoddard broke with the decision of 1662 and admitted to the Lord's Supper all those who had been baptized, without asking for public expression of a "change of heart."

In 1687 he published *The Safety of Appearing at the Day of Judgment* which was a justification for opening the Lord's Supper to all members of the church. Stoddard's essay was largely theological. He sought to recapture Calvin's doctrine of the inscrutable nature of God's will. We have noted that as New England covenant theology changed character it came to stress man's role in salvation, of discovering and carrying out God's will. The idea that God's dealings with man are unfathomable tended to be lost. Stoddard insisted that since God is arbitrary and inscrutable, man cannot pretend to

---

29. Williston Walker, *Creeds and Platforms of Congregationalism*, 423.

know His will; neither can man pretend to know who make up the "elect." "Because the covenant is dispensed by an arbitrary and unpredictable divinity, because it definitely is not reasonable, it is open to all and no man can tell who is really a saint."[30] There was no justification for set rules and regulations governing attendance at the Lord's Supper. "The call is to every one that will. . . . So that they that are at a loss about their present condition, have free liberty to come as well as others."[31] Thus, Stoddard moved far beyond the Synod of 1662 by removing the barriers to the Lord's Supper. What a change he brought to the secure, certain covenanted church!

In 1700 Stoddard published *The Doctrine of Instituted Churches*. In it he amplified his reinterpretation of the idea of church covenant. He rejected the idea of a particular covenant, for "this Doctrine of the particular Covenant which is wholly unscriptural, is the reason that many among us are shut out of the Church, to whom Church Privileges do belong."[32] Stoddard would accept into church membership all those in Northampton who accepted the jurisdiction of the church and its leaders, who showed knowledge of the Christian faith, and who were not scandalous in the conduct of their everyday lives. He made no requirement for a "change of heart." "All such Professors of the Christian Faith, as are of blameless Conversation, and have Knowledge to examine themselves, and discern the Lord's Body, are to be admitted to the Lord's Supper."[33] The requirements for church membership and admission to the Lord's Supper were one and the same.

Stoddard's skill as a revivalist was connected to his pronouncements regarding the Lord's Supper. Revivalistic measures were needed to bring people to the church, and Stoddard viewed the Lord's Supper as a means of regeneration, of completing the work of conversion. Accepting the offer of church membership was man's responsibility; in turn, God offered "saving regeneration" through

---

30. Solomon Stoddard, *The Safety of Appearing at the Day of Judgment* (Boston: D. Henchman, 1729), 275. Perry Miller called this essay "the only speculative treatise since the founders and before Edwards that makes any constructive contribution to New England theology." Perry Miller, *The New England Mind: From Colony to Province* (Cambridge: Harvard University Press, 1953), 233.

31. Stoddard, *The Safety of Appearing*, 279–280.

32. Solomon Stoddard, *The Doctrine of Instituted Churches Explained and Proved from the Word of God* (London: 1700), 8.

33. Stoddard, *The Doctrine of Instituted Churches*, 18.

the "means" which He had established, primarily the Lord's Supper. In New England these were heretical pronouncements. Mather felt that Stoddard was "giving away the whole Congregational cause at once."[34]

Leaders at Harvard College, then the center of theological education in the colonies, sought to put similar principles to work in eastern Massachusetts. In 1699, two tutors, William Brattle and John Leverett, together with the treasurer of the college, Thomas Brattle, formed the Brattle Street Church. In November, 1699, they circulated a document which they called *The Manifesto* and which proposed some concrete changes in common church practices. Though an opening article of the *Manifesto* affirmed subscription to the Westminster Confession of Faith, the succeeding articles diverged sharply from other accepted standards. The *Manifesto* explicitly refused to ask those partaking of the Lord's Supper to declare their "experience" publicly.

> But we assume not to our selves to impose upon any a Publick Relation of their experience; however, if anyone think himself bound in Conscience to make such a Relation, let him do it.[35]

The *Manifesto* also gave every "Baptised Adult Person" who contributed to the maintenance of the church the right to vote in the election of the minister. Throughout, stress was placed upon the church's independence from external control, be it "consociation" or civil power. The Brattle Street Church elected Benjamin Colman, a former resident of Boston and a student of Leverett at Harvard, to be its minister. In disregard of another New England principle, he was ordained as a Presbyterian in England, perhaps to escape the difficulty he might encounter in securing ordination in Boston. By 1707 the Brattles, Leverett, and Colman had even wrested control of Harvard away from the Mathers.

The formation of the Brattle Street Church was a clear sign of the disruption of unity in Boston Congregationalism; it was a revolt against the ruling powers. The accusation against the dissenters,

---

34. Increase Mather, *The Order of the Gospel, Professed and Preach'd by the Churches of Christ in New England* (Boston: 1708), 8.

35. Samuel K. Lothrop, *A History of the Church in Brattle Street* (Boston: W. Crosby and H.P. Nichols, 1851), 23. The Text of the *Manifesto* is contained in this volume.

that they were hospitable to new ideas coming by way of Boston harbor, particularly latitudinarian theology, brought the rebels into closer alliance with John Mico and other Boston merchants. One may even say that this was the beginning of Boston as the center of "liberal" Congregationalism. In one generation the fears which Davenport, Chauncy, and Increase Mather expressed in 1662 over the acceptance of the "Half Way Covenant" had been realized.

During these same years a controversy, connected to the changes in Harvard College and the formation of the Brattle Street Church, arose over polity, particularly the question of the jurisdiction of an association of churches over a particular church. The Synods of 1637, 1662, and 1679–80 had acted on the theory that the Synod was an advisory organ for the churches, but as the number of churches grew there came to be more frequent dissension and controversy. In September of 1705 the Mathers and a group of Boston area ministers offered the *Proposals* to clarify and correct the situation. The *Proposals* called for an association of ministers whose function would be to settle disputes within churches, to examine candidates for ordination, and to act as a clearing house for acceptable candidates for vacant churches. It also proposed the formation of consociations, which were to be representative bodies of laymen and clergy that would supervise the churches. These *Proposals* were not accepted.[36]

The developing schism in Massachusetts Congregationalism contributed to the unacceptability of the *Proposals*. Their most competent and vocal critic was John Wise (1652–1725), who opposed any type of consociation. He insisted on the sole authority of the individual church, but not for the reasons adduced by radical Independents. The argument in his two major works, *The Churches Quarrel Espoused* (1715) and *A Vindication of the Government of New England Churches* (1717), emphasized the role of reason and natural law; Wise viewed reason and revelation as equal emanations of Divine wisdom. He based his attack on the *Proposals* on four supports: church fathers, the "Light of Nature," Scripture, and "the Noble Nature of the

---

36. Here the influence of the "Heads of Agreement" of 1691 formulated by English Congregationalists and Presbyterians was important. It was not until 1790 that any of the *Proposals* was adopted, and then only the article providing for the examination of ministerial candidates. See Williston Walker, "Why Did not Massachusetts Have a Saybrook Platform?" *The Yale Review* (May, 1892), 68–86.

Cambridge Platform."[37] Arguing for the need to preserve the liberty of each church against the control of a consociation, he asked his reader to rely on his rights as an English gentleman, and on the wisdom of the fathers of New England, to preserve the rights which Wise contended belonged to "our churches."[38] Though it is questionable that Wise's theological convictions had much effect on New England Congregationalism, his attack on the *Proposals* was indirectly an attack on the Mathers, and hence another important challenge to the authority of the ruling order within the churches. His contentions portended the increased importance which arguments from reason were to have in ecclesiastical discussions in New England.

In the early 1700's work was also begun (independently of the Massachusetts quarrels) to secure a stricter form of church government in the Connecticut colony. In 1707, the appointment of Rev. Gurdon Saltonstall, pastor of the New London Church, to be Governor of the colony opened the door for the acceptance of measures for stronger ecclesiastical control which had been suggested by the clergy. Representatives from the churches met at Saybrook in September of 1708. The preface to the articles of the Saybrook Platform stated the two goals sought in the deliberations of the Synod:

> the one holding forth the power of particular churches in the Management of Discipline confirmed by Scripture [and the other] to preserve, promote or recover the Peace and Edification of the Churches by Means of a Consociation of the Elders, and Churches or of an Association of Elders.[39]

The articles provided for the formation of county ministerial associations, for the formation of all churches within a county into a consociation, for the consociation's decision to be binding in the event of disputes, for the elder or elders of a church to exercise discipline within that church, and for an annual meeting of all associations within the General Association.[40] Basically, this was a modified form of Presbyterian polity.

---

37. John Wise, *A Vindication of the Government of New-England Churches* (Boston: John Boyles, 1772), 3, 20ff, 46, 56.

38. John Wise, *The Churches Quarrel Espoused* (Boston: John Boyles, 1715), "The Epistle Dedicatory," 5–26.

39. Text in Williston Walker, *Creeds and Platforms of Congregationalism*, 517–523.

40. Williston Walker, *Creeds and Platforms of Congregationalism*, 502ff.

The Saybrook Platform, although not totally accepted by all the churches in Connecticut, made the distinction between the Congregationalists of Connecticut and the Presbyterians of the middle colonies largely geographical; polity differences were not great. During and after the Great Awakening the work of itinerant revivalists was to be facilitated by this lack of clear denominational differences.

All of these changes in New England Congregationalism were related to the revivals of religion which occurred frequently during the 1730's and 1740's. Though the first Great Awakening only lasted from approximately 1735 to 1745, the dissension created by these revivals was to affect the course of New England Congregationalism for the remainder of the eighteenth century.

There was general agreement among the clergy of New England that the state of religion in the colonies during the early decades of the eighteenth century was at a low ebb.[41] The church declined in membership; the zeal of its members lessened. Solomon Stoddard's efforts to revive the piety of church members by insisting that the Lord's Supper was a means of regeneration, was part of a total effort to reinvigorate the New England churches. His efforts resulted in Northampton revivals in 1679, 1683, 1712, and 1718. Sporadic revivals were common throughout New England in the early years of the eighteenth century.

When Jonathan Edwards, Sr. was called to Northampton in 1727 to be the associate of his grandfather, Solomon Stoddard, he faced several challenges. Stoddard was the leader of a large segment of New England Congregationalism and it would not be easy to succeed such a commanding figure. When Stoddard died in 1729 Edwards took charge of one of the most important churches in New England. Naturally, the clergy of eastern Massachusetts wanted to meet this new parson, and, if possible, align him with their interests.

Edwards was invited to lecture in Boston in the spring of 1731, and he faced a difficult audience there. Besides the social-clerical alliances forming in the Boston area, there was increasing regional

---

41. George Leon Walker, *Some Aspects of Religious Life of New England* (New York: Silver, Burdett and Co., 1897), Ch II. "The Puritan Decline." Walker cites numerous sermon references pointing to this "decline of piety."

rivalry between the churches of Connecticut-western Massachusetts and those of eastern Massachusetts. A different religious response seemed to be characteristic of each. The unemotional, "catholic" religion of the upper class clergy (illustrated by those who formed the Brattle Street Church) had come to dominate Boston thinking. A spirit of tolerance for religious differences prevailed. On the other hand, the concern for personal piety and for revivalism, which Solomon Stoddard exemplified, dominated the western Massachusetts-Connecticut region. The "westerners" distrusted the mood of the Boston clergy.[42] The unexpressed mutual suspicion between the two areas was reflected in the two colleges, Yale and Harvard, each of which became symbolic of the spirit dominating its region.[43]

Edwards' address at Boston in 1731, "God Glorified in Man's Dependence," was published in the same year and evoked considerable debate. Edwards sought to recall the churches to a sense of

> an absolute and universal dependence of the redeemed on God . . . that the redeemed are in every thing directly, immediately, and entirely dependent on God: they are dependent on him for all, and are dependent on him every way.[44]

It was not new doctrine, but it marked a departure from the steadily increasing emphasis on human endeavor which was taking place in New England theology.

A few years after his public introduction to the Boston audience, Edwards noticed that Northampton "seemed to be full of the presence of God. There were remarkable tokens of God's presence in almost every house."[45] By 1740 the revival of religion had become widespread throughout the colonies. When George Whitefield arrived in New England in 1740, fresh from a journey through the middle colonies, the "awakening" took on a more controversial character. His theological convictions and his revivalistic measures

---

42. See Conrad Wright, *The Beginnings of Unitarianism in America* (Boston: Starr King Press, 1958), 33ff.

43. The resignation of Rector Timothy Cutler of Yale and two of his tutors in 1722 because of their "conversion" to the Anglican Church, brought the institution under great suspicion.

44. Jonathan Edwards, Sr., "God Glorified in Man's Dependence," *The Works of President Edwards, in Four Volumes* (New York: Leavitt, Trow & Co., 1844), Vol. IV.

45. Edwards, Sr., "A Narrative of Surprising Conversions," *Works*, Vol. III, 235.

soon brought latent hostility into the open. Soon after Whitefield left, Gilbert Tennent came on a preaching tour. Tennent had already rent the Presbyterian Church that same year by preaching his sermon, "The Danger of an Unconverted Ministry." James Davenport followed Tennent to New England, and it was mainly his influence that brought the revival to a crisis. The fact that he censured all ministers who disagreed with him doctrinally aroused resistance among the clergy. He was forced to leave New Haven in 1742 because he was "under the influence of enthusiastical impressions and impulses, and thereby disturbed in the rational faculties of his mind, and therefore to be pitied and compassionated. . . ."[46] He journeyed to Boston, where he was again made unwelcome, and when he refused to leave he was jailed and put on trial. The verdict was that he was *noncompos mentis* and therefore not guilty.[47] Each of these three men—Whitefield, Tennent, and Davenport—appealed to the less privileged social class and directed their abuse against the standing order. Their criticism of an educated ministry, attacks on the regular clergy, and itinerant preaching further broadened social divisions in New England.

Among the regular clergy of New England the controversy over the Great Awakening centered on two men: Jonathan Edwards, Sr. and Charles Chauncy; their doctrinal disagreements illuminate the theological divisions in eighteenth century American Congregationalism.[48]

Chauncy's dislike for the revivalistic techniques of the itinerant evangelists prompted him to collect material for an essay on the revival, which was published as *Seasonable Thoughts on the State of Religion in New England*.[49] Chauncy noted that the practices of the revivalists tended to undermine the religious unity of New England. His criticism of itineracy was based on his belief that it was an

---

46. Quoted in Joseph Tracy, *The Great Awakening. A History of the Revival of Religion in the Time of Edwards and Whitefield* (Boston: Tappan and Dennet, 1842), 240. See also Edwin Gaustad, *The Great Awakening in New England* (New York: Harper, 1957).

47. Quoted in Tracy, 248.

48. Chauncy did not speak for all of eastern Massachusetts; nor Edwards for all of western Massachusetts-Connecticut. They represent, however, a decided theological division within the churches which, later, became more pronounced.

49. Charles Chauncy, *Seasonable Thoughts on the State of Religion in New England* (Boston: Printed by Rogers and Fowle, for Samuel Eliot, 1743).

indirect criticism of the established clergy and, therefore, caused confusion and disorder.[50]

> There never was a Time, since the Settlement of New England, wherein there was so much bitter and rash judging; Parents condemning Their Children, and Children their Parents; Husbands their Wives and Wives their Husbands; Masters their Servants, and Servants their Masters; Ministers their People, and People their Ministers. Censoriousness, to a high degree, is indeed the constant Appendage of this religious Commotion.[51]

This fear that the standing order would be permanently disrupted caused some of Chauncy's colleagues, who had earlier shown sympathy with the revival, to lose their ardor for it. Chauncy and those who opposed the revival felt themselves to be the real defenders of the Congregational way, both in ecclesiastical and doctrinal matters.

Differing views on the nature of conversion plagued the entire first century of New England Congregationalism. Chauncy affirmed that the first step in conversion was an awareness of one's sinful condition. This conviction could be sudden or quite general. Even though emotional outbreaks might accompany the conviction, "this is only the first step towards it, a preparation of mind making way for it: Nor unless it end in this blessed change, will it signify anything, if persons are under ever so deep distress."[52] The process of conversion "means that glorious change, whereby men are turned from darkness to light; whereby of slaves to diverse lusts and pleasures, they are made the servants of God and righteousness."[53]

There was a noticeable shift from Edwards' early enthusiasm for the revivals to his later views. In his *Distinguishing Marks of a Work of the Spirit of God,* written in 1741, he found little to criticize in the revival which took place in Northampton. The *Thoughts on the Revival in New England,* 1742, was a more cautious endorsement of revivalistic measures. By the time that he published his *Treatise on Religious Affections* in 1746, his opponents were no longer the critics,

---

50. Chauncy, *Seasonable Thoughts,* 51.

51. Chauncy, *Seasonable Thoughts,* 168–170.

52. Charles Chauncy, *The Out-pouring of the Holy Spirit* (Boston: Printed by T. Fleet for D. Henchman and S. Eliot, 1742), 13.

53. Charles Chauncy, *The New Creature Describ'd* (Boston: Printed by G. Rogers for J. Edwards and S. Eliot, 1741), 18.

but the extreme proponents, of the revivals. Edwards, like Chauncy, said that the degree of emotional upheaval was no criterion of conversion: "There are many affections which do not arise from any light in the understanding."[54] Edwards' *Treatise on Religious Affections* was a prolonged discussion of the nature of religious experience. None of Edwards' works, however, expressed anything similar to Chauncy's fear of the methods of the revivalists. Nor did he share Chauncy's concern for the stability of the standing order in the face of the attack by Davenport, Tennent, Whitefield, and the like. Conrad Wright is essentially correct when he suggests that "between Chauncy and Edwards, therefore, the dividing line was at least as much one of temperament and diverse traditions as anything."[55]

There were many defenders of the techniques of the enthusiasts in eastern and southern Connecticut. Several churches encouraged itineracy, emotional extravagances, and the condemnation of the clergy. In November of 1741 a general Consociation meeting was called to deal with such dissent. The Separates, or Strict Congregationalists, as the supporters of the revivals were called, rejected the Saybrook Platform of 1708 and its control over individual churches and asserted their allegiance only to the Cambridge Platform.[56] The result of the Consociation of 1741 was that it became a penal offense for ministers or laymen, "or any foreigner," to go into the parish of any clergyman and preach without his invitation.[57] The extreme position of the Separates contributed to their extinction within a comparatively short time.

The terms, New Light and Old Light, ascribed to the defenders and opponents of the revivals, respectively, were common in the arguments of the day. Edwards, the leader of the New Lights, and Chauncy, the leader of the Old Lights, were the focal figures in a theological division in New England Congregationalism. The concerns of eastern Massachusetts and more particularly of the urban

---

54. Edwards, Sr., "Treatise on Religious Affections," *Works,* Vol. III, 109. See the introduction by John E. Smith in the Yale Edition of Edwards' *Works* (1960).

55. Wright, 25.

56. See S.L.Blake, *The Separates; or, Strict Congregationalists of New England* (Boston: The Pilgrim Press, 1902), and C.C.Goen, *Revivalism and Separatism in New England, 1740–1800* (New Haven: Yale University Press, 1962).

57. Blake, 43–45. Blake has quoted the essence of the "Act for Regulating Abuses and Correcting disorders in Ecclesiastical Affairs."

areas along the coast, where Old Light men were in the majority, were the stability of the standing order and the fear of political intrusion by foreign powers. The rural and inland areas, where the New Light men were in the majority, turned more attention to theological matters, for the isolation of western Massachusetts and Connecticut cushioned the fears which affected the coastal region. The reactions to the growth of Anglican churches illustrated this difference in concern. The urban Old Light men saw the Anglican invasion mainly as a political danger; the inland New Light men saw it as a theological danger, for the Anglican Church was thought to be a stronghold of Arminianism.[58]

The transformation of covenant theology, the innovations proposed by Solomon Stoddard, the break in the solidarity of Massachusetts Congregationalism, the developing bifurcation of New England along economic, social, and geographical lines, the alliance of the merchant class with dissenters, the distinction in polity structure between western Massachusetts and Connecticut Congregationalism, the theological issues raised by the Great Awakening—all these factors became intertwined and by the middle of the eighteenth century produced new problems for the church.

58. See J. H. Allen, "The Ecclesiastical Situation in New England Prior to the Revolution." *Papers of the American Society of Church History,* Vol. VIII (1897), 67–80.

CHAPTER THREE

The Theological Heritage of Jonathan Edwards the Younger

Jonathan Edwards the Younger accepted a parish of his own late in 1768, but for a little more than a year before that he served as a tutor at the College of New Jersey. In the same year that he joined the faculty, the college was looking for a President to succeed Samuel Finley. The tensions between the Old Side and the New Side Presbyterians were involved in the choice to be made. Since the uncomfortable reunion of the two groups ten years earlier, efforts had been made to placate the Old Side wing of the church and to win their support for the college. Now, the Old Side men sought to have one of their number, Francis Allison, elected President of the school. The New Side men who controlled the Board of Trustees felt that to elect such a man would be to betray the founders of the school, yet there was no outstanding New Side man who was satisfactory to the conservative wing of the church. The trustees, therefore, looked to Scotland and England for a man who was not embroiled in the division within American Presbyterianism. The name of John Witherspoon was chosen and in November, 1766, he was elected President of the College. However, Witherspoon's wife was reluctant to leave Scotland, and he declined the invitation, much to the chagrin of the trustees, who believed that he would be a healing agent for the church.[1] In September, 1767, the trustees elected Samuel Blair

---

1. *John Witherspoon Comes to America,* ed. L. H. Butterfield (Princeton: Princeton University Press, 1953). This volume is largely a collection of letters pertaining to the invitation of Witherspoon to assume the Presidency of the college. See Witherspoon's refusal, 37ff.

President. Blair was pastor of the Old South Church in Boston, and a 1760 graduate of the college. They also elected Hugh Williamson, an Old Side man, Professor of Mathematics and Moral Philosophy, and John Blair Professor of Divinity and Moral Philosophy. However, before Samuel Blair assumed the Presidency word reached the trustees that Witherspoon had found his way clear to accept it himself, and in December, 1767, after Blair graciously withdrew, the invitation was again extended to Witherspoon. In August, 1768, the new President arrived in Princetown. He became a symbol of the church's willingness to unite, insofar as basic ecclesiastical and theological differences would permit.

There is little extant evidence concerning Edwards' role as tutor during the period from November, 1767, to January, 1769, though we know he was responsible for training students in languages and advising in the minor crises which plague students of any generation. He must have made contacts throughout New Jersey and Connecticut because he preached frequently in New Brunswick, Maidenhead, Woodbridge, Elizabethtown, Kingston, and Trenton in New Jersey, and the White Haven Church in New Haven, Connecticut; these contacts were no doubt important for his later career. Certainly the contact at New Haven was. In 1769 he became pastor of the White Haven Church.

By now Edwards the Younger was well immersed in the theological and ecclesiastical problems of the American Reformed tradition. As a boy he had suffered through his father's dismissal from the Northampton Church; during succeeding years he was made aware that Edwardsean thought had avid and vocal supporters within the New England churches and within Presbyterianism. His eleven years among the Presbyterians made him intimately aware of the problems of that church. He was primarily acquainted with the New Side party, but could not escape a confrontation with Old Side principles.

In 1769, when Jonathan Edwards the Younger began his pastorate in New Haven, signs of political discontent were evident everywhere. The New Haven newspaper kept the citizens of the village aware of new demands laid upon the colonies by their mother country. Though many colonists were restive about England's colonial policies, the New World was not yet prepared to assume control of its own destiny. No united course of action had developed; the colonists were too busy quarreling among themselves. In 1765 James Otis remarked: "were these colonists left to themselves tomorrow, America would be a mere shambles of blood and confusion."[2]

The colonists only developed a sense of identity, separating them from their Old World ties, gradually. When England began to impose stricter demands on the colonies, common resentment shaped a spirit of independence. In 1764 Parliament passed the Sugar Act, laying a tax on imports. The primary aim of this bill was, of course, to provide revenue for the treasury, but in carrying out the act new and odious restrictions were made on the colonists; involved book-keeping was necessitated and the income from the tax was used to maintain troops in the colonies. The sore point was that the colonists had had no voice in the passage of the Sugar Act.

In the following year, 1765, the Stamp Act was passed. This bill went far beyond the Sugar Act and became a burden the Americans were not willing to bear. The paper needed for formal documents, newsprint, and playing cards was levied with a tax. Riots and plain disregard forced the distributors of the stamped paper out of business. Such outside restrictions on their freedom, imposed without their consent, brought the colonists into session at New York in October, 1765, to protest Parliament's actions.

The Stamp Act was repealed in March, 1766, but other repugnant impositions followed. In 1767 the Townshend Acts taxed imports into America, and the duties were collected at the ports of entry. Thus, the colonists' money was going into the pockets of tax commissioners living in their own midst. There was increasingly united and forceful rebellion against such taxation, and in 1768 British reinforcement troops arrived in America. It was obvious that armed conflict would soon erupt. On March 5, 1770, the Boston Massacre occurred; five colonists died and eight were wounded. No British troops suffered injury. News of the incident reached into all corners of the New World. In 1774, fifty-five representatives of the colonies met in Philadelphia and constituted the first Continental Congress.

The ensuing revolution and final victory left many problems for

---

2. James Otis, quoted in Edmund S. Morgan, *The Birth of the Republic, 1763–89* (Chicago: University of Chicago Press, 1956), 5.

the diplomats and statesmen. A workable form of government had to be devised and its ratification had to be won. Underlying the complicated and crucial debates over the formation of the nation were the obvious, yet hard-won, assumptions governing the minds of the colonists, that men had a right to happiness and self-government and should be free to determine their own destiny, without the pressures and controls of foreign power. From the revolution, a new humanized and secular spirit emerged.

The course of the American Reformed tradition did not escape the influence of this new spirit; the political theory of the day influenced the day's theology. The jurisdiction of King and Parliament was not, in theory, intolerable to the colonists. The King and those he governed had mutual obligations. The people could expect aid and protection if they adhered to the government; the government could expect the allegiance of the colonists if it did not transgress the natural rights of free Englishmen. Such political theory led to a powerful, if sometimes unstated, theological analogy. God, the sovereign ruler of the universe, could expect the loyalty and respect of His people; if man fulfilled his responsibility as a loyal church member, he could expect the blessings of God. But a God who damned and chose, irrespective of an individual's efforts, found little loyalty in revolutionary America.

Calvinism was on the defensive; the times demanded a theology stressing man's power and freedom, not his inability and sin. This caused two major problems for American Reformed theology. First of all, there were efforts to liberalize, gloss over, or openly attack the root structure of Calvinistic theology. The second problem, ironically, arose from efforts to defend the long-standing New England theology. Defense of a belief invariably brings a rigid re-shaping of that which is meant to be preserved. Thus, Edwards the Younger—who became a central figure in the defense of Calvinism and a critic of the liberalizing tendency of Reformed theology—and his colleagues, believing full well no doubt that they were working to preserve their tradition, and particularly to preserve the vision of Edwards, Sr., were themselves undermining both the tradition and vision, by casting them so rigidly that, in fact, they offered a new vision and pointed the American Reformed tradition in a new direction.

1. The Sources of Theological Change

Though the new nationalist spirit and assertion of independence and freedom were part and parcel of the shift away from the issues of the late seventeenth century in New England theology, the change in theological perspective was specifically brought about by a coalescence of thought involving three major theological issues: the effects of eighteenth century rationalism in England, with its expressions in Deism and the Arminian-Arian controversies; the Great Awakening and resulting debates over the nature of man; and the thought of Jonathan Edwards, Sr. with his re-interpretation of Calvinism in the light of rationalistic and Neo-Platonic thought.

A. *The English Rationalistic Strain*

In the Old World, intellectual changes which would lay the foundation for American dissent occurred during the late seventeenth and early eighteenth centuries. The work of Isaac Newton, the Deists, and John Locke placed new emphasis on the power of man's reason and expressed distrust for dogmatics and metaphysical speculation.

Newton's scientific work helped bring about a revolution in theology; his view of nature, not as a "given group of objects," but as "a certain 'horizon of Knowledge', of the comprehension of reality," enhanced the prestige of natural religion.[3] The time was marked by a changing focus of interest which shifted from the transcendental to the natural, the immanent, and the knowable. The Deists stressed the power of man's reason, and this is illustrated by John Toland's *Christianity Not Mysterious,* published in 1696. Toland insisted that there is nothing above reason in the Christian gospel. We are not required to believe contradictory and inconceivable doctrines; religious truths are mysterious only insofar as scientific truths are mysterious. In Toland's view, "that which is in every aspect mysterious and by definition beyond all understanding, must therefore remain as alien to faith as to knowledge."[4] Toland was joined in

---

3. Ernst Cassirer, *The Philosophy of the Enlightenment,* tr. F.C.A. Koelln and V.P. Pettigrove (Boston: Beacon Press, 1955), 55. See also R. S. Westfall, *Science and Religion in Seventeenth-Century England* (New Haven: Yale University Press, 1958).

4. John Toland, *Christianity Not Mysterious* (London: 1696), 133.

a deistic chorus by men such as Tindal, Chubb, Collins, and Shaftesbury.

Though John Locke was not a Deist, his voice was added to those who sought to emphasize the importance of reason in religious discourse. Reason was to be the judge of revelation. "Whatever God hath revealed is certainly true; no doubt can be made of it. This is the proper object of faith; but whether it be a divine revelation or no, reason must judge."[5] But, for Locke, reason was not the only test of right belief. Scripture, particularly the gospels, was equally important. His simple reliance on Scripture was characteristic of the thought of the period.

The emphasis on reason, the distrust of doctrine and metaphysics, the reliance on individual authority and interpretation, the new dependence on the simple words of Scripture, the need for demonstration and analysis, the conception of "natural religion"—these all came to shape the course of American thought.[6] Out of this general mood came the debates over Arianism and Arminianism which were to be of special importance for American theology.[7]

In 1712 the publication of Samuel Clarke's *The Scripture-Doctrine of the Trinity* marked the formal opening of the eighteenth century Arian controversy. In this particular essay Clarke attempted to determine if the orthodox interpretation of the Trinity was that of the New Testament. His criticism of the doctrine centered on its metaphysical presuppositions, which were, in his view, unscriptural. "The word, God, in Scripture, never signifies a complex Notion of *more persons than one;* but always means one *Person only, viz.,* either

---

5. John Locke, *An Essay Concerning Human Understanding,* ed. A. C. Fraser (Oxford: Clarendon Press, 1894), Book IV, Ch. XVIII, Sect. 10.

6. For further studies of this period see Basil Willey, *The Seventeenth Century Background* (London: Chatto & Windus, 1934); G. Cragg, *From Puritanism to the Age of Reason* (Cambridge, Eng.: Cambridge University Press, 1950), particularly the chapter entitled "The Religious Significance of John Locke"; R.I. Aaron, "Limits of Locke's Rationalism," in H.J.C. Grierson, *Seventeenth Century Studies* (Oxford: The Clarendon Press, 1938); Leslie Stephen, *History of English Thought in the Eighteenth Century* (New York: G. Putnam's Sons, 1876), Vols. I and II.

7. Throughout this study the term Arminianism refers to the movement in eighteenth century theology. The Arminianism of Charles Chauncy is not the same as that of the Remonstrants at the Synod of Dort; the term is used as it was in the context of eighteenth century thought and, therefore, I have not used quotation marks to distinguish the later development from the original expression in Jacob Arminius. For the origin of the movement see Carl Bangs, *Arminius: A Study in the Dutch Reformation* (Nashville: Abingdon Press, 1971).

the person of the Father singly or the person of the Son singly."[8] The Son is subordinate to the Father, for he derives His very being and His attributes from the Father and "the Father nothing from Him."[9]

Clarke's methodology is evidence of his relationship to the general theological mood of the early eighteenth century. He insisted, like many others of his time, that "a constant and sincere observance of all the Laws of Reason and obligations of Natural Religion, will unavoidably lead a man to Christianity."[10] The utter reasonableness and simplicity of Christianity stripped of orthodox accretions which covered scriptural truths, if re-established, would attract countless numbers. It was this belief in the power of reason, and the simplicity of Scripture and scriptural truth, which was so influential in eighteenth century theology, not only in England but also in America. Clarke, nevertheless, was attacked from all sides: orthodox and Unitarian alike, and the Arian controversy had begun.

The opening of the Arminian controversy in England can best be dated with the publication of John Taylor's *The Scripture Doctrine of Original Sin* in 1738.[11] Taylor denied outright that men are totally depraved by nature.[12] Because of Adam's sin men were "sub-

---

8. Samuel Clarke, *The Scripture-Doctrine of the Trinity* (London: James Knapton, 1712), 304.

9. Clarke, *The Scripture-Doctrine*, 304.

10. Samuel Clarke, *A Discourse Concerning the Unchangeable Obligations of Natural Religion, and the Truth and Certainty of the Christian Revelation* (London: Printed by W. Botham for J. Knapton, 1719), 15.

11. It is interesting to note the similar titles of the two books, *The Scripture-Doctrine of the Trinity* and *The Scripture Doctrine of Original Sin;* they are indicative of the method of approach of both men and of the general over-all interest of the period. In Europe the Arminians had been condemned at the Synod of Dort in 1619. Though this Synod had great effect on the continent, particularly in Holland where the leaders of Arminianism were located, it had comparatively little immediate influence in England. By the third decade of the eighteenth century, Arminianism of a far more liberal character than that of the Remonstrants became, in England, not heresy but orthodoxy. (R. Stromberg, *Religious Liberalism in Eighteenth-Century England* [London: Oxford University Press, 1954], 110.) In an age which felt comfortable with its own capabilities it was not surprising that a new impetus was given to Arminian theology. (See Paul Hazard, *European Thought in the Eighteenth Century* [New Haven: Yale University Press, 1954], Ch. 11, "Happiness.") The two major objections which rational theology had against Calvinism were that it made God author of evil, and that by denying free will it wrecked moral responsibility. These two issues determined the arguments of eighteenth century Arminian thought.

12. John Taylor, *Supplement to the Scripture Doctrine of Original Sin* (London: J. Waugh, 1767), 74ff.

jected to temporal Sorrow, Labour, and Death."[13] There was, however, no imputation of Adam's *guilt* to us for *"man's sinfulness consisting in* the Guilt of Adam's first Sin is language the Scripture no where useth."[14] Taylor argued that the doctrine of original sin contradicted belief in man's moral nature. If men were universally "disabled and opposed to Actions spiritually good, and wholly and continually inclined to all Evil, how are we moral agents? How are we capable of performing duty?"[15] So Taylor dismissed the idea that our nature is in any way to blame for our sin.

> ...If our Faculties are neglected, and run wild, we have no more Reason to blame our Nature, than the careless, slothful Indians, inhabiting a fruitful Country, have to quarrel with Providence for not furnishing them with the Conveniences which the ingenious and industrious European enjoyeth.[16]

He solved the question whether infants are inherently sinful by saying that "ignorance, and the absence of virtuous action in an Infant, is no Sin, because in that State it is incapable of it, through a natural Defect of Power."[17]

Taylor's method was the same as Samuel Clarke's. Both examined Scripture to determine the validity of doctrine. Taylor undertook the added task of confuting the deliberations of the Westminster Assembly, and a substantial part of his essay was devoted to a refutation of its doctrinal formulations. The tone of his approach to their deliberations is illustrated by the following passage.

> But lo! Men, met together in solemn Assembly, to settle religious truths, have pointed out these Texts to prove, that Christ will or may justly, condemn us to all Tortures to Body and Mind In Hell-First without Intermission, to all Eternity, only for One Sin committed thousands of Years before we had a Being, without taking into the Account of any of our personal Iniquities. This is perfectly astonishing. Surely the heavenly Rule of our Faith shall not always be thus trampled upon.[18]

13. John Taylor, *The Scripture Doctrine of Original Sin* (London: J. Waugh, 1738), 69.
14. Taylor, *The Scripture Doctrine,* 101.
15. Taylor, *The Scripture Doctrine,* 127.
16. Taylor, *The Scripture Doctrine*, 195.
17. Taylor, *The Scripture Doctrine,* 100.
18. Taylor, *The Scripture Doctrine,* 162.

The denial of original sin, the emphasis on moral responsibility and the concomitant assertion that the doctrine of total depravity denies moral responsibility, the rejection of creed and confession as legitimate bases for theological formulation, the stress on moral living, the reliance upon Scripture as a prime authority—these were the central contentions of Arminian theology in eighteenth century England. Little constructive interpretation of Christian doctrine was offered, but John Taylor did raise the issue to be discussed by the theologians of the day. He also set the stage for Jonathan Edwards, Sr., who would give the controversy metaphysical and theological depth.

B. The Great Awakening

These ideas and issues became important to Christians in the American colonies largely because of the Great Awakening. The revivals of 1734–35 and 1739–40 were begun on the frontier of New England, and were not well received by the more sophisticated and cosmopolitan churches of eastern Massachusetts. Earlier we noted the developing bifurcation of New England into two areas: eastern Massachusetts, and western Massachusetts-Connecticut. By this point in the eighteenth century the influence of the Boston elite had narrowed considerably, and the influence of the inland region had begun to reach eastward and northward. Until then, the western New England area had been isolated because of threatening local wars between Indians and white settlers, and because of the natural isolation of frontier communities. The inland areas were not hospitable to new currents of thought coming by way of Boston harbor. Thus, a geographical dividing line became a theological border as well, with the coastal ports as the "liberal" centers and the exponents of orthodoxy being found in the interior. This theological division of New England continued throughout the remainder of the century.

Theologically, the central issue raised by the Awakening concerned the relationship of "consistent" Calvinism with the call to repentance and the "new life." How does the preacher justify calling men to repent if they are predestined to election or damnation? Many of the eastern Massachusetts clergy who were critical of the revivals insisted that the demand for immediate conversion is not a necessary element in the message of the church, for God works gradually as well as instantaneously. One need not, then, become a "regenerate" member of the church, but rather attend to the "means of regeneration" with the expectation that at some future time one might be ready to publicly "own the covenant." It was not far from this to the affirmation that church membership was a natural action for a respectable member of the community. In contrast to the great revivalists, many came to assert that man has freedom to accept or reject; one's call is not predestined by God. The doctrine of predestination did not jibe with a rationalistic temper of mind.

C. Jonathan Edwards, Sr.

The work of Jonathan Edwards, Sr. brought the issues of the day into sharp focus. His theology was in part an effort to interpret the canons of the Synod of Dort (1619) to his age. The influence of John Locke, Isaac Newton, the Cambridge Platonists, and the stimulation from John Taylor and Samuel Clarke are clearly discernible in his writing, as is his New England theological heritage. Because of Edwards' position of influence at the time of great theological change in America, it was natural for him to set the pattern of issues for the debates of the later eighteenth century.

Edwards, Sr. brought new interpretations to the issues of New England theology, particularly regarding the nature and extent of sin and the question of man's responsibility. He sought a strict but reasoned acceptance of the Westminster formularies regarding original sin, and resisted modifications of the Puritan tradition which had occurred under covenant theology. During his time that tradition was even more immediately threatened by Arminian doctrine. Edwards reasserted the doctrine of the total depravity of man and radically re-interpreted the traditional theory of the imputation of Adam's sin to men, explaining the relationship of Adam and his descendants through a metaphysical theory of identity, an identity which makes Adam's sin truly man's sin. Men are not charged with the guilt of Adam's sin because it is imputed to them, but because it is actually *their* sin. This interpretation of the doctrine was resisted by the Old Calvinist party.[19] Intimately tied to this doctrine was the

---

19. See below, pp. 120ff.

problem of free will, one which had been raised numerous times in Christian history, but never so loudly as by the Arminians. Edwards tried to preserve the doctrine of the sovereignty of God as well as that of the responsibility of man by distinguishing between natural ability and moral inability. Man has the natural ability to fulfill the commands of God, but he is morally unable to turn to God because of his sin. The will is determined by the strongest motive which, because of man's sinful state, is always a corrupt motive. Therein lies man's inability to obey and to have any "hold" on God. Man is lost, and only the mercy and completely free action of God can save him. Thus, any "means of regeneration" are totally impossible, for God cannot be bound by any restrictions on his sovereignty.

These theological problems, the nature and extent of sin and the question of man's responsibility, were paramount in Edwards' thought and became the occasion for further debate during the last half of the eighteenth century.

2. Party Structure of New England Theology

As we turn specifically to the articles of debate which Jonathan Edwards the Younger inherited, we should note the developing party structure of New England theology during this period.

New interests shattered old alignments and three parties emerged, each of which had its roots in seventeenth century New England theology. The effect of the liberal theological movements in England was felt most strongly in the group labeled Arminian, whose representative figures included Charles Chauncy and Jonathan Mayhew. As the eighteenth century passed, Arminian thought, which was widespread in eastern Massachusetts, turned radically away from its Calvinistic base and eventually gave birth to the Unitarian movement in America.[20] It should be noted that the label Arminian suggested more than a particular view of human nature; these men reflected a new theological movement which involved greater reliance on human reason, an appreciation of natural religion, and a distrust for traditional formulations of doctrine.

A second party has traditionally been called the Old Calvinist,

---

20. See Conrad Wright, *The Beginnings of Unitarianism in America* (Boston: Starr King Press, 1955).

or moderate Calvinist, group. These men were concerned to preserve the theological traditions that had developed in New England during its first century and a half; they were strongly opposed to the "new" divinity of Jonathan Edwards, and they defended the Half Way Covenant. The preaching of the Old Calvinists placed less emphasis on the utter sovereignty and arbitrariness of God; rather, it stressed the ways to know God, the "means of regeneration." Less concern was expressed for the total and immediate conversion of the Christian; more emphasis was placed on the gradual transformation of the mind and heart of the unconverted. Thus, the Old Calvinist party was generally unenthusiastic about the revivals of religion which occurred in the 1730's and 1740's. Such representative Old Calvinists as Moses Hemmenway and William Hart were suspicious of hasty and extreme revivalistic measures. Through the latter half of the eighteenth century this general perspective continued to denote a separate party within the New England churches.

A third party—which was actually in sharper contrast to the other parties, Arminian and Old Calvinist, than they were to each other—was termed the New Divinity or Consistent Calvinist group. The most marked feature of the sermons and publications of the spokesmen of this group was the doctrine of the utter sovereignty of God over all aspects of creation. According to them, nothing is done without the grace of God; the world would crumble in an instant if God withdrew His sustaining hand. In the late seventeenth century Solomon Stoddard tried to recall New England Congregationalists to this belief, though he also stressed the "means of regeneration." Jonathan Edwards, who is usually regarded as the father of this New Divinity group, swept away the vestiges of the modified Calvinism of late seventeenth century New England. Stoddard and the New Divinity men who succeeded him possessed a revivalistic fervor which was a natural outgrowth of their distrust of anything man can do for his own salvation. Man needs to be regenerated, and they believed that God does this immediately.

The strain of New England theology represented by Edwards the Younger, Joseph Bellamy, and Samuel Hopkins took its departure from the theological labors of Jonathan Edwards, Sr. This New Divinity tradition remained in the forefront of the later eighteenth century theological debates, but these men departed subtly from the central thrust of their teacher's thought. All of them honed their dialectical skills on specific issues raised by Edwards, Sr. and challenged by the deviationists. But they were first of all defenders of Edwardsean theology, not original thinkers themselves, and in defending his thought they gave it a new and legalistic character.

An example of the rigidity into which New Divinity doctrine declined can be found in discussions of the nature of virtue. Between 1755 and 1758, Edwards, Sr. wrote the essay, "The Nature of True Virtue," suggesting that

> true virtue most essentially consists in benevolence to Being in General; or perhaps to speak more accurately, it is that consent, propensity and union of heart to Being in General, that is immediately exercised in a general goodwill. . . . Nothing is of the nature of true virtue in which God is not the first and the last.[21]

Any action of the heart not directed to God is sin; man's sin lies in his selfishness, or more particularly, in his self-love. Acts which are undertaken to soothe a bad conscience are not virtuous, but only illustrations of self-love. In his discussion, the distinctly Edwardsean mystic apprehension of God is presupposed. Elsewhere Edwards wrote:

> He that truly sees the divine, transcendent, supreme glory of those things which are divine, does as it were know their divinity intuitively; he not only argues that they are divine, but he sees that they are divine. . . . God is God, and distinguished from all other things, and exalted above them, chiefly by his divine beauty, which is infinitely diverse from all other beauty.—They therefore that see the stamp of this glory in divine things, they see divinity in them, they see God in them, and see them to be divine; because they see that in them wherein the truest idea of divinity does consist . . . a soul may have a kind of intuitive knowledge of the divinity of the things exhibited in the gospel. . . .[22]

Quite simply, the Neo-Platonic and mystic frame of mind from which Edwards, Sr. considered theological issues is absent in the work of his disciples, particularly in the work of his son. Whereas

---

21. Jonathan Edwards, Sr., "The Nature of True Virtue," *The Works of President Edwards, in Four Volumes* (New York: Leavitt, Trow and Co., 1844), Vol. II, 122.

22. Edwards, Sr., "Treatise Concerning Religious Affections," *Works*, Vol. II, 129.

Edwards, Sr. wrote about "disinterested benevolence" and "union of heart to Being in general," in the work of his disciples these concepts deteriorated into legal images.

Bellamy, Hopkins, and Edwards the Younger conceived of God as the "moral governor," "glorious monarch of the universe"; one finds in their work the image of God as King, ruler, magistrate—none of their teacher's Neo-Platonism. They spoke, therefore, of virtue in terms of the law. In the Biblical record they found the demands of the King of Kings; it is to these clearly and authoritatively stated injunctions that man must conform if he is to be virtuous. The law, Hopkins wrote,

> is the eternal rule of righteousness, which is essential to the being and glory of God's moral government and kingdom, and is in a sense the foundation of it, pointing out and declaring the duty of rational creatures, or moral agents, as what is fit and proper to be required of them, and containing the rule of God's conduct towards them, as their moral governor.[23]

Adherence to the law became the mark of true virtue. Sin, wrote Bellamy, "is a transgression of the law."[24] The effect of this subtle but far-reaching change in the understanding of virtue evolved the New Divinity theology into what might be called Calvinistic legalism. Their opponents did not have a radically different position which they sought to promulgate, but attacked the "consistent Calvinists" on the ground that their legalism, tied to reaffirmations of predestination, was unfit for the revolutionary era. The Arminian, for example, also thought in vaguely legalistic terms but stressed the benevolent, merciful, loving God, not the omnipotent King, while doing so.

This general tendency of the New Divinity, Old Calvinist, and Arminian pastors to stress the requirements of the Christian life, was perhaps inevitable given the changing and disrupting events of the day. Attacks on Christian doctrine were becoming more numerous during those revolutionary years. The influx of French deism, the essay of Ethan Allen, *Reason the Only Oracle of Man*

---

23. Samuel Hopkins, *The Works of Samuel Hopkins, D.D.*, ed. E. A. Park (Boston: Doctrinal Tract and Book Society, 1854), Vol. II, 522.

24. Joseph Bellamy, *An Essay on the Nature of Glory of the Gospel of Jesus Christ* (Washington: John Colerick, 1798), 113.

(1784), Tom Paine's *The Age of Reason* (1794), the rise of Republicanism, and the outspoken deism of some of its major leaders were all concrete evidence of threats to the "grand errand." Yale College, that bulwark of orthodoxy, was shaken by inroads of the Illuminati, Tom Paine, and general infidelity. Wine, liquor, and gambling found their way into Connecticut Hall. Thus, circumstances of the time encouraged emphasis on the duties and demands of Christian life. Sermons were preached to bring these matters to the attention of the people. In 1792, Edwards the Younger wrote:

> Never at least in this country was it so necessary as at the present time, that ministers be well skilled in the whole system of Christian theology; and that for these three reasons: that the country was never so knowing; that there were never so many heresies and erroneous opinions in the country; and that irreligion and profaneness never prevailed to so great a degree.[25]

"Opposition to Christianity both in faith and practice was never, at least in our country, so great and so increasing, as at the present day."[26] Edwards' friend and colleague, Benjamin Trumbull, put the cause for the moral decline succinctly:

> A state of war is peculiarly unfriendly to religion. It dissipates the mind, diminishes the degree of instruction, removes great numbers almost wholly from it, connects them with the most dangerous company, and presents them with the worst examples. It hardens and emboldens men in sin; is productive of profaneness, intemperance, disregard to property, violence and all licentious living.[27]

It is not, therefore, difficult to understand the fact that these theologians stressed requirements and duties. Christianity was seen as the bulwark of moral order, good government, and political prosperity. Edwards wrote: "Christianity . . . is most excellently adapted to the ends of restraining men from vice and promoting that general practice of strict morality, which is so essential to the political prosperity of any people."[28] Here again, when he came to the

---

25. Jonathan Edwards the Younger, "All Divine Truth Profitable," *The Works of Jonathan Edwards, D.D., with a Memoir of his Life and Character by Tyron Edwards* (Andover: Allen, Morrill and Wardwell, 1842), Vol. II, 118.

26. Edwards the Younger, *The Necessity of the Belief of Christianity by the Citizens of the State in order to our Political Prosperity* (Hartford: Hudson & Godwin, 1794), 43.

27. Benjamin Trumbull, *A Complete History of Connecticut, Civil and Ecclesiastical* (Hartford: Hudson & Goodwin, 1797), Vol. II, 18.

28. Edwards the Younger, *The Necessity of Belief*, 8–9.

question of virtue he saw it as a legalistic matter of "strict morality," and that is a radical change of perspective from his father's more philosophical discussions of the subject. In *The Necessity of Belief of Christianity by the Citizens of the State,* Edwards the Younger wrote,

> On the plan of the gospel the motive [to virtue] is endless misery, proportioned in degree to the demerit of the person punished. On the infidel plan it is a merciful chastisement, which is to continue no longer than till the subject shall repent. And as every sinner will naturally flatter himself, that he shall repent as soon as he shall find his punishment to be intolerable; so all the punishment, which in this plan he will expect, is one that shall continue but for a moment, after it have become extreme or intolerable. And whether this momentary extreme punishment be an equal restraint or vice, as the endless misery threatened in the gospel, let every man judge. . . . Therefore as even this, the most plausible scheme of infidelity, cuts the sinews of morality and opens the flood-gates of vice; the prevalence of it in our state would be a very great political evil.[29]

One must sympathize with the dilemma of the New Divinity men. They had to defend Calvinism against the encroachments of Arminianism and also had to preach a relevant word to their congregations who were living in an era which emphasized man's freedom and desire for self-determination. The circumstances of the time made the decline of New Divinity doctrine almost inevitable.

Jonathan Edwards the Younger regarded himself as a faithful member of the New Divinity tradition and was convinced that the group was dominant.

> I believe a majority of the ministers mean to embrace the system of my father and Dr. Bellamy, a few are in Whitby's, Taylor's, and Clarke's scheme; a number mean to think, & preach after the manner of Watts and Doddridge; and a considerable number do not think or study enough to have any distinct scheme at all.[30]

His "Remarks on the Improvement in Theology Made by His Father, President Edwards" shows clearly that he saw no conflict between his theological position and that of his illustrious father. However, he also noted with favor the additional interpretations

---

29. Edwards the Younger, *The Necessity of Belief,* 13–14.
30. Ms. letter of February 8, 1787, from Jonathan Edwards the Younger to John Erskine (Andover–Newton Seminary Library).

made by Samuel Hopkins and Joseph Bellamy. We can probably assume that he himself did not understand the subtler distinctions between the thought of his father and that which he and his colleagues were practicing.

In actuality, Edwards the Younger did not always observe the three-fold distinction between Arminian, Old Calvinist, and New Divinity. In a letter to his niece, Sarah Burr, his underlying conviction that one was either of the Edwardsean stamp or an Arminian is evident.

> ... I am pleased wh the notice wh you have taken of the difference between Arminians & Calvinists in two important respects. There are many other marks of distinction. Particularly it is worthy of notice that they have always differed upon five particular points of doctrine wh are therefore by way of eminence [?] called the *Five Points*. They are these, *election, original sin, special grace in conversion, justification by faith alone, saints perseverance*. Each of these all the thorough Calvinists hold, & all thorough Arminians deny. There are also many half-way Calvinists & half-way Arminians, who endeavor to halve matters, but one really as far from the true & as dangerous in their tenets as any.[31]

Within the New Divinity circle there was real *esprit de corps*. Edwards would frequently counsel and exchange books and theological gossip with other men of this tradition. From extant correspondence among these New England clergy we learn that they would parcel out assignments of theological rebuttal to works which had just appeared, and pass around new books with comments about weak and strong points of a particular essay. Many of the theological discussions of the day were carried on by mail. In the early 1780's Edwards and Samuel Hopkins had been discussing a theological point when, with an almost audible sigh of relief, Edwards brought the discussion to a close.

New Haven Oct 12, 1785

Revd Sir

In the midst of the bustle of commencement I had not time to write even a short letter. Immediately after commencement, I went a long journey & am but lately returned & now I embrace this first opportunity to acknowledge your favor of Aug 16th. You say "adieu

---

31. Ms. letter of March 17, 1770, from Jonathan Edwards the Younger to Sarah Burr (Yale University Library).

once more to this controversy on my part", & I echo the voice. I am fond of correspondence with my friends, & not adverse, as you perhaps will allow to disputation. But when a controversy is run out, it is not worth while to continue it for the sake of having the *last word.* I do not see yt in your last letter the argument is carried on to any further steps, or yt the ground of it is materially shifted, from that on which it stood in some of our former epistles. Of course, if I were to make a particular answer, it must for substance be a repetition of what I have already sent you this being the case, it is high time to drop the subject, & accordingly I do drop it.

What is become of the controversy between Messrs Tappan & Spring. I have not heard. If Mr. Tappan has answered the Dialogue on Duty, I wish to see it; & if you will send it me, I will remit you the money.

With proper salutations to Mrs. Hopkins Miss Bertha & c I am,

Your brother & servant,
Jona Edwards[32]

An illustration of Edwards the Younger in an apologetic role, illustrating his desire not to unnecessarily offend those who might otherwise be sympathetic to the New Divinity perspective, is his attempt to convince Samuel Hopkins that the section on "willing to be damned for the glory of God" be excluded from the latter's *System of Doctrines.*[33] We should understand that these personal relationships helped to cement the theological tradition of New Divinity men.

This was, in brief, the theological heritage of Jonathan Edwards the Younger.

---

32. Ms. Letter of Oct. 12, 1785, from Jonathan Edwards the Younger to Samuel Hopkins (Yale University Library). Samuel Spring, a graduate of Princeton in 1771, and a student of Bellamy and Hopkins, was an ardent New Divinity spokesman. David Tappan, appointed as Hollis Professor of Divinity at Harvard, was more properly called an Old Calvinist.

33. Ms. Letter of October 29, 1795, from Jonathan Edwards the Younger to Samuel Hopkins (Yale University Library).

... I hear you intend to insert your section on Being willing to be damned. I have mentioned it to all the ministers of this neighbourhood, friendly to the System, they all wish it may not be inserted, particular[ly] Mr. Upson. The System is now in credit & I wish nothing may done to hurt the credit of it & to prevent its doing good. The enemy of the truth will take advantage of that section & triumph. Now they are silent. Besides, it would be an injury to the property of Thomas Andrews [publisher]; & certainly they will be asking you to correct it, do not imagine that you are empowered to hurt the sale of the work; if they did, they wo'd not suffer you to meddle with it. Indeed I think you cannot insert that section consistently with justice to them. I will subscribe for one half a dozen, if you will print that section in a separate pamphlet. ...

——————————————————

CHAPTER FOUR

The White Haven Church

To be pastor to a congregation in eighteenth century New England involved responsibilities which are not always duplicated today. Certainly one visited the sick, participated in civic functions, spoke to the particular social issues of the day, and attempted to bring unity to frequently warring factions. But beyond these duties, a church expected its pastor to be a theologian who would meet the theological needs of the particular congregation and lead them in time of controversy. Fulfillment of such a duty could bring dissension, however, if the desires of the congregation altered, or if the perspective of the minister changed.

In December, 1768, Jonathan Edwards the Younger, then twenty-three years old, was called to be pastor of the White Haven Church in New Haven, Connecticut, where he had preached several times after his graduation from the College of New Jersey in 1765. The congregation knew well the theological heritage from which their new pastor came. The White Haven Church had been formed during the heat of the Great Awakening. Before 1742, New Haven had only one Congregational Church. Joseph Noyes became its minister in 1715 and won recognition as a leading Congregational churchman.

Trouble began in New Haven with the coming of the itinerant revivalists. When George Whitefield stopped at New Haven during his New England tour in 1740, Noyes invited him to his pulpit, though he was unenthusiastic about Whitefield's revival work. Shortly after Whitefield's visit, James Davenport came uninvited on a missionary tour of New England and also visited New Haven. Because Noyes received the work of the itinerant evangelists coolly,

Davenport, speaking from Noyes' own pulpit, denounced him as an "unconverted man, a wolf in sheep's clothing and a destroyer of souls."[1] Suspicion about their pastor's religious zeal, which Whitefield had sown in the minds of Noyes' congregation, was thus cultivated by Davenport. The visits of these two men caused some of Noyes' parishioners to question his leadership, for his "religious fervor" compared quite unfavorably with that of the two revivalists. At a meeting on September 21, 1741, Noyes challenged Davenport to substantiate the charges which he had made. Davenport answered by reasserting that Noyes was "an unconverted man and his people to be as sheep without a shepherd, and prayed that what he had now said, might be a means of his and their conversion. . . ."[2]

The ultimate result of this controversy was a request by thirty-eight members for a division of the society.

> A Considerable number of the Brethren of the first Church of Christ in New Haven being agreaved with the conduct and preaching of the Revd Mr. Joseph Noyes the then Pastor of Said Church the Church being then Congregational as it had even been from its beginning Said agreaved sought a redress of their greavances according to the Congregational Rule of Discipline but could not obtain one but instead Revd. Mr. Noyes lead the remaining Body of the Church or the Greater part thereof to Vote in a different rule of discipline whereby all hopes of a redress of greavance in the Congregational way was frustrated upon which said Secluded members more agreaved after many difficulties called on a Council of ministers to advise and direct them under their distressed Circumstances who came accordingly and having searched the record of Said first Church came to Sundry conclusions and restablished them upon the Antient Basis of the first Church of Christ in New Haven upon their assenting and consenting to the Doctrine of faith antiently embraced by said Church and renewing their covent [sic]. . . .[3]

The protestors wished to have their complaints against their minister investigated either by the church itself or by a council agreed

1. Quoted in Samuel Dutton, *History of the North Church in New Haven* (New Haven: A. H. Maltby, 1842), 24.

2. Leonard Bacon, *Thirteen Historical Discourses, on the Completion of Two Hundred Years, From the Beginning of the First Church in New Haven* (New Haven: Durrie and Peck, 1839), 217. See also Mary H. Mitchell, *History of the United Church of New Haven* (New Haven: The United Church, 1942).

3. *Records of the White Haven Church,* 1. These manuscript records are in the possession of the United Church, New Haven, Connecticut.

upon by the two parties. The Noyes faction, however, sought to bring the matter before the Consociation, a majority of whose members favored the pastor. Since the Noyes faction still controlled the deliberations of the society, the dissenters felt compelled to withdraw from the church and establish their own place of meeting. On May 7, 1742, these New Lights were constituted a Congregational Church—called the White Haven Church—by four ministers who supported their position: Samuel Cook, John Graham, Elisha Kent, and Joseph Bellamy.[4] At the same time, efforts were made in the still-undivided Society to call a colleague to assist Noyes. The dissenters wanted someone who would support their views but Noyes resisted these efforts. The plans of the separate White Haven Church went forward and in 1744 a meeting house was erected on the south-east corner of Elm and Church streets. For the ensuing fifteen years there were continuous efforts to unite or divide the Society as a whole, but it was not until 1759 that the division was formalized.[5]

---

4. It is important to keep in mind the distinction between Society and Church. As long as New Haven had only one Congregational Church there was only one Society. The members of the Society were taxed for the support of the minister and the various expenses of the Church. The Toleration proviso of 1708 gave other religious groups freedom from ecclesiastical taxation. Yet, when the White Haven Church split from the First Church, the Society was not divided and thus members of the schism group were still called upon for the financial support of Mr. Noyes. It was not until 1759 that the White Haven *Society* was formed and given the approval of the legislature.

5. In an effort to prevent the secession of New Light factions from the Churches of Connecticut the legislature passed a law which would prevent uninvited clergymen from entering the various parishes of the state (Benjamin Trumbull, *A Complete History of Connecticut, Civil and Ecclesiastical* [New Haven: Maltby, Goldsmith and Co., 1818], Vol. II, 163ff). Trumbull believed that this law was formulated by the New Haven Church (165n). One of the first clergymen accused of breaking this law was Samuel Finley, later to become President of the College of New Jersey, who was forcibly removed from the state after preaching at a secession church in Milford. Finley's repeated visits to Connecticut forced the Association of New Haven to state that no member of the Presbytery of New Brunswick should be admitted into any of their pulpits, until satisfaction had been made for Mr. Finley's preaching within their bounds. Trumbull, *A Complete History of Connecticut*, Vol. II, 263; Also, Joseph Tracy, *The Great Awakening* (Boston: Tappan & Dennet, 1842), 308.

A specific prohibition of Whitefield was passed by the General Association of Connecticut:
Whereas there has of late years been many errors in doctrine and disorders in practice, prevailing in the churches in this land, which seem to have a threatening aspect upon the churches; and whereas Mr. George Whitefield has been the promoter, or at least the faulty occasion, of many of these errors and disorders; this association think it needful for them to declare, that if the said Mr. Whitefield should make his progress through this government, it would by no means be advisable for any of our ministers to admit him into their pulpits, or for any of our people to attend his administrations. *The Records of the General Association of ye Colony of Connecticut, 1738–1799* (Hartford: Case, Lockwood and Brainerd Company, 1888), 17–18.

In the meantime, visiting clergymen of New Light sympathies supplied the pulpit of the secession church until September of 1751. At that time the new church called Samuel Bird, who had been dismissed from the church at Dunstable, Massachusetts, for his New Light sympathies, to be their pastor. A council composed of Edwardsean men installed Mr. Bird. In the meantime, Yale College established its own church, perhaps to escape involvement in these ecclesiastical dissensions, but probably also to provide a more student-oriented program.[6]

The increasing strength of the New Light faction in New Haven prompted the First Church to petition the Assembly to decree either:

1) that those persons who have dissented as aforesaid, and their adherents, be disenabled to act or vote in any meeting of this society, in any matter that respects the ministry and the buildings or repairing the meeting house of the society; or

2) that the said dissenters and their adherents be set off from this Society, so as that Said Society may need and vote respecting the matters aforesaid, exclusive of and without taxing or having regard to said dissenters and their adherents in such way and manner as said General Assembly shall see fit.[7]

Because of New Light objection the Assembly refused to grant either motion. One of the issues at stake was the disposition of the property of the First Church; the secession church wanted its share of the Society's holdings. This issue could not be decided until the formal division of the Society was completed.

In January, 1757, a new request for the division of the Society into two distinct bodies was sent to the Assembly. Members of the two churches were requested to declare themselves in either "Mr. Noyes' party" or "Mr. Bird's party." The result of this poll indicated

---

6. Though Mr. Noyes' church had been the College Church, the officials of Yale felt that the dissension between the Congregational Churches of New Haven was affecting the life of the school. Thus, a college church was formed in 1757. Concurrent efforts were made to establish a Professorship of Divinity, whose occupant would also serve as college pastor. In 1757 Naphtali Daggett was chosen to fill both positions. See Ralph H. Gabriel, *Religion and Learning at Yale; The Church of Christ in the College and University, 1757–1957* (New Haven: Yale University Press, 1958).

7. Bacon, 235.

the great growth of the New Light party, for it outnumbered the Noyes' group, 212 to 111.[8] Surprised at their support, the New Light majority withdrew the division petition and proceeded to elect Mr. Bird the minister of the whole society. It was voted that thereafter society meetings would be held in the secession church and that, since Mr. Noyes had not attended public worship at the place appointed by the society, "it is the desire of this society that he would desist from his ministerial labors in this place, and that no farther [sic] provision will be made by this society for his support and maintenance."[9]

In the following year, 1758, over the objection of the society Mr. Chauncey Whittelsey was installed as Noyes' colleague in the First Church.[10] This move, together with the First Church's refusal to admit that the property of the church belonged to the Society, prompted the Society to renew its appeal to the Assembly for a formal division. In January, 1759, this request was granted, and the division was formalized. Noyes' Church was called the First Society and the secession church was named the White Haven Society; the two churches had no communion in the immediate years following. Noyes died in 1761 and Whittelsey assumed charge of the First Church. In 1768 Bird asked to be relieved of his duties at the White Haven Church and Jonathan Edwards the Younger was chosen as his successor.[11]

The call extended to Jonathan Edwards in 1768 was not unanimous; he was invited only after a long debate within the church. The controversy involved the church's acceptance of the Half Way

---

8. Dutton, 57.

9. Bacon, 237.

10. Chauncey Whittelsey, a tutor at Yale College, had been involved in the New Light-Old Light controversy for some time. The remark made by David Brainerd, the young missionary friend of the Edwards' family, about Whittelsey, "I believe he has no more grace than the chair I am leaning upon," resulted in Brainerd's dismissal from the College. The incident increased the tension between the two factions.

11. Notation in the *Records of the White Haven Church*.

At a meeting of the Church in White Haven Sept 16th 1768—Mr. Jonathan Edwards a Candidate for the Ministry having for some time past been preaching the Gospel among us and this Church being well satisfied with his Ministerial Gifts & Accomplishments Voted, that an Invitation be given to him the Mr. Edwards, to settle in the work of the Ministry among us as the Pastor of this Church & that the Necessary Steps in order to accomplish it be taken as soon as prudence shall direct. . . .

Covenant. It had debated the issue in 1760 and a majority of the
members had decided to accept its practice.[12] Before Edwards
agreed to accept the call to the White Haven Church it re-opened
the question and rescinded its previous action rejecting the Covenant.

> Whereas on the 6th Day of August in the Year 1760 it was voted by
> this Church that the Infants of such as own the Covenant (being civil
> and moral persons) shall be admitted to baptism—upon further Con-
> sideration and Enquiry into the Qualifications, required by the Gos-
> pel of Christ for admission to Baptism this Church is of opinion that
> the same Qualifications are Necessary for Admitting Persons to re-
> ceive Baptism for themselves or Children as for admission to full
> communion, and that none ought to be admitted but those who made
> a Credible Profession of real Christianity.
>
> Test. Daniel Lyman Moderator[13]
> (6th Dec., 1768)

There is no certain evidence that this was done at Edwards' request,
but it is quite probable. With the way thus cleared, Edwards accepted the call.

> To the Church of Christ in New Haven
> Dearly Beloved Brethren
> Whereas it hath pleased our common Lord & Master to incline
> your hearts to invite & elect me to the Pastoral Office in this Church;
> I would hereby signify to you that after much solemn Consideration
> and earnest application to the *Wonderful Counsellor* for his guidance in
> this important Matter I have been inclined to accept your Invitation;
> devoting myself wholly to the Great Work & begging as with your
> Assistance both by Prayer and Counsel, as the Assistance of him *who*

---

12. *Records of the White Haven Church.* The notation regarding the acceptance of the
Half Way Covenant is in the minutes of the church for August 6, 1760.

> The Church being meet to consider & determine what is duty concerning Children's
> being admitted to Baptism upon their Parents owning & consenting to the covenant
> which shall be agreed upon by this Church. Voted & determined by a great majority:
> that the Infants of such as own the Covenant (being civil & moral persons) shall be
> admitted to baptism.
>
> Test. Samuel Bird Pastor

13. *Records of the White Haven Church,* December 6, 1768.

is made Head over all things to the church Wishing that Grace Mercy & Peace may be multiplied unto you.

> I am Brethren Yours in the Gospel of our common Lord
>
> Jonathan Edwards

New Haven, December 15th, 1768.[14]

Not all the members of the White Haven Church supported the rejection of the Half Way Covenant, and when Edwards was ordained on January 5, 1769, a group protested his installation as pastor. The dissenters attempted to install a colleague pastor more in sympathy with their views, but this was resisted by the Edwards faction. Therefore, in September, 1769, eight months after Edwards was installed, the advocates of the Half Way Covenant withdrew and were constituted in June of 1771 as the Fair Haven Church.[15] In that same year Ezra Stiles estimated the membership of the Fair Haven Church at 200 members, which was considerably smaller than the 480 members at the White Haven Church and the 500 members of the First Congregational Church.[16]

---

14. *Records of the White Haven Church,* December 15, 1768.

15. *Records of the Fair Haven Church,* in possession of the United Church, New Haven. Note that the council which ordained Edwards heard the objection offered by those who opposed him. The council agreed that it would "set them off if upon trial they could not be edified or contented under his ministry." F. Writing in 1770 Edwards indicated that the new Fair Haven Church was a zealous group. (The addressee of the following letter is unknown; it may have been written to Joseph Hawley of Hadley, Massachusetts.)

Northampton June 27, 1770

Revd Sir,

Being at this town, & having this opportunity to write at last so as yt it will probably reach you, I gladly embrace it, to keep up the acquaintance, wh once subsisted between you & our family. —you have doubtless heard of my settlement at New Haven & of the difficulties wh have obtained there. Mr. Bird is a preaching there in the [undecipherable] & trades in the week-time. His party is but small, but he has infused zeal into em to that degree that they are about building a meeting house. As to my own friends they appear firmly attached to me & that upon principle; therefore I esteem their friendship proper to be relied on.

You cannot have remained wholly ignorant of the controversies which have appeared generally thro our colony. . . . There seems to be a vigorous attack from all quarters on the truth. But might is the power of truth & I hope will prevail.

If I have not acted impertinently in writing to you, I shod be glad whenever you have a leisure hour, wh you cannot better emply, yt you would also write me a line. With due respect to Mrs. Hawley,

I am, your humble sert.

Jona Edwards.

Ms. letter of June 27, 1770, from Jonathan Edwards to J. Hawley (?) (Harvard University Library).

16. *The Literary Diary of Ezra Stiles,* ed. Franklin B. Dexter (New York: C. Scribner's Sons, 1901), Vol. I, 283–284; and *Extracts From the Itineraries and Other Miscellanies of Ezra Stiles,* ed. Franklin B. Dexter (New Haven: Yale University Press, 1916), 42–50.

The issue of "owning the covenant" remained a point of contention throughout Edwards' ministry. He insisted that each new member of the church give public testimony of his experience of regeneration; he would allow no private testimonies. The account of one's religious experience was a necessary corollary to accepting the covenant of the church. The minutes of a church meeting in January, 1771, indicate that this issue had come up for discussion and that the church reaffirmed its belief that "owning the covenant" involved public expression of regeneration.

> It was considered whether the church could not allow persons of civil moral lives to own the *covenant of grace* & also have their children baptised. Upon this it was observed that to own the covenant of grace implies grace in the heart, which no unregenerate person hath. But that if a person is possessed of true grace, he ought not only to own the covenant of grace & have his children baptised, but also to come into full communion.[17]

No exceptions were to be made, even if full members of the First Church or the Fair Haven Church wished to join the White Haven Church.

So Edwards began his ministry in a difficult situation. Though, at the time of his call, the majority of the members of the White Haven Church desired the kind of leadership and theological perspective that Edwards the Younger could give, theological debate was to dominate his ministry.

---

17. *Records of the White Haven Church,* January 22, 1771.

CHAPTER FIVE

Pastoral Labors

It was not until well into the eighteenth century that New Haven became an important economic and cultural center in New England. In earlier years the growth of the village was hampered by its inadequate harbor and the scarcity of roads leading inland. As New England developed its commercial potential, New Haven grew, and its facilities expanded. By the pre-revolutionary war years it was a thriving coastal town. New roads were built and the harbor improved. Ties with sister ports and with inland markets were increased and more foreign ships made New Haven a port of call.[1] Prominent citizens of the town also participated in plans to colonize the "west." As a result of these new activities an increasing number of rural New Englanders entered New Haven and other coastal towns to undertake commercial ventures. There evolved among the citizenry a social distinction between the "town born" and the "interlopers," and the resultant competition in business and the professions gave the town's commercial life new vitality.[2] These factors contributed to New Haven's growth from a village of 1400 in 1748, to a town of 8,000 in 1774.[3]

By the 1780's the physical facilities of the town had expanded greatly. All the important buildings were located around the green. At the recent site of the Schubert Theatre were the post office and

---

1. Rollin Osterweis, *Three Centuries of New Haven, 1638–1938* (New Haven: Yale University Press, 1953), Chapters X and XI.
2. Osterweis, Chapters X, XI, XII are particularly illuminating concerning the growing self-consciousness of the New Haven people.
3. Osterweis, 102.

general store; nearby, on the corner of Church and Chapel Streets, was the combination inn and book store. On the western edge of the green were Hopkins Grammar School and the city jail. Two of the three traditional churches—First Church and Fair Haven (North) Church—were in positions similar to those which they occupy today. The Courthouse stood at the present location of Trinity Church. On the south-east corner of Church and Elm was the White Haven Church. Yale College, which had 260 undergraduates in 1784, was composed of three buildings and occupied an imposing place in the center of the town. By modern standards the town of New Haven was rural in character; its contacts with surrounding centers were still limited, but it was increasing in importance as a center of Connecticut life.[4]

The parsonage of the White Haven Church was located just off the central green, north of the intersection of Elm and Church Streets; it was here that Edwards brought his new wife late in 1770. He had met Mary Porter in the summer of 1765 while he was a student of Samuel Hopkins in Great Barrington, Massachusetts. Though little of their correspondence is extant, we do know that they wrote frequently during the years after their first meeting. A letter, written shortly before their marriage, offers rich insight into an episode in eighteenth century romance.

New Haven, July 25, 1770

Dear Miss Polly,

You doubtless remember that just before we last parted, I told you that if a safe opportunity had [occurred, in] fulness to my own word, & especially from the strong affection, which I have not only professed, but do daily feel for you, I have been constantly looking out for a safe opportunity. Hitherto I have looked out in vain, but now one offers altogether such as I desire with eagerness therefore do I embrace it—Why? to flatter you—to send you a formal love letter, stuffed with the ordinary compliments, which one delivered forth on such occasions, as mere matter of form? or with the most high strained gyricks, which however extravagant, one frequently uttered

4. For detailed descriptions of the physical characteristics of New Haven in this period see Osterweis, 157ff; also F. Dexter, "New Haven in 1784," in *A Selection from the Miscellaneous Historical Papers of Fifty Years* (New Haven: Tuttle, Morehouse & Taylor Company, 1918), 116–132.

with an heart as indifferent as the most ordinary chit-chat—No—
these things are for the most part said or written by pretended lovers
because they know not what else to say, not having affection enough
to excite them to utter themselves with unadorned simplicity which
over more attends & cannot but express a sincere love. But I write to
let you know that I neither have nor can forget you. How often, do
my thoughts recur to her, whose esteem at least, I hope I have
gained, & whom ere long I hope to embrace as my bosom friend. O
How tedius is the time! how fully & heavely do the hours move
along, which intervene & prevent the arrival of the happy day!—
Patience in other things is a virtue. But can it be a virtue in such a
case as this? Can it be a virtue to be willing that the time should be
protracted?—No—such willingness would argue the offence of an
affection which I am proud to own & free to boast of—this affection
give me leave to assure you, is in my breast, kindled even into a
flame, an affection founded in virtue & true friendship and purified I
hope by the exercise of true religion. O my dear Polly may I not
flatter myself that there is something corresponding to it, in your
heart. If there is then I have a happiness, which all the gold of Ophir
is not sufficient to purchase Yea I enjoy a happiness even in the
imagination & hope of it. This happiness I shall for the present take
to myself; hoping for yet more demonstrative evidence of the reality
of that upon which it is founded.

As [my] state since I left you, I have been well, till last week,
which by an illness occasioned as I suppose by, a cold, I was confined
for several days, but th'o divine goodness am now in a great measure
recovered. By the [. . .] of providence I shall be with you on the 19th
or 14th of August—In the meantime if you have an opportunity, I
hope I shall receive in a letter a testimony of your regard for me. Be
assured nothing at present could be more acceptable to me—With
the strongest assurance of friendship, affection, & the most tender
love permit me to subscribe myself,

Your constant admirer & most
obedient humble servant
Jona Edwards.[5]

This formal display of warmth was characteristic of Edwards
throughout his life. A letter from his bride-to-be showed similar
reserve.

---

5. Ms. Letter of July 25, 1770, from Jonathan Edwards the Younger to Mary Porter
(Yale University Library).

Hadley, Sept 23, 1770

Dear Sir

If I could flatter myself that a letter from me, would be as agreeable to you, as you seem to think it will, I should with double pleasure, write to you;—but I am fully sensible that there will be nothing, to recommend it to you—I received your kind letters by your Brother & you may believe they was welcome to me; I assure you nothing could be more agreeable to me at present; than to receive those [evidences] of an unfeigned Love & friendship which you so often profess—you may believe, that you have not bestowed your love where you do not meet with an equal return—but why do I tell you of that; I hope you have a better opinion of me, than to suppose I should consent to give my hand, where I had not first given my heart.—yea Dear Sir I am not ashamed to own, that I am yours—what tho the sacred ceremony is not past; that it is true [it] can bind us more closely together—but the want of it cannot part us.

I shall send this by the waggon that caries [sic] my things & shall expect a letter by him if he returns this way as I propose he will

Your affectionate friend
Mary Porter[6]

Later in the same year Jonathan Edwards and Mary Porter were married in Hadley, Massachusetts, by Samuel Hopkins.

The Edwardses had four children but we know little about them; the name of one child who died in infancy is even lost. Their daughters, Jerusha and Mary, were married rather late in life. Their son, Jonathan Walter, became a successful lawyer in Hartford and advised his father in financial matters.[7]

A tragedy occurred twelve years after their marriage when Mrs. Edwards was drowned while riding in her buggy to do some family chores. The account of the accident in the New Haven newspaper, *The Connecticut Journal,* for July 4, 1782, reads in part:

> . . . She rode out in a chair, with a view to transact some domestic affairs with a family about two miles from Town, and coming to the

6. Ms. Letter of September 23, 1770, from Mary Porter to Jonathan Edwards the Younger (Yale University Library).

7. Their birthdates: Mary, July 11, 1773; Jonathan Walter, February 26, 1775; Jerusha, February 4, 1776. Jerusha's husband was Calvin Chapin, minister of the Congregational Church in Rocky Hill, Connecticut, and an active participant in the Second Great Awakening.

Pond, appears to have turned the Horse, with a view to water him, at a place which appeared smothe and convenient for the purpose; but the shore only a few feet from the edge of the Pond was uncommonly steep, descending at once, and the horse probably eager for drink and pressing forward too far plunged instantly into eight or ten feet water. No person saw Mrs. Edwards when she was drowning . . . the waters were so deep and muddy that it was an hour and a half before she was found tho' the utmost exertions were made. . . .

Edwards' own account of the accident, written in a letter to his nephew, Timothy Dwight, indicated the circumstance of the tragedy and the grief it brought to him.

New Haven, July 18, 1782

Dear Sir

I thank you for kind & sympathising Yea comforting letter of the 13th. . . , & for the valuable hints it contains, tending both to my edification & relief under my affliction. My trials are indeed great, but I hope I do not murmer against God or call in question his righteousness; yet I am afraid I shall not be quickened to duty, I know I ought to be by this particular dispensation. I think I have some desire, that I may hereby be made a better man & a better minister & I ask your prayers that that may indeed be the case.— And, oh my dear children; what a loss to them! O may God be their father! Dear Sir, pray for them.

You say, you are ignorant of most of the circumstance wh attended you ant' death, I suppose you had not seen my letter to Major Porter, wh I desired him to communicate to you, or share the contents. The principal circumstance known are contained in the printed account wh I inclose,—The Sabbath, being the day before her decease, she attended public worship all day & it was remarked by many how much better in health she appeared to be, both by her countenance & walk. The evening of the Same Sabbath the Doctor was here & remarked the same, particularly from her pulse. The next morning between 8 & 9 o'clock we rode together, as far as my lot in the mill lane. She choosing to ride further, determined to go as far as over Mr. Ford's & do an errand. She had often rid to the same house alone, as we had a part of our clothes and furniture deposited there. I staid at my lot to direct and assist about some hay. In her way to Mr. Ford's the fatal disaster befell her. Just before she arrived at the place where she watered her horse she was met by a lad who also met, a little behind her, the other lad who first discovered the dire event. There were two houses within call of the spot & the lad immediately gave the proper notice but too late! It is supposed that she never rose out of the water, after She was once plunged. When the body was found there was a wound just above her left ear, supposed to be made by falling suddenly & violently on the fore part of the carriage, in consequence of the horse's plunging instantly into deep water. This probably stunned her so as to prevent the usual exertions. These I think are all circumstance we know, besides those contained in the printed account. I have received expressions of tender sympathy from all, as they have had opportunity, especially from our own congregation; which have greatly comforted me. But I am still more affected to observe the expressions of esteem for the deceased. This at once excites pleasure & grief; pleasure to see justice so fare done to a character most amicable to me & grief at the greatness of my own loss. But I pray that all my grief & sorrow, may be after a godly sort.

Your sincere Friend & Servant
Jona Edwards[8]

Mr. T. Dwight

Left with three children between the ages of six and nine the burden of grief must have been all the more difficult to bear. The following year, however, Edwards became attracted to Mercy Sabin, daughter of Mr. Hezekiah Sabin, a New Haven merchant, and in December of 1783 they were married. She outlived her husband, and in the course of her life earned the affection and devotion of the children.

The family remained closely knit and devoted to one another. Edwards corresponded frequently with his children and advised them concerning various decisions and problems. The letter below contains fatherly counsel given to Jonathan Walter who had written about his approaching marriage.

New Haven, Aug 5, 1795

Dear Son

Yours of the 28th ult, has just now reached me. I have found the papers to wh you refer, & shall send them by a safe hand.

The remaining subject of your letter is very important; & I am pleased, that you have written to me on it, both because it appears

---

8. Ms. Letter of July 18, 1782, from Jonathan Edwards the Younger to Timothy Dwight (Andover-Newton Seminary Library).

that you have a sense of the importance & one not likely to act in that matter from blind feeling or sudden emotion; but with consideration & reason; & also because you show a dutiful regard to your father. You know that I have never undertaken to prescribe to my children very strict rules as to marriage. Still it is both my duty & inclination to give them my best advice; & it is proper for them to ask it, as you have done. . . .

The most essential things in a wife are good sense, good nature & virtue; the next one to be considered a good constitution & decent appearance, with a proper education; & lastly her family & connections. . . . As to form & beauty, I leave these to your own taste; & I think that as to these you cannot very widely err. . . .[9]

His daughter, Jerusha, wrote him often concerning the "state of her soul."

Rocky Hill, March 18, 1797

. . . If I could answer your letter so as to give any satisfaction, or make you less anxious for the state of my soul how great would be my lot but I fear I cannot. Far be it from me to wish to conceal the truth. The thoughts of death & eternity are often in my mind, that I am a sinner, & unworthy of the least of God's mercies I daily feel. That I am not thoughtless I think I can say, & that I do sincerely wish to do my duty with respect to God and man.

I endeavour to watch over & guard myself from sin & I daily pray for light and instruction to walk in the way of my duty.

Besides praying daily to God and an endeavor so far as in me doeth to keep his commands, what can I do to be saved? This question I have often asked myself. But I do not talk so freely as I ought to upon these subjects with any one I acknowledge.

How can I know whether God has ever bestowed his grace on me or not? If I could answer that to my own satisfaction, to myself, I could answer it to you Sir, but I can not.

I fear death because I fear I am not prepared, what would I not give to be sure of the favour of God in the world to come. I have often thought I would give worlds had I them in my possession for the salvation of my soul. Do write to me Sir and in the plainest Manner tell me my duty and the way to eternal life. . . .[10]

---

9. Ms. letter of August 4, 1795, from Jonathan Edwards the Younger to Jonathan W. Edwards (Yale University Library).

10. Ms. letter of March 18, 1797, from Jerusha Edwards to Jonathan Edwards the Younger (Yale University Library).

Her father willingly and repeatedly encouraged her to continue her search.[11]

Even his nieces and nephews received his counsel. In 1770 he wrote a few words of admonition to Sarah Burr, who could not have been more than seventeen.

New Haven Feb. 21, 1770

My Dear Niece
... That I may not write you a letter wholly about nothing, I will make so free as to desire that in your next [letter] you give me your sentiments concerning the principles of the Arminians, wherein they differ from the Calvinists. Perhaps this may seem a dry question. However, I think it will not be a useless one. Many people use the name Arminian & Calvinist, who perhaps know nothing of the meaning of these words, or so much as whence they derived their origin. But to have clear & distinct notions of the opposite principles embraced by these two parties is absolutely necessary in order to be able to judge concerning the truth & falsehood of the one scheme or the other. And I think it of great importance that young minds be early accustomed to attend to these things. By this means a habit of attention to em will be acquired, which will be much more easy to maintain afterwards than to acquire it. Besides youth is the very best time of life to acquire knowledge of all sorts. Then we not only more caply [sic] imbibe it, but that which is imbibed then, we shall retain the longest. Hence it is that [saying] of Solomon, *train up a child in the way he sho'd go, & when he is old, he will not depart from it.*
Please to make my compliments acceptable to Mr. & Mrs. Burr & believe me to be

Your sincerely affectte uncle,
Jonathan Edwards[12]

The sentiments expressed in this letter are representative of similar letters sent to other young members of the Edwards clan.

The impression of Edwards that comes from his correspondence is of one devoted to those close to him, yet stern in appearance, formal in action, precise in speech, and humorless in disposition.

---

11. This correspondence is found in the Yale University Library.
12. Ms. letter of February 21, 1770, from Jonathan Edwards the Younger to Sarah Burr (Historical Society of Pennsylvania, Library). *Cf.* page 66.

Excerpts from his "Memoranda in Temporal Affairs" display a very business-like attitude, even toward matters of small significance.

> In getting a chair see that both ends of the springs are bound with iron,—that there are plates of iron under all the nuts of the screws.
> Make no bargain suddenly & beware of given [sic] peremptory answers.
> In planting a garden, plant your peases beans cucumbers & lettuce & turnip . . . at different times that there may be an aportment.
> In purchasing a cow see that she not only give a good quantity of milk but that the milk is good. Of colour a brinted . . . or darkened or black hoofs are said to be the best, a brown colour is also recommended. But in all colours it is said that it is best that the bag be yellow, this being a material circumstance; & that the hind-quarters of a cow be much the largest.[13]

Recollections of those who knew him, and observations that he made about himself, add to our picture. A contemporary described him as a short, dark-complected man, with a "severe countenance" and "piercing eye." It was said that "he seemed to have no small talk for anybody; being probably opposed to it, as well from principle as taste." This same account described him as a very irritable man, using as an example the time Edwards "once called at Mr. Atwater's at Westfield, and having occasion to get his horse shod, lost all patience with the blacksmith, who had either made a blundering job of it, or in some other way had dissatisfied him."[14] His son-in-law, Calvin Chapin, had frequent talks with Edwards and remembered the pastor's sense of regret and self-condemnation over this trait. "He watched, and prayed, and struggled, against it, as the besetting infirmity of his nature."[15]

Edwards did not easily give himself in close friendships. From contemporary descriptions we see a man rather aloof, seemingly cold and distant. He certainly was not a man of the world.

> . . . In every day conversation, his habits were removed, as far as possible, from every thing low and vulgar. And if others, as some-

---

13. Jonathan Edwards the Younger, "Memoranda in Temporal Affairs," Undated Manuscript (Andover-Newton Seminary Library).

14. Recollection of Timothy M. Cooley in W. B. Sprague, *Annals of the American Pulpit* (New York: R. Carter and Brothers, 1859), Vol. I, 659.

15. Recollection of Calvin Chapin in Sprague, Vol. I, 658.

times occurred amidst the incautious hilarities of mixed company, came too near the verge of propriety, his frown was sure to be expressed, either by a significant and piercing look, or by well chosen words of merited rebuke.[16]

An incident related by a contemporary is illustrative of Edwards' whole character. President George Washington was visiting in New Haven and attended the meetings of both the Episcopal Church and the White Haven Church. A large number of townspeople, expecting a timely message, had gathered for the service at which Edwards was to speak. Edwards, however, used as his text, "Train up a child in the way he should go, and when he is old he will not depart from it." He was quoted as saying: "In speaking from these words I shall direct my remarks principally to the children in the galleries." The commentator remarked that Edwards "doubtless thought that the services of the sanctuary of the King of Kings should not be changed on account of the entrance of an earthly magistrate."[17]

In the pulpit Edwards was not a sparkling orator. Preaching was serious business; there was no time for the well-turned phrase, the pithy illustration, or moralizing discourse. One of his contemporaries described his manner of delivery.

> In the pulpit, he was too profound to be interesting, or always intelligible to ordinary minds. His own mind was so trained to philosophical disquisitions that he seemed sometimes to forget that the multitude whom he was addressing were not also metaphysicians. A portion of his preaching, however, was highly practical, and sometimes it was irresistibly impressive and even terrible. His manner was the opposite of attractive. In his voice there was a nasal twang which diminished the effect of his utterance. He had little or no gestures,

---

16. Quoted in Sprague, Vol. I, 658. His grandson, Tryon Edwards, recounted an impression of Edwards given to him by one who knew his grandfather.
One individual who remembers him, says of his eye, 'that it seemed as if it would look him through and through—as if it could absolutely read his thoughts.' That after he first saw it, its calm and intensely penetrating look haunted him for weeks.
Tyron Edwards, "Memoir of Jonathan Edwards," in *Works of Jonathan Edwards D.D.* (Andover: Allen, Morrill and Wardwell, 1842), Vol. I, xxv.
17. Samuel Dutton, *History of the North Church in New Haven* (New Haven: A. H. Maltby, 1842), 72n. On October 17, 1789, Edwards had joined with Stiles and three other leading citizens of New Haven in a letter of congratulations to George Washington on his election to the presidency (Ms. letter in Yale University Library).

looked about but little upon his audience, and seemed like a man who was conscious that he was dealing in abstractions. Nevertheless he was uttering great and profound thoughts; and those who were capable to estimating them, went away admiring the power of his genius, and edified by the striking and original views which had been presented to them.[18]

Edwards was well aware of his severe and formal style. On one occasion he wrote down a list of stylistic faults which he needed to correct: speaking too fast in preaching and prayer, having too much action in the argumentative part of a discourse, speaking on too high a key, neglecting the spirit in preaching, preaching legally, not caring for fools, preaching metaphysically, spending too much time in telling others' sentiments, and having too much of a sameness in the argumentative part of the discourse and in the application.[19] His self-criticism coincided with that offered by his listeners. Despite his pulpit manner, however, he was frequently invited to speak in other churches.

In the pulpit Edwards was a theologian. Most of his sermons are left only in note form, minus titles and scriptural text, yet even these are well-organized theological treatises. His sermon subjects indicate his concerns: "Depravity the Source of Infidelity," "Mere Repentance No Ground of Pardon," "Universal Salvation Inconsistent with Salvation by Christ," "The Acceptance and Safety of the Elect," "The Law Not made Void Through Faith," "God the Author of all Good Volitions and Actions." These sermons were undoubtedly delivered in as serious a vein as they were conceived.[20]

---

18. Recollections of Timothy Cooley, in Sprague, Vol. I, 659–660. A student at Yale remarked after hearing Edwards speak to the College that

Mr Edwards improves greatly in his delivery that is in his gesture and emphasis—he appears posest [possessed] of more animation & energy than formerly—he has yet however a poor elecution—and this I believe remediless. . . .

John Cotton Smith, "Diary," Jan. 26, 1783. (Connecticut Historical Society, Hartford, Connecticut. For this reference I am indebted to Professor Edmund Morgan, Yale University.)

19. Edwards the Younger, "Corrigenda," Undated Manuscript (Andover-Newton Seminary Library).

20. On one occasion Edwards called upon one of his colleagues, Benjamin Trumbull of North Haven, to preach to his congregation on a specific doctrinal issue which he felt needed more explication.

New Haven April 10, 1770

Revd and Dear Sir

Our people want much to be instructed upon the subject of moral inability. I have endeavored to lead 'em into that doctrine; but have not succeeded according to my

As was customary for nearly every minister of the period, Edwards had a share in training the next generation of clergy. Like Nathaniel Emmons, Samuel Hopkins, Joseph Bellamy and others, he conducted a "school for prophets," that is, he accepted certain young men into his home in order to guide their theological education. Though the number of Edwards' students was not large, their quality was excellent. Among his more illustrious pupils were his nephew, Timothy Dwight, later President of Yale College; Samuel Austin, pastor of Fair Haven Church and later President of the University of Vermont; Jedidiah Morse, defender of orthodox doctrine in the controversy involving Harvard, and a moving force in the formation of Andover Theological Seminary; Edward Dorr Griffin, minister of the Park Street Church, Boston, teacher at Andover Seminary and later President of Williams College; and Samuel Nott, pastor of the church in Norwich, Connecticut, in whose home were trained nearly 300 theological students, and who was later director of the Missionary Society of Connecticut. A manuscript, left by Maltby Gelston, a pupil of Edwards, indicates the type of training his students received.[21] They were required to become familiar with a series of theological questions, and the appropriate answers to enable them to understand and attack heretical sentiments. Naturally, the topics under examination were those which were dominant in New England theology during this period, and the answers offered were those consistent with the New Divinity theological tradition.[22]

Edwards also served as a critic of the preaching abilities of his

---

desires. But what deacon Bishop has told me of your sermons, I believe they are well calculated further to instruct 'em. If therefore you will be so good as to bring them with you, & preach 'em, you will much oblige me & many of our people—I mean not, Sir, to prescribe to you, but only to ask a favor.

—With complements to Mrs. Trumble [sic],

    I am

        Your real friend, brother & humble servant

                            Jonathan Edwards

Ms. letter of April 10, 1770, from Jonathan Edwards the Younger to Benjamin Trumbull (Yale University Library).

    21. Edwards the Younger, "A Systematic Collection of Questions and Answers in Divinity," Ms., January 22, 1974, copied by Maltby Gelston (Yale University Library).

    22. The term, New Divinity, refers to the school of thought stemming from Jonathan Edwards, Sr. and having as its leading exponents Samuel Hopkins, Joseph Bellamy, and Jonathan Edwards the Younger. See Chapter III.

young students. His "Miscellaneous Observations on Preaching" was undoubtedly written for the edification of the young clergymen who came to study with him. The following selections from these "Observations" indicate some of the more important homiletical principles which he wished his students to observe.

1. Avoid an argumentative strain of preaching & a frequent use of the particles thereof, so then, consequently.

3. Avoid new phrases, where not necessary, & setting of common docts, in a new light unless some advantage is to be obtained by it.

6. Nothing seems more necessary either to please a popular auditory or to do 'em good than zeal & devotion, & an appearance of it in all public performances.

9. The Antinomians are the most devout & zealous in the country & in the world. The Edwardsean almost all fail thr'o want of zeal & devotion. Theref. the zeal of the former is worthy of being imitated by the latter.

10. The Edwardseans are too apt to run into an argumentative & what is commonly called a metaphysical way of preaching.

11. It is a great fault in preaching to speak so as not to give to the audience an idea of tender concern in the preacher for their good. Some men preach as if they were angry at em, & delighted to tease em, with horrible descriptions of their sins & ill desert, which I have heard called a *fancy way of preaching.* They seem to domineer & lord it over their hearers, treating em very roughly & to appearance proudly.

15. In extemporizing beware of expletives i.e. superlative, needless, epithets, adverbs, etc. They obscure the sense, or drown it, protract the discourse & seem to indicate a want of tho't. Beware also of too frequent an use of some particular phrases.[23]

These "Observations" may give us a picture of Edwards' own sermons to his White Haven Congregation, though some accounts suggest that he formulated principles better than he carried them out.

Besides this private tutoring Edwards participated in some of the functions of Yale College. Ezra Stiles, who was President of Yale

---

23. Edwards the Younger, "Miscellaneous Observations on Preaching," Undated Manuscript (Andover-Newton Seminary Library).

during most of Edwards' tenure in New Haven, was more liberal than he on many points of doctrine. Yet Stiles, superb diplomat that he was, called upon Edwards to participate in the public examination of Yale students. Edwards acquired a reputation among the students for being extremely thorough and strict. A contemporary account recalls that he would often call out "haud recte" (not correct) to the student's remarks, and thus acquired the nickname, "Old Haud Recte."[24]

It was undoubtedly because of his theological position that Edwards was never asked to have an official connection with the college. His name was considered for the position of Professor of Divinity in 1781, but the suggestion never received much support. When his name was suggested, in 1782, for election as a fellow of Yale College, Stiles commented: "why not at once choose Dr. B.[ellamy] Prest., Mr. H.[opkins] Prof Divy, etc."[25] Yet Edwards' presence in New Haven was undoubtedly felt by many of the budding theologians at Yale.

Social and political change were evident as Edwards began his ministry in New Haven. The commercial and cultural transformation of New England brought a sense of self-awareness to its people, and a spirit of self-sufficiency and independence grew. The colonists were becoming more vocal and forceful in resisting English efforts to force them to contribute to the financial well-being of the Empire. As in other areas of the New World, many people in New Haven became outspokenly critical of English policies. The New Haven newspaper, *The Connecticut Journal and New Haven Post-Boy,* filled its pages with accounts of the rising colonial resentment against the unfair impositions placed upon them by their mother country.

> Every new piece of intelligence, from England, is more alarming than the last. Luxury, Venality, and corruption are arrived in that enormous height, that Great Britain, like antient Rome, seems ready to sink under her own weight.[26]

Waves of indignation spread throughout the colonies.

---

24. Quoted in Dutton, 72n.
25. *The Literary Diary of Ezra Stiles,* ed. Franklin B. Dexter (New York: C. Scribner's Sons, 1901), Vol. III, 317. Edwards was granted an honorary M.A. degree by Yale in 1769.
26. *Connecticut Journal and New Haven Post-Boy,* Friday, June 2, 1769.

The churches of New Haven saw the approaching conflict as a judgment from God. One of the few times that the congregations of the First Church, Fair Haven Church, and White Haven Church met together occurred during the 1770's, when they assembled for a prayer meeting, to ask divine protection and favor. The White Haven Church had to hold its own meeting to decide whether such a meeting would be proper; few had forgotten the dissension caused by the earlier division of the New Haven churches.

> At the same time was laid before the church a motion, which was lately made to some of the members of this church, by some of the members of the other churches in town, to this effect: that instead of our next sacramental lecture, we should spend the time in prayer, upon the account of the threatening aspects of divine providence with respect to this land; that in this exercise we should join with the other churches & societies in town & meet in the brick meeting house; the meeting to begin at 4 o'clock p.m. After some conversation upon it, the question was put, passed in the affirmative.[27]

Though it was in opposition to his policy, the pastor supported the decision of the congregation.

Jonathan Edwards shared in the efforts of the clergy to explain and justify the right of the colonists to govern themselves.[28] He advocated rebellion on the grounds that it can promote the greatest good for God's system.

> Whosoever . . . shall in ordinary cases resist the established supreme authority resists the ordinances of God, and is guilty before him. [Yet] it must always be considered whether the evil consequences of resistance be not likely to overbalance the good; and then only is resistance justifiable, when the rulers rule tyrannically, and there is also a good prospect that the public good will be promoted, more than injured, by resistance.[29]

To resist rulers who do not act "in fear of God and for the good of the people" is to do God's service.[30] Edwards' hearty support of the

---

27. *Records of the White Haven Church,* April 30, 1775, 55.

28. Alice Baldwin, *The New England Clergy and the American Revolution* (Durham, N.C.: Duke University Press, 1928).

29. Edwards the Younger, sermon, "Submission to Rulers," preached at the Annual Freemen's meeting for Voting in 1775. *The Works of Jonathan Edwards, D.D., with a Memoir of his life and Character by Tyron Edwards* (Andover: Allen, Morrill and Wardwell, 1842), Vol. II, 240.

30. Edwards the Younger, "Submission to Rulers," 245.

Revolution was shared by his congregation at the White Haven Church, and in this instance the congregation of the Fair Haven Church backed him as well. The First Congregational Church, however, was hopelessly divided between loyalists and patriots.[31]

When the revolution began, New Haven was not immediately affected. Though its citizens were made painfully aware of the conflict when young men left to serve in the continental army and when their port was blockaded, it was not till July 5, 1779, that the citizenry had a first-hand view of war.[32] The invasion of New Haven was part of a series of coastal raids designed to entice General Washington away from his position near West Point. New Haven was caught unaware; there was only time to collect an ill-trained group to offer token resistance to the British troops. Naphtali Daggett, Professor of Divinity in Yale College, led a force to meet the British, but it was quickly dispersed and Daggett was taken prisoner. Though little damage was done, the attack gave the town a taste of war. For the most part, the Revolution was over in 1781, though its effects were to be felt for years to come. The social changes which had begun to manifest themselves in the pre-war period gained new force. Large numbers of emigrants left for the "west." In New England the rate of population increase dropped nearly in half.[33] The quest for richer lands forced many in rural New England to leave their homes for New York, Pennsylvania, and the western reserve.[34] It appears to be true that the "Ohio wheat and corn were among the many things that contributed much toward the decay of rural New England."[35] Many from southern New England also moved northward into Vermont.[36]

The churches felt compelled to send missionaries to work in the

---

31. See Osterweis, 128.

32. Chauncy Goodrich, "Invasion of New Haven by the British Troops," *Papers of the New Haven Historical Society,* Vol. II (July 5, 1779).

33. Percy Bidwell, *Rural Economy in New England at the Beginning of the Nineteenth Century,* Transactions of the Connecticut Academy of Arts and Sciences, Vol. XX (New Haven: 1916), stated that where before the Revolution the rate of population increase per decade was 28.4%, in the period from 1774–1790 the rate of increase dropped to 11.9%; 386ff.

34. Lois Mathews, *The Expansion of New England* (Boston: Houghton-Mifflin Company, 1909), has charted this emigration on maps, pages 150 and 154.

35. Stewart Holbrook, *The Yankee Exodus, an Account of Migration from New England* (New York: Macmillan Co., 1950), 36.

36. See David Ludlum, *Social Ferment in Vermont, 1791–1850,* Columbia Studies in American Culture, No. 5 (New York: Columbia University Press, 1939).

new settlements. Missionary efforts had long been part of the New England scene. The Society for the Propagation of the Gospel in New England (founded in 1649) had sent several men to work among the colonists and supported the mission at Stockbridge where Edwards, Sr. served; in 1730 the Society in Scotland for Propagating Christian Knowledge (1709) established a Board of Correspondents in Boston to guide their work in the new land. In 1769 the College of New Jersey, its Board of Trustees acting as the representative of the Scottish SPCK, sent missionaries to the Indians in New York. In 1787 the Massachusetts Legislature gave legal status to the first voluntary missionary organization of American origin, the American Society for Propagating the Gospel Among the Indians and others in North America.[37]

The Connecticut churches shared this enthusiasm. The General Association voted, in 1774, to support frontier missionaries, but the effort was interrupted by the Revolution. By the early 1780's requests were made to various congregations to release their ministers for six months or a year so they could undertake mission work in the newly settled frontier areas. Since many of the former Connecticut settlers had gone to Vermont and New York, these areas received the greatest number of itinerant clergy. The records of the Connecticut Missionary Society contain scores of letters from Vermont and New York churches to prominent Connecticut clergymen, thanking them for efforts to secure ministers for their churches.[38] Jonathan Edwards was one of the leading figures in this work. Together with Benjamin Trumbull, pastor of the church in North Haven, and Ezra Stiles, he contacted numerous Connecticut clergymen, asking them to serve a term in Vermont or New York. There is clear indication, however, that it was very difficult to "procure settled ministers," for churches were reluctant to have their ministers leave.[39]

It appears that men of New Divinity persuasion controlled the policy of the New England missionary societies.[40] Edwards and

---

37. See O. W. Elsbree, *The Rise of the Missionary Spirit in America, 1790–1815* (Williamsport, Penna: The Williamsport Printing and Binding Co., 1928).

38. It was not until 1798 that the missionary work of the General Association was centered in the Connecticut Missionary Society.

39. The manuscript materials of the Connecticut Missionary Society (Hartford, Conn.) are valuable sources of information concerning the missionary work of the Connecticut churches.

40. Letter of October 15, 1799, from Samuel Hopkins to Andrew Fuller, quoted in *The Works of Samuel Hopkins* (Boston: Doctrinal Tract and Book Society, 1854), Vol. I, 236.

Benjamin Trumbull played leading roles in the Connecticut organization; Edwards and Samuel Hopkins shared in the work of the Rhode Island missionary society. In 1799 a group of New Divinity men formed the Massachusetts Missionary Society.[41] It was at the instigation of Samuel Hopkins that the missionary efforts of the New England clergy were directed to the foreign field; his early concern for the negro aroused his interest in African missionary work. Jonathan Edwards' work was directed primarily toward the communities on the American frontier.

Related to this missionary work was the increasing concern of the New England clergy for the negroes in their society. The churches slowly became aware of a missionary obligation to this group. The issue of slavery was not a new one to New England; in the earliest colonial settlements Indians had been used as slaves. The Articles of Confederation of the United New England Colonies (1634) included a fugitive slave law. By 1660 there were references to negro slaves in the Connecticut Records. In 1690 Connecticut passed a law providing that if a negro were found wandering outside of town without a proper pass he was to be considered a runaway slave.[42]

It was not until after the Revolution that real efforts were made to put an end to slavery. In 1784 the General Assembly of Connecticut passed a bill which proposed gradual emancipation. It provided that no Indian or black child under seven years of age should be held in slavery beyond his twenty-eighth year, but the fact that slavery was not absolutely forbidden until 1848 indicates that this gradual emancipation law was not adhered to fully. Jonathan Edwards stands out as the leading Connecticut anti-slavery advocate of this period.[43]

Samuel Hopkins is usually regarded as the first strong anti-slavery advocate among the New England clergy. Hopkins began his

---

41. The leaders of this Society were Nathaniel Emmons, Samuel Austin, Samuel Niles, Samuel Spring, and Jonathan Strong.

42. For further literature on this subject see: B.C. Steiner, "History of Slavery in Connecticut," in *Labor, Slavery and Self Government*, ed. H.B.Adams. Johns Hopkins Studies in History and Political Science, Vol. XI (Baltimore: Johns Hopkins Press, 1893), 10ff; L. Greene, *The Negro in Colonial New England, 1620–1776* (New York: Columbia University Press, 1942); F.R. Weld, "Slavery in Connecticut," *Publications of the Tercentenary Commission of the State of Connecticut*, Vol. 35 (New Haven: 1935); M.H.Mitchell, "Slavery in Connecticut and Especially in New Haven," *Papers of the New Haven Historical Society*, Vol. X (New Haven: 1951).

43. R.C. Senior, "New England Congregationalism and the Anti-Slavery Movement 1830–1860," Unpublished Ph.D. dissertation, Yale University, 1954, 16.

work in the New England emancipation movement in 1776 when he moved to Newport, the center of the slave market in America.[44] Edwards' efforts ran concurrently with Hopkins'. The New Haven newspaper carried a series of outspoken anonymous articles entitled "Some Observations upon the Slavery of Negroes" in October, November, and December of 1773. These articles follow very closely Edwards' later sermon (1791) "The Injustice and Impolicy of the Slave Trade and Slavery." In fact, they even use some of the same wording, and there is little doubt that they are the work of Jonathan Edwards the Younger. The 1791 sermon was "published and republished, achieving a wide circulation and providing prime ammunition even for the abolitionists of Garrison's generation."[45] Edwards analyzed all the possible justifications for slavery; after demolishing them he insisted, on theological and political grounds, that freedom for all men in bondage was the only alternative. "To steal a man or to rob him of his liberty is a greater sin, than to steal his property, or to take it by violence."[46] Slavery itself was unjust, not only because of the cruel way in which it was conducted but because it was contrary to "the law of nature and . . . the law of God."[47] It was harmful to the people and the country, for it destroyed morality, discouraged industry, promoted indolence, and encouraged pride. There could be no biblical justification for the enslavement of any race. "Every man who cannot show, that his negro hath by his voluntary conduct forfeited his liberty, is obligated immediately to manumit him."[48] Edwards' sermon was delivered before the "Connecticut Society for the Promotion of Freedom, and for the Relief of Persons unlawfully holden in Bondage," whose purpose was to end the slave trade, to defend those who were legally held in bondage, and to prepare the way for total abolition.[49]

---

44. For a full analysis of Samuel Hopkins' contribution to the anti-slavery movement in New England see Dick L. Van Halsema, "Samuel Hopkins 1721–1803: New England Calvinist," unpublished Th.D. thesis, Union Theological Seminary, New York, Ch. VIII, "Disinterested Benevolence in Action," 240–277.

45. Van Halsema, 15.

46. Edwards the Younger, "The Injustice and Impolicy of the Slave Trade and of Slavery," *Works*, Vol. II, 90.

47. Edwards the Younger, "The Injustice and Impolicy," 79.

48. Edwards the Younger, "The Injustice and Impolicy," 89.

49. Edwards the Younger, "The Injustice and Impolicy," 92ff. This Society, in which Edwards actively participated throughout his New Haven pastorate, did much more

In succeeding years Edwards and Hopkins were joined by Ezra Stiles, Joseph Bellamy, and other leading New England clergymen to form a strong front against the proponents of slavery. Delegates from New England and the middle colonies held periodic conventions to consolidate their work. Edwards was a delegate to such a convention in Philadelphia in 1794; its purpose was "to consult on measures favorable to the abolition of African slavery."[50]

Edwards' pastoral labors reached far beyond the needs of the White Haven Church. In fact, his wide interests prevented him from devoting as much time to caring for his flock as his parishioners felt was necessary. As he made frequent requests to be absent in

---

than carry on a pamphlet war. The following letter from Benjamin Trumbull to the Reverend John Lewes of Cheshire, Conn., indicates clearly that direct efforts were made to free slaves.

North Haven March 12, 1792

Revd Sir,

The Committee of Connecticut for the promotion of freedom and for the relief of persons holden in bondage, at one of our meetings, sometime since, were informed, that a Negro girl belonging to a family of free Negroes in Cheshire, was under the cover of Night carried off from her fathers house, by a number of persons unknown entirely either to that family, or to any person in that town. We have since been informed that it was by your order that she was carried off in this extraordinary manner; and that she is now holden in your service.

. . . in the name and at the desire of said Committee to acquaint you that the honourable Superior Court have twice given it as their opinion that the family of which said girl is a member is free. Esq. Daggett who managed the case before said court judges it to be a clear case, and that the girl ought by no means to be holden in bondage. We have understood that Mr. Robbins gave her a manumission to prevent a process against him and the recovery of damages for her Services.

We consider her as a free girl, and wish you Sir to discharge her from your service and suffer her to return without fear or molestation to her fathers house.

Otherwise the very design of our Society, and the nature of our appointment, will lay us under the disagreeable necessity of commencing a suit against you for the recovery of the girl.

Should we be put to this necessity, we shall think it our duty to take every legal measure, not for her liberation, but for the recovery of damage. We desire you as soon as may be to communicate to us your views and purposes relative to the affair, that we may know what course to pursue, Meanwhile I am Revd Sir, your friend, brother, and humble servant.

Benjamin Trumbull

The Revd. John Lewes.

Ms. Letter of March 12, 1792, from Benjamin Trumbull to John Lewes (Yale University Library).

50. Ms. Letter of November 10, 1749, from Jonathan Edwards the Younger to Stephen West (Yale University Library). In that same year Edwards wrote: ". . . to our shame, and to the shame of humanity, and the scandal of Christianity, a slavery and a treatment of slaves similar to what existed among the Romans, exist and are tolerated in some parts of America." *The Necessity of the Belief of Christianity* (Hartford: Hudson & Godwin, 1794), 27.

order to attend meetings of the various groups to which he belonged, resentment grew against him in the White Haven Church.

In addition, he was embroiled in the theological discussions current in New England; no one gave more time or energy to these matters. Such work also imposed on his time and diminished the extent of his specifically pastoral work. Nevertheless, it was during these years, while engaging in the many other activities which attracted his interest, that he made his own distinctive contribution to American theology.

Three main issues occupied the attention of the theologians of this period: the "means" of regeneration, the issue of universal salvation, and the nature and extent of sin; these issues, and Edwards' contribution to the discussion regarding them will be discussed in the three succeeding chapters.

CHAPTER SIX

The Means of Regeneration

The place of the "means of regeneration" in the work of redemption was one of the most important issues in New England theology.[1] The revivalist called for men to repent. Yet how was this consistent with New Divinity theology? If man were so totally corrupt, how could he even understand, let alone try to fulfill, the will of God? The Old Calvinist was ready to allow the proper use of the "means of regeneration"; this had become an accepted part of seventeenth century New England theology. God's call to men to accept the means which He has instituted for their salvation was an important article of Calvinist thought. The Arminian was ready to rely much more openly on "means"; this was consistent with his conviction that man has an important part in his own salvation.

Arminian theologians denied the doctrine of election, and relied on the universal grace which God extends to all men. They taught that men are only required to fulfill the duties of religion which they are capable of fulfilling. God gives grace "as may be sufficient to what is nextly and immediately required of him; on a man's improving of which he may from the divine goodness hope for more, according to future needs."[2] Jonathan Mayhew's famous sermon, *Striving to Enter in at the Strait Gate,* was a plea for his congregation to attend to all their duties as church members.[3] In the face

---

1. The "means" of regeneration include everything from "striving after holiness" to attendance at worship service and participation in the sacramental life of the church.

2. *Letters from the First Church in Gloucester to the Second in Bradford, with their Answers* (Boston: 1774), 26, quoted in Conrad Wright, *The Beginnings of Unitarianism in America* (Boston: Starr King Press, 1955), 124–125.

3. Jonathan Mayhew, *Striving to Enter in at the Strait Gate Explain'd and Inculcated* (Boston: R. Draper, Edes & Gill and T. & J. Fleet, 1761).

of strong objections from their more orthodox critics, the Arminians relied openly on man's role in salvation. Chauncy wrote that both man's spiritual and intellectual powers must be exercised;

> they are small, and weak, in their beginnings; but capable of growth, and naturally tend to it; and will, under the influence of heaven, continually increase in strength, and go on towards perfection, if they are duly exercised.[4]

Here was a clear assertion of man's ability to progress in salvation by using the means of regeneration.

Neither the Old Calvinist nor the New Divinity men were so certain about the "spiritual progression" which supposedly came from man's manipulation of the "means of regeneration." Neither group would accept the Arminian position, but they were divided between themselves about what there is in man that needs regeneration; as a result, their different estimates of the "means of regeneration" became more sharply defined. In general, the Old Calvinist was concerned with the *mind* of the unbeliever, that true doctrine might illumine his understanding. The New Divinity man was concerned with the "new man," and looked for a transformation of the heart of man which only God might effect. Hopkins, following Edwards, Sr., insisted that the depravity of man lies in his heart and "so regeneration must begin there—not in the understanding."[5] "Men in natural state are blind to inner light because of the state of their heart—not because of any natural defect in reasoning and intellectual faculties of the soul."[6] This same emphasis is present in the work of Smalley, Emmons, and West, other New Divinity spokesmen.[7]

---

4. Charles Chauncy, *Twelve Sermons* (Boston: Printed by D. and J. Kneeland, for T. Leverett, 1765), 314. Also his *Five Dissertations on the Scripture Account of the Fall* (London: C. Dilly, 1785), 30.

5. Samuel Hopkins, "Systems of Doctrines," *The Works of Samuel Hopkins* (Boston: Doctrinal Tract and Book Society, 1854), Vol. I, 370.

6. Hopkins, *Works,* Vol. I, 416. Here again, Jonathan Edwards, Sr. was inclined to place a different interpretation on the doctrine than the majority of the New Divinity men. Edwards stressed the need for the regeneration of heart and mind, as distinct from reliance on one or the other. "Two things in saving faith: belief of the truth and answerable disposition of the heart," *Observations Concerning Faith, The Works of President Edwards, in Four Volumes* (New York: Leavitt, Trow & Co., 1844), Vol. II, 625. See also John E. Smith, "Introduction" to Edwards, Sr's. *Religious Affections* (New Haven: Yale University Press, 1960).

7. John Smalley, Sermon I in *Sermons, Essays, Extracts* (New York: George Forman, 1811); Nathaniel Emmons, *The Works of Nathaniel Emmons,* ed. Jacob Ide (Boston: Congregational Board of Publication, 1860), Vol. II, 700ff; Stephen West, *An Essay on Moral Agency* (Salem: 1794).

The Old Calvinist had a different concern.

> When we duely understand, and firmly believe the truth, then it
> exerts its quickening, and purifying influence upon all the pores of
> our Souls; and so, conforms our whole spirits unto God, and gradu-
> ally perfects the renovation of his image in us.[8]

Even the work of the Holy Spirit is not primarily to renovate man's
heart, but rather to bring light to his understanding.

> In order to bring us to a regenerating knowledge of belief of God and
> Jesus Christ, or the great Doctrines of salvation, the Holy Spirit
> excites in us, a honest and touchable disposition, a hearty desire for
> knowing the truth.[9]

Another Old Calvinist wrote,

> there are those things especially which have a manifest tendency to
> hinder a man's turning to God, thro' faith in Christ; namely, gross
> ignorance and error, and stupid inconsiderateness and wilful opposi-
> tion to the dictates of conscience.[10]

These differences in opinion over the need for regeneration, and the
forms which regeneration might take, accounted for different views
concerning the use of the "means of regeneration."

In many ways the Old Calvinists absorbed much of the Arminian argument. They attempted to preserve for man some action in
his own salvation, though insisting, as both Arminian and New
Divinity men also did, that salvation ultimately comes from God
alone. The preaching of the Old Calvinists stressed man's need to use
the means of regeneration.

> ... hearers of the gospel, antecedent to their believing in Christ
> savingly, are commended and encouraged, to make it their chief
> concern and endeavour, to obtain that faith and grace of the Holy
> Spirit, which is necessary to justification and salvation.[11]

They assured their listeners that God would act to save those who

---

8. William Hart, *A Discourse Concerning the Nature of Regeneration and, the Way
Wherein it is Wrought* (New London: T. Green, 1742), 11.

9. Hart, *A Discourse*, 13.

10. Moses Hemmenway, *Seven Sermons, on the Obligation and Encouragement of the Unregenerate, to Labour for the Meat which Endureth to Everlasting Life* (Boston: Kneeland and Adams,
1767), 12.

11. Hemmenway, *Seven Sermons*, 10.

were sincere believers and doers of his word. Men were ignorant of
the commands of God; they needed to be enlightened and this was
accomplished through the means of regeneration.[12] "Though the
best actions of the unregenerate are sinfully defective, yet there is in
them something good and right in its proper place and kind."[13]
Because of their conviction that the understanding needed to be
enlightened and that this was not done in a cataclysmic way, they
were, as a group, never ardent revivalists. William Hart made the
reason for this clear.

> Now every body that understands Human Nature knows, that our
> understandings are in the best Disposition and Capacity to attend to,
> to apprehend and receive the great Truths of religion, and so convey
> their vital and purifying Influences to the Heart; When our minds are
> most free from the Influence of wild and vehement imaginations, and
> our Passions are Calm and undisturbed. . . . A more meek, gentle and
> alluring Method is uncontestably more Agreeable to the Spirit of the
> Gospel.[14]

In *Freedom of the Will* Jonathan Edwards, Sr. made an effort to
reconcile the call to repentance with the doctrine of total depravity.
He distinguished between man's moral inability and his natural
ability to comply with the commands of God. By "natural ability"
Edwards meant that man has no physical defects which prevent him
from turning to God. Yet, man is so totally corrupt that he is
morally unable to obey God. The strongest motive, by which the
will is determined, is always a corrupt motive. Therefore, the heart
of depraved man is turned from God, and there is no way by which
he can turn himself to God. Any use of the "means of regeneration"
would be vain, for man would only use them for a corrupt purpose.
But this does not mean that man should give up prayer, church
attendance, or striving after holiness, for even if man has no part in
it, God can use these things to help in the work of regeneration.

The idea that the "means" might be the primary element in the
work of redemption was resisted by all of the New Divinity men.
Smalley insisted that nothing man can do to improve himself has any

---

12. Hemmenway, *Seven Sermons,* 162ff.
13. Hemmenway, *Seven Sermons,* 170.
14. Hart, *A Discourse,* 54, 56.

effect on God. "No light, no conviction of the understanding, which the natural man is capable of receiving, can be sufficient to draw or drive him into a true compliance with the gospel."[15] Man must be born again. "If mankind have lost the moral image of God entirely, it is easy to see that nothing short of a new creation can restore it to him."[16] None of this implies, however, that the accepted means should be totally neglected; Smalley relied on the judgment of probability. "It is not necessarily implied . . . that the externally moral, and those who are in the diligent use of the outward and ordinary means of grace are no more likely to be saved, than the immoral, the careless and inattentive."[17] Hopkins insisted that man should be acquainted with the "means" instituted by God so that he might know how to act when he is regenerated. However, this exercise has no effect on his salvation.[18] Hopkins spelled out the New Divinity distinction between regeneration and conversion in order to allow, and to justify, some effort on man's part.

> . . . Regeneration does not produce any new natural capacity or faculty in the soul [but] wholly consists in the change and renewal of the will. In the Change . . . the spirit of God is the only agent; and man, the subject, is wholly passive, does not act, but is acted upon.[19] Man is so far from being active in producing this change, or having any hand in it by voluntarily falling in with, or submitting to, the divine operation, or cooperating with the spirit of God, that the whole strength of his heart opposed it, until it is affected and actually takes place. . . .[20]

Thus, the New Divinity theologians saw conversion as man's response to the regenerating work of God.

Outlining the substance of Christian faith in his personal notebook, Hopkins made clear his belief that the means of regeneration are simply withheld from the non-elect.

---

15. Smalley, in *Sermons, Essays, Extracts*, 25.
16. Smalley, in *Sermons, Essays, Extracts*, 50.
17. John Smalley, *Sermons, On a Number of Connected Subjects* (Hartford: Printed for Oliver D. Cooke; Lincoln and Gleason, Printers, 1803), 253. Hopkins argued that if the churchman knew of the instituted means of grace and did not attend diligently to them, that he was worse off than the man who had never heard of Christ.
18. Hopkins, "The Cause, Nature, and Means of Regeneration," *Works*, III.
19. Hopkins, "The Cause, Nature, and Means," *Works*, III, 552, 554.
20. Hopkins, "The Cause, Nature, and Means," *Works*, III, 554.

God 1st proposed to himself to manifest the Glory of his Grace and justice. Hence 2ly he proposed to create man in his own image; and after he had created him, to enter into a covenant of works with him and to suffer him to break this covenant by falling. Hence 3ly he determined to chuse out of a created and fallen man, this particular one and to reject another particular one Wherefore 4ly he determined to bestow the means of salvation upon the Elect (viz) Redemption; which was to be procured by faith—and to deny, on the other hand, the Means of Salvation to the reprobate, and so leave them in their sins—and to 5ly eternally to save the Elect by faith on the account of Christ; and eternally to condemn the reprobate for their sins.[21]

The uncertainty of knowing on which side one fell kept the issue alive.

The controversy had more than theoretical interest. In early American Puritanism the lines of separation between the saved and the damned were not always clear, though the attempt was made to clarify them. But, as we have noted, the development of Congregationalism broke down this sharp division. The Half Way Covenant of 1662 and the innovations of Solomon Stoddard had blurred the issue, and this blurring had become part of the heritage of the New England churches. Edwards' father had sought return to the earlier views, but his vision of the church as a visible communion of the regenerate led to his dismissal from the Northampton Church.

Other factors clouded the picture. As Anglican and Baptist churches began to appear in New England, the Congregationalists could no longer claim absolute authority, though disestablishment did not occur until 1818 in Connecticut and until 1838 in Massachusetts. But now new church members had to be cultivated; unpopular restrictions on church membership would lead only to the withering of the church.

It was in this context that the controversy over the means of regeneration assumed practical significance for the churches of New England. The Arminians could appeal to a broad spectrum of people; the Old Calvinists had not insisted on public testimony of regeneration in order to insure a regenerate church membership, but

---

21. Samuel Hopkins, "His Book," Ms. in Huntington Library, San Marino, California.

rather that attendance on the "means" would assist in the regeneration of the unconverted.

But the position of the New Divinity men put them in a difficult situation. The "means of regeneration" were not converting ordinances; they were, despite the efforts to make them appear otherwise, part of the process of conversion and development of the Christian life. But regeneration had to come first—for that the "means" were of no avail. Put bluntly, the New Divinity men did not view the "means of regeneration" as means of regeneration at all.

The situation of Edwards the Younger illustrates their dilemma. In 1787 he refused communion to a member of a local church who was active in the White Haven Church until the man gave public testimony of regeneration. It was the same decision his father had made forty-three years earlier. While Edwards wrestled with this problem, his own church was in the throes of dissension. Membership had declined; he was being criticized openly. The resentment against his theological position and personal character must have weighed heavily on his mind.

He sought to justify the "means," while making clear that, unless God had first regenerated a person, their use did not effect his salvation. His dilemma was not a happy one.

> But how is a man in duty bound to believe, when God hath not decreed that he shall believe, but has decreed to leave him without the gift of faith? Answer. Notwithstanding any divine decree, it is our duty to believe for the same reason as it is our duty to do anything else, which God has not decreed to give us an inclination to do: for instance to read the scriptures, to pray, to worship God in any form, to pay our just debts, to speak the truth, etc. If any man neglect any of these duties, this very neglect proves, that God did not decree to influence him to perform the duty neglected, but did decree to permit the neglect of it. 'For God decrees whatsoever cometh to pass.' Yet no man will hence argue, that the man who neglects those duties, commits no sin in that neglect.[22]

In his words at the ordination of a "fellow laborer" he carried on the same theme.

---

22. Jonathan Edwards the Younger, "Faith and a Good Conscience Illustrated," *The Works of Jonathan Edwards, D.D., with a Memoir of his Life and Character by Tyron Edwards* (Andover: Allen, Morrill and Wardwell, 1842), Vol. II, 156.

> ... Preach those doctrines and those duties which are immediately connected with [faith]; such as the new birth, conversion, repentance unto life, Supreme love to God, real and direct benevolence to mankind, the divine efficacious grace and the sovereignty of it, the saint's perseverance, and endless rewards and punishments. Preach the dependence of man on God for faith as well as for grace in general; yet preach the *duty* of faith, even the duty of all men to whom the gospel is preached, to repent and believe the gospel, and that no man hath a right to procrastinate this duty at all. ... .[23]

The means of regeneration were of no ultimate use, but this did not excuse man from attending to them; man was not entirely passive in the work of redemption. Obedience to the will of God was the Christian's duty, required by the gospel.[24] One could not be certain who were among the elect; therefore, one must act. "Though Christ has already died, yet no man will escape the curse of the law on that account, unless he repent and forsake sin and walk in newness of life."[25] And though there is no absolute promise to the sinner who strives to fulfill the will of God, "the experience of all ages shows that while thus seriously pursuing and attending to the solemn truths of the gospel, he is in the most likely way that he can be in, to obtain the saving grace of God."[26]

The battle goes on. "Even the Christian is like one rowing against the stream. He has need of constant and vigorous exertion; and if he slackens his stroke he is carried backward in the swift current driving him towards the wide gate of destruction."[27] If one does not pursue the "means," the fact that he does not is unmistakable evidence that God has not decreed his salvation. God has withheld from the non-elect a "willingness" to pursue the means which he has instituted for their salvation.

> God has furnished them [non-elect] with such means for salvation that if they were heartily willing to accept the offer, no real obstacle would be in the way. Except giving them a willingness, he has done everything he could be expected to do, were he ever so desirous they

23. Edwards the Younger, "Faith and a Good Conscience," *Works,* Vol. II, 159.
24. Edwards the Younger, "Christ Crucified," *Works,* Vol. II, 275.
25. Edwards the Younger, "Thoughts on the Atonement," *Works,* Vol. I, 503.
26. Edwards the Younger, "The Glory of the Gospel," *Works,* Vol. II, 409.
27. Edwards the Younger, "The Broad Way," *Works,* Vol. II, 417.

would accept. But he is under no obligation to give them a willingness.[28]

The motive for attending the "means" was clearly stated.

To be prepared for heaven a man ought to be of an holy heart; otherwise he cannot take pleasure in the displays of the divine holiness there exhibited; or in the holy inhabitants, or in the holy employment and holy pleasures of that holy world.[29]

Thus, the purpose of the means of regeneration is to prepare the already regenerate for the life to come. For that reason Edwards saw no justification for allowing the unregenerate to participate in the "means of regeneration."

While other churches were discarding the Half Way Covenant and replacing it with a general requirement of moral rectitude for church membership, Edwards and other New Divinity men, also rejecting the Half Way Covenant, substituted for it the more rigorous requirement of a public testimony of regeneration. Here, again, we find the theology and polity of the New Divinity tradition hardening in such a way that it offered little attraction to men of the revolutionary era, confident of their power, cognizant of their freedom.

---

28. Edwards the Younger, "A Systematic Collection of Questions and Answers in Divinity," Ms., January 22, 1794, copied by Maltby Gelston (Yale University Library), Question 169, p. 227. Gelston was a student in the home of Edwards. The manuscript is in the Yale University library. A typewritten copy of the document has been prepared by Wesley Ewarts and is deposited in the Hartford Seminary Library.

29. Edwards the Younger, "Faith and a Good Conscience," *Works*, Vol. II, 148.

CHAPTER SEVEN

Universal Salvation

It is impossible to fix firmly in time the beginning of the debate in New England concerning universal salvation. In the 1750's Charles Chauncy had written *The Mystery Hid From Ages and Generations, Made Manifest by the Gospel-Revelation: Or, the Salvation of All Men the Grand Thing Aimed at in the Scheme of God.* Chauncy made even a sharper break with New England theological tradition than a venturesome Arminian theologian like himself dared express publicly at that time. The work was not published until 1784, and even then in London and anonymously.[1] The base for acceptance of such ideas might have been there, but more time was needed for the issue to be brought into the open.

In the 1770's a new figure appeared on the New England scene—John Murray began his preaching tours throughout New England and the middle colonies in 1772. Murray was an ardent and outspoken Universalist.[2] He had been brought up in England, in the Presbyterian Church, and had experienced a religious conversion prompted by the preaching of John Wesley.[3] In Murray's view,

---

1. Charles Chauncy, *The Mystery Hid From Ages and Generations, Made Manifest by the Gospel-Revelation: Or, the Salvation of All Men* (London: C. Dilly, 1784).

2. Universalism is the position which holds that all men will be saved.

3. See John Murray, *The Life of Rev. John Murray, Preacher of Universal Salvation. Written by himself* (Boston: Universalist Publishing House, 1869). This autobiography is an excellent study of the phase of English and American religious thought to which Murray was so intimately tied. See also: J.H. Allen and R. Eddy, *A History of the Unitarians and Universalists in the United States* (New York: The Christian Literature Co., 1894). It is important to note that the universalism of Murray was primarily influenced by the Wesleyan notions of abounding grace and unlimited atonement, while Chauncy's universalism had its roots more directly in 18th century rationalism.

Christ had suffered all the punishment due to mankind. To say that man must undergo further punishment for his sins would be to ignore the work that Christ had already done. Murray was reacting against a view of the atonement which saw Christ's work as the payment of a debt, as a work of satisfaction to God, limited in scope.

In the early 1770's Murray visited New Haven and spoke to a large gathering near the New Haven green. The effect of his message must have been felt immediately in the White Haven Church, for it was not long afterward that Jonathan Edwards the Younger published his "Brief Observations on the Doctrine of Universal Salvation, As Lately Promulgated at New Haven."[4] Edwards' reply to Murray's views prefigured the more extensive controversy on the subject, later in the century. He believed that Murray's view of universal salvation denied the grace of God operating in the world. If man does not face punishment for his sin because Christ has already taken the punishment upon himself, "it follows from this system, that grace is in a great measure, excluded from the plan of salvation published in the gospel."[5] Though Edwards did not, at that time, fully spell out his opposition to Universalism, his basic objections were stated. In essence, he found in Universalism a misconception concerning the extent of human sin, a faulty view of the atoning work of Christ, and a total neglect of God as the moral governor of the universe.

When Chauncy's essay was finally published in 1784, the issue was brought to the forefront of New England theological debate. Arminians split with Arminians; Old Calvinists split with Edwardseans; and even more significantly, many, perhaps because of hidden yet hesitant sympathy with the argument of the Universalists, remained silent.

Chauncy's thesis rested on the basic views of Arminian theology. God, the benevolent, wise, moral father of all men, could not leave some men to eternal punishment. Eternal damnation is incon-

---

4. Jonathan Edwards the Younger, *The Works of Jonathan Edwards, D.D., with a Memoir of his Life and Character by Tyron Edwards* (Andover: Allen, Morrill and Wardwell, 1842), Vol. I. This essay, "Brief Observations," appears to have been published in 1772; to my knowledge the original is not extant. A controversy over this issue provoked intense debate within the White Haven Congregation at this time and for several succeeding years. See pp. 141ff.

5. Edwards the Younger, "Brief Observations," *Works*, Vol. I, 279ff.

sistent with the very character of God. Even sinful man could not obstruct the final purpose of God—the happiness of His creation.[6] In the end, all men will come to see the folly of their ways and turn to God, for the heart of man is not unalterably fixed for all time. Christ not only suffered for man, but also serves as his guide. Through Christ, men are saved from themselves, and from sin.[7] But unlike Murray, Chauncy did not see this happy termination during the immediate course of life, at least not during everyone's life. Some obstinate sinners would suffer through a time of torment and hell "in proportion to the number and greatness of their vices."[8] Chauncy never minimized the sufferings which the sinner must endure, but he insisted that the purpose of this suffering was to change the heart of man so that he could accept God's will. The idea of hell as upholding God's justice was foreign to Chauncy. In the end, all men would acknowledge God and be reconciled to Him; all men would be saved. The chief points of Chauncy's argument were that man is not so unalterably opposed to God that no reconciliation is possible; that God's goal is the happiness of His creation, not the satisfaction of His justice; that punishment of man is meant to encourage his reformation; and that the true power and glory of God is seen in His work to save all men, and in the final reconciliation of man to God.

Jonathan Edwards' essay, *The Salvation of All Men Strictly Examined* (1790), was written in rebuttal to Charles Chauncy. In it we see clearly the mind and method of a man schooled in "consistent Calvinism." On page after page Edwards accused Chauncy of inconsistency. For example, on the issue of the purpose of divine punishment, Edwards argued that Chauncy proposed two mutually exclusive ideas of punishment. On the one hand, Chauncy said that punishment is vindictive, that man is punished because he has sinned. On the other hand, he contended that punishment is reformatory, that man is punished so that he will reform and turn to God. In Edwards' view "Dr. C. was compelled by necessity to associate in his scheme, principles which will wage eternal war with each other."[9] Chauncy, of course, admitted no contradictory prin-

---

6. Chauncy, *The Mystery Hid*, 2.
7. Chauncy, *The Mystery Hid*, 220ff.
8. Chauncy, *The Mystery Hid*, 10.
9. Edwards the Younger, "The Salvation of All Men Strictly Examined," *Works*, Vol. I, 15.

ciples. He believed that God is offended by sin, but strives to turn men from their sinful ways because their happiness is His goal.

Edwards' view of the nature of sin brought him to disavow any notion that God administered punishment for simple disciplinary reasons. Sin is a moral evil; it deserves the most severe manifestation of God's wrath.[10] ". . . If sin do not by its general nature deserve the manifestation of divine displeasure, it does not by its general nature deserve displeasure itself; and if so, it is not by its general nature a moral evil."[11] Edwards asserted that the logical result of the Universalist position was the belief that the only proper punishment due men was the removal of the very punishment which they deserved.

> The hypothesis which we are opposing . . . is that the only just ends of punishment, are the repentance and good of the sinner himself; that is, the removal or prevention of personal evil to the sinner, is the only just end of punishing him.[12]

If punishment be only disciplinary, then it is true

> . . . that the greatest end which God can consistently with justice inflict on the greatest and most obdurate enemy of himself, of his Son our glorious Saviour, of his law, of his grace, and of mankind, is, to put him under the best possible advantages to secure and promote his highest everlasting happiness.[13]

Yet, if sin be truly hated by God, this could not be so. The Universalist is mistaken about the true extent of sin. Sin is a moral evil; it

---

10. In this connection it is interesting to note one of Edwards' earliest sermons, written while he was under the watchful eye of Joseph Bellamy in August of 1766.

> It is the very nature of all men, in their original state, to live in sin; their whole hearts are set upon it; they are as naturally inclined to it, & as much act out their very nature in sinning, as a dog in returning to his vomit & a sow in wallowing in mire. . . . They have no taste, bias, or inclination for virtue & holiness; but their whole souls are corrupted. . . . [The reason why some people do not always fall into open sin] is not because they have not a taste and inclination for them; but by reason of something foreign, some cause *ab extra;* which either lays a nat. impediment in their way, so that they cannot, if they will; or else influences some other principle. . . . The dog or sow may for the present be diverted from their vomit & mire, by food thrown them by their master; but this is but for the present; they soon dispack their food and then away to their darling delights.

These are strong words for today but they were staple diet for men of the Edwardsean stamp. This ms. sermon was preached at Great Barrington in October, 1766, in Bethlehem, Conn., in November, 1766, and in Princeton on Christmas Day, 1766! (Hartford Seminary Library).

11. Edwards the Younger, "Salvation of All Men," *Works,* Vol. I, 40.
12. Edwards the Younger, "Salvation of All Men," *Works,* Vol. I, 34.
13. Edwards the Younger, "Salvation of All Men," *Works,* Vol. I, 27–28.

deserves greater punishment than the human mind can comprehend. Scripture declares that sin deserves much more than mere disciplinary punishment. It says "that those who die impenitent are lost, are cast away, perish, suffer perdition, are destroyed, suffer everlasting destruction."[14] Chauncy argued that some men would turn from their sinful ways sooner than others. But, to Edwards, this view ignored the fact that according to Scripture the smallest sin deserves everlasting punishment.

Man's mere repentance cannot repair the damage to God's moral government or His glory.[15] Repentance only deals with sins to come; it "makes no alteration in the nature of the sin which is past; nor is it any satisfaction for that sin."[16] For, if divine goodness allowed exemption from punishment on the basis of repentance alone, then sin could not be a moral evil.[17]

It is clear that these two men saw a different purpose in divine punishment.

> If it be consistent with the divine perfection to subject a sinner to misery, for the sake of advancing his own good, as is implied in the very idea of disciplinary punishment; why is it not equally consistent with the same perfections, to subject a sinner to misery, for the sake of promoting the good of the system?[18]

For Edwards, the purpose of divine punishment was not the happiness of God's creation, but to uphold divine government.[19]

> Moral evil is a damage to the universe, as it is a violation of the law, an opposition to the authority and government of the God of nature, and as it dissolves and weakens that government. Therefore satisfac-

---

14. Edwards the Younger, "Salvation of All Men," *Works,* Vol. I, 58.

15. Edwards the Younger, "The Glory of God, and the Greatest Happiness of the System of the Universe, and even of the Created System, mutually imply each other." *Works,* Vol. II, 121.

16. Edwards the Younger, "Salvation of All Men," *Works,* Vol. I, 39. See also his sermon "Mere Repentance No Ground of Pardon," *Works,* Vol. II, 248–257. "Now it is not the dictate of reason that sin deserves nothing but repentance, or beneficial discipline; but it is the dictate of reason that it deserves some real and proper token of displeasure—something that on the whole shall be a real evil and displeasure to the sinner." 251.

17. Edwards the Younger, "Salvation of All Men," *Works,* Vol. I, 138.

18. Edwards the Younger, "Salvation of All Men," *Works,* Vol. I, 59.

19. Another of Edwards' early sermons written while he was studying with Joseph Bellamy and Samuel Hopkins in 1766 indicates the way in which he was trained.

Everyone that believeth in JX shall be treated as if he stood perfectly right with respect to the Law. . . . A person is said to be justified when he is in certain respects esteemed,

tion is due to that authority and government, and the good of the system requires that by something done to support the government, to restore its tone, and to deter others from future transgressions, reparation be made of the injury done by moral evil.[20]

Edwards repeatedly accused his opponents of minimizing the effect of man's sin. He saw sin as a transgression of the law of God, and therefore as a breach in divine government.

The demerit of sin is in proportion to the obligation violated. The obligation is measured, by the dignity and excellence of God. As therefore, he is infinite, in every perfection and excellence, the obligation is infinite, and the violation of it, is a sin infinitely criminal. As also, all sin is, in effect, of this description, the demerit of all sin is infinitely great.[21]

To Edwards, this view of the nature of sin obviated any notion of punishment as disciplinary. Rather, punishment for sin is

that which is deserved by the sinner and is necessary to support the divine law and moral government in proper dignity, and thus to promote the general good; and this surely is opposed to no attribute of God, whether justice or goodness.[22]

Chauncy, however, regarded endless punishment as contrary to the justice of God. The infinitely wise, benevolent God would not allow eternal damnation for any of His creatures. Edwards answered this charge with an elaborate discussion of the nature of justice itself. There were, in Edwards' view, three kinds of justice: commutative justice, which applies only to the exchange of property; public jus-

---

looked upon, approved as just; or as one that has never sinned; and so in certain respects is treated accordingly; not that God will ever look upon, or suppose a person who has once sinned, never to have sinned; no, it is impossible that God should ever be so deceived, or view things as contrary to what they really are in fact. . . . For everyone who has the righteousness of the law, is entitled, by the promise of God, to eternal rewards; as will accordingly be so rewarded by him . . . when men fell there was no way by which a pardon could be granted consistent with the honor of the government or consistent with his glorious perfection.

Ms. Sermon written at Bethlehem, Connecticut, in October, 1766 (Yale University Library).

20. Edwards the Younger, "Mere Repentance No Ground of Pardon," *Works*, Vol. II, 252.

21. Edwards the Younger, "A Systematic Collection of Questions and Answers in Divinity," Ms., January 22, 1794, copied by Maltby Gelston (Yale University Library), Question 132, p. 177.

22. Edwards the Younger, "Salvation of All Men," *Works*, Vol. I, 68.

tice, which protects the rights of the community or the state; and distributive justice, which is concerned with an equal distribution of rewards and punishments. Regarding the question of endless punishment we are concerned with distributive justice alone. Edwards insisted, "we do not plead for endless punishment on any other grounds, than that it is just; that is, on the grounds of distributive justice, of rewards and punishments."[23] Sin is an infinite evil; it deserves an infinite punishment.

> But whatever punishment the wicked justly deserve, they will in fact suffer; they will have to pay the uttermost farthing; they will suffer judgement without mercy. Therefore, they will suffer not only in endless punishment, but an endless misery or torment.[24]

But God is good as well as just.

> The divine justice promotes the happiness of the universal system, implying the divine glory, by treating a person strictly according to his own character; the divine goodness promotes the same important object, by treating a person more favorably than is according to his own character or conduct.[25]

However, it appears that only the elect come to know the goodness of God; the damned are aware only of His justice. Those who are delivered from the curse of the law know the goodness of God; those who remain under the curse of the law are merely treated justly. Divine goodness does not require the salvation of all men. The Universalists, Edwards argued, never questioned the justice or goodness of God in permitting earthly calamities, so "why may not the general good be promoted, as well by endless misery, as by the miseries of this life?"[26]

> The very idea of salvation is deliverance from the curse of the law. But if the pains of hell for ages of ages be the curse of the law, they who suffer those pains are not saved; they are damned to the highest possible degree consistent with law and justice, which is all the damnation for which any man can argue.[27]

---

23. Edwards the Younger, "Salvation of All Men," *Works*, Vol. I, 86, 74.
24. Edwards the Younger, "Salvation of All Men," *Works*, Vol. I, 259.
25. Edwards the Younger, "Salvation of All Men," *Works*, Vol. I, 121.
26. Edwards the Younger, "Salvation of All Men," *Works*, Vol. I, 123.
27. Edwards the Younger, "Salvation of All Men," *Works*, Vol. I, 106.

Men are delivered from the curse of the law by the goodness of God, by His grace. Only if divine punishment is endless and just does God show grace by saving men. To say that one is saved by God's grace implies that endless punishment would have been just. If it were unjust, man's salvation would not be an act of grace.[28] Edwards' insistence that endless punishment is just can be summed up in one sentence: "The salvation of the sinner consists in deliverance from the curse of the law; the curse of the law is endless punishment; and to be delivered from this by free grace, implies, that the endless punishment of the sinner is just."[29]

In Edwards' mind the Universalist position, that all men will be saved from eternal punishment, was neither theologically intelligent nor logically defensible.

> Therefore I wish to ask them from what they believe all men are, according to these words, to be saved? From an endless punishment? then they were by a divine constitution exposed to an endless punishment; then sin is an infinite evil; which to them is an infinitely horrible doctrine. But let them if they can, avoid it, once allowing that all men are to be saved from an endless punishment; or are all men, according to these words, to be saved from a temporary punishment? What temporary punishment? Not that which is to continue for ages of ages; some will suffer that. Not from a longer temporary punishment; because none such is threatened; and sinners are not exposed to a punishment greater than that which is threatened in the divine law. On the whole, according to universalism, these words mean, that all men shall be saved, indeed, but shall be saved from—NOTHING.[30]

In point of fact Chauncy and Edwards could not argue effectively against each other. Their conceptions of God and His relationship to the created world were simply too disparate, and implied differing conceptions of the work of salvation. When we turn to Edwards' interpretations of the specific work of Christ in atoning for man's sin we see the further development of his ideas relating to these issues.

---

28. Edwards the Younger, "Salvation of All Men," *Works,* Vol. I, 108.
29. Edwards the Younger, "Salvation of All Men," *Works,* Vol. I, 259.
30. Edwards the Younger, "Salvation of All Men," *Works,* Vol. I, 191.

The Atonement

Students of Christian thought have often attributed to New England theology a particular view of the atonement—the governmental theory. It was not until the time of the younger Edwards, however, that this view was expressed in full detail by an American theologian.

Hugo Grotius (1583–1645), the Dutch jurist, is credited with originating and developing the governmental theory of the atonement. His effort was in part an answer to the Socinian movement which had directed its fire against traditional theories concerning the atonement. The Socinians suggested that Christ's life and death were an example of true obedience to the will of God, and not the payment of a debt, or an effort to satisfy an offended deity. The effect of Christ's death could not be transferred, but man could imitate His life.

Grotius proposed quite different meaning for the event. A jurist of considerable fame, he thought in terms of law, justice, and government; he applied the thought of his profession to interpreting the atonement, seeking to avoid both the position of the Socinians, and the substitutionary and propitiatory interpretations of the doctrine.[31] Grotius's sympathy lay with the original Arminian movement of his native country, and he insisted that traditional theories of the atonement conflicted with any view of God as forgiving and merciful. He suggested that God as ruler of the world had established certain laws, including the divine law expressed in Scripture, for the maintenance of peace and harmony. When man sins he acts both against the law established by God and against God Himself. God acted in Christ to show man that, though forgiveness is granted, the order and peace of the world must be upheld. Contending against the Socinian view that Christ did not undergo punishment Grotius wrote:

> . . . Since the Scripture says that Christ was chastised by God, i.e., punished; that Christ bore our sins, i.e., the punishment of sins; was made sin, i.e. was subjected to the penalty of sins; was made a curse with God, or was exposed to the curse, that is, the penalty of the law; since, moreover, the very suffering of Christ, full of torture, bloody,

---

31. Hugo Grotius, *A Defense of the Catholic Faith Concerning the Satisfaction of Christ, Against Faustus Socinus*, tr. F. H. Foster (Andover: F. Draper, 1889).

ignominious, is most appropriate matter of punishment; since again, the Scripture says that these were inflicted on him by God on account of our sins, i.e. our sins so deserving; since death itself is said to be the wages, i.e. the punishment of sin; certainly it can by no means be doubted that with reference to God the suffering and death of Christ has the character of a punishment.[32]

The laws of God could not be relaxed. Punishment must be inflicted; divine government must be upheld.

For to inflict punishment, or to liberate anyone from punishment whom you can punish (which the Scripture calls justifying), is only the prerogative of the ruler as such, primarily and *per se;* as, for example, of a father in a family, of the king in a state, of God in the universe.[33]

Once the law has been upheld by the atonement, God can forgive the damage being done to His moral order.

Until Jonathan Edwards the Younger, New England theologians had not accepted this conception of the atonement. Jonathan Edwards, Sr. viewed the work of Christ as the payment of a debt, not as the upholding of divine government. In his mind, the atonement was an act of glory to God. "It is manifest from Scripture that God's glory is the last end of that great work of providence, the work of redemption by Jesus Christ."[34] Hopkins and Bellamy began to shift away from Edwards' interpretation. Hopkins suggested that not only the work of redemption but sin itself promotes the "greatest good" of the created order.[35] The atonement is designed to this end; but it does not primarily express God's glory or uphold divine government. Bellamy was most clearly an American precursor for the governmental theory of the atonement.[36] He combined the

---

32. Grotius, 32.

33. Grotius, 51.

34. Jonathan Edwards, Sr., "Dissertation Concerning the End for Which God Created the World," *The Works of President Edwards, in Four Volumes* (New York: Leavitt, Trow & Co., 1844), Vol. II, 232. This oft neglected work of Edwards' shows explicitly that he believed that the glory of God's own character was the purpose for the creation and redemption of the world.

35. Samuel Hopkins, "Sin Thro' Divine Interposition," *The Works of Samuel Hopkins* (Boston: Doctrinal Tract and Book Society, 1854), Vol. II, 503ff.

36. Bellamy's remark that "the whole mediational scheme is designed, and in its own nature adapted, to do honour to the divine law" (*Nature and Glory of The Gospel,* 41), reflects the governmental interpretation. Edwards the Younger gave the theory its first elaborate statement.

two interpretations.[37] Like Edwards, Sr., he insisted that God must punish to vindicate His own character, but he also believed that God acts to uphold His divine government, a view first articulated in America by Jonathan Edwards the Younger.

Edwards did not view his acceptance of the Grotian formulation as a deviation from his New Divinity predecessors.

> The followers of Mr. Edwards have proved, that the atonement does not consist in the payment of a debt, properly so called. It consists rather in doing that, which for the purposes of establishing the authority of the divine government is equivalent to the punishment of the sinner according to the letter of the law.[38]

The ease with which this interpretation of the atonement appeared to fit into the New Divinity scheme indicates how far the disciples of Edwards, Sr. had moved from his thought. The governmental theory was out of character with the total theological effort of Edwards, Sr., even though one can refer to parts of his *Dissertation Concerning the End For Which God Created the World* and *Miscellaneous Observations Concerning the Divine Decree in General and Election in Particular* for support for it.

In 1785 Edwards the Younger was invited to deliver three sermons at the opening meetings of the Connecticut General Assembly. He chose to speak about the atonement.[39] In his opening sermon he made his position clear: the atonement was designed to uphold the divine law and government. Mere reformation of one's ways could not repair the damage to divine government.[40]

> The atonement is the substitute for the punishment threatened in the law, and was designed to answer the same ends of supporting the authority of the law, the dignity of the divine moral government, and the consistency of the divine conduct in legislation and execution.[41]

---

37. See Joseph Bellamy, "True Religion Delineated," *The Works of Joseph Bellamy, D.D.* (Boston: Doctrinal Tract and Book Society, 1853), Vol. I, 275ff.

38. Edwards the Younger, "Remarks on the Improvements Made in Theology by His Father, President Edwards," *Works*, Vol. I, 486. Part of the original manuscript of this short essay can be found in the Hartford Seminary Library, though about one-third of it has been lost.

39. Edwards the Younger, "Three Sermons on the Necessity of the Atonement, and Its Consistency with Free Grace in Forgiveness," *Works*, Vol. II. See also *Sermons, Essays, Extracts, by Various Authors* (New York: George Forman, 1811).

40. Edwards the Younger, "Three Sermons," *Works*, Vol. II, 18.

41. Edwards the Younger, "Three Sermons," *Works*, Vol. II, 17. See also "Thoughts on the Atonement," *Works*, Vol. I, 493.

It cannot properly be conceived as the payment of a debt.

> That if the atonement of Christ be considered as the payment of a debt, the release of the sinner seems not to be an act of grace, although the payment be made by Christ, and not by the sinner personally. . . . But, the fact is, that Christ has not, in the literal and proper sense, paid the debt for us. . . . The sense of this is, that since the atonement consists, not in the payment of a debt, but in the vindication of the divine law and character; therefore it is not at all opposed to free grace in pardon.[42]

Christ has restored the divine government; this is an act of grace.[43] In Edwards' mind, if Christ only paid man's debt to God, the atonement would merely be an act of justice, not of grace. "Grace is ever so opposed to justice, that they mutually limited each other; wherever grace begins, justice ends; and wherever justice begins, grace ends."[44]

The argument often used by the opponents of the governmental theory of the atonement centered on the supposition that the grace of God would show much more clearly if men were pardoned freely without an atonement. Edwards' doctrine, the argument continued, showed God as an unmerciful, legalistic deity who extracted every last ounce of punishment. Edwards' rebuttal, quite consistently, emphasized the need to uphold the general good of the created order. Viewed in that light, he contended, God's mercy shows much more clearly than it could in any other way.

> Therefore, so far is the doctrine of atonement from representing the Deity, as implacable and unmerciful, that since the atonement is no more than a measure taken by infinite wisdom to prepare the way for pardon consistently with the general good, it represents God to be as placable and as ready to show mercy as is consistent with the general good and happiness.[45]

To Edwards, belief in the endless punishment of man was the only view consistent with belief in the divinity of Christ.

> If Christ were a mere creature we might well disbelieve either the scriptural doctrine of endless punishment, or the sufficiency of the

---

42. Edwards the Younger, "Three Sermons," *Works,* Vol. II, 25–27.
43. See Ms. Sermon, composed at New Haven, December, 1768 (Hartford Seminary Library).
44. Edwards the Younger, "Three Sermons," *Works,* Vol. II, 30.
45. Edwards the Younger, "Christ Crucified," *Works,* Vol. II, 287.

Redeemer. . . . No wonder, therefore, that those who disbelieve the divinity of Christ, do generally, if not universally, disbelieve the endless misery of those who die impenitent.[46]

No one other than Christ could have upheld the divine government and secured man's redemption.

For God never, consistently with his own glory, could have pardoned any one sin, had not Christ died. The nature then of every sin being such that it requires an infinite atonement, it must certainly justly deserve an infinite punishment, and the sentence which condemned to it, is a just, righteous and holy sentence; and were it not for the mere grace of God it would be actually executed upon everyone of our race.[47]

Thus, the atonement must be made by Christ, because Christ alone can uphold God's law and government and show the infinite grace that God has bestowed upon man.

If an atonement be necessary to support the authority of the law and of the moral government of God, it is doubtless necessary to the public good of the moral system, or to the general good of the universe and to the divine glory. This being granted or established, the question just now stated, comes to this simply, whether it exhibits greater grace and goodness in the divine mind, and secures greater good to the universe, to pardon sin in such a mode, as is consistent with the general good of the universe; or in such a mode as is inconsistent with that important object;—a question which no man, from regard to his own reputation, would choose to propose.[48]

God has acted in the only way possible to uphold His rule. If God could conceivably pardon without an atonement, "it would prove that he is destitute of goodness and regardless, not only of his own glory, but of the true happiness of the system of his moral creatures."[49]

What Edwards did to the doctrine of the atonement seems a long way from the Pauline phrase: "God was in Christ reconciling

46. Edwards the Younger, "All Divine Truth Profitable," *Works*, Vol. II, 101.
47. Edwards the Younger, "The Law Not Made Void Through Faith," *Works*, Vol. II, 370.
48. Edwards the Younger, "Three Sermons," *Works*, Vol. II, 37.
49. Edwards the Younger, "Three Sermons," *Works*, Vol. II, 52.

the world unto himself." Instead we find a neat scheme. The Christian life is obedience to the moral law, fitting in with divine government. The death of Christ is clear and unmistakable evidence that God will punish wrongdoing. Divine government must be upheld at any cost, and fear of vindictive justice becomes the weapon to enforce obedience. Paradoxically, however much other items of New Divinity dogma offended the spirit of the time, this theory blended well with the current political temper. Edwards himself wrote: ". . . So long as the established powers rule according to law, justice, and the constitution, none can pretend that it is lawful to resist them."[50] But "the apostle [Paul] did not mean to teach that it is never lawful to resist the higher powers";[51] "the truth is, and the whole spirit of scripture sustains it, that rulers are bound to rule in the fear of God and for the good of the people; and if they do not, then in resisting them we are doing God's service."[52] If God's government is not justly upheld by the King, armed rebellion and "vindictive" punishment is not just desirable but necessary. If God's government is not upheld by man, vindictive punishment is necessary for those who transgress His law.

---

50. Edwards the Younger, "Submission to Rulers," *Works,* Vol. II, 240.
51. Edwards the Younger, "Submission to Rulers," *Works,* Vol. II, 243.
52. Edwards the Younger, "Submission to Rulers," *Works,* Vol. II, 245.

CHAPTER EIGHT

The Nature and Extent of Sin

The nature and extent of sin was the one issue at the heart of the theological debates in New England during the latter half of the eighteenth century. The other major problems—"liberty and necessity," the means of regeneration, universal salvation—all had their roots in this central concern. The problem is, of course, a perennial one in Christian theology, but the particular catalyst for these debates, Jonathan Edwards, Sr., and the growing bravado of Arminianism, made the issue paramount.

In general, there were three explanations of the relationship between Adam and his descendants. The Arminians held that Adam's personal example in rejecting God has been followed throughout human history.[1] Their concern to preserve man's responsibility for sin prompted their denial of any legal or constitutional relationship between Adam and his posterity. The similarity between their position and the arguments of John Taylor is striking.[2] Though there are certain physical inheritances, such as "pain, sickness, labour, sorrow and death,"[3] which come to men because of Adam's sin, man's moral defects are his own, and are brought about by his own action. But although man is corrupted by sin, his good actions do not go unnoticed by the benevolent God. Thus, the

---

1. Samuel Webster, *A Winter Evening's Conversation Upon the Doctrine of Original Sin* (New Haven: James Parker, and Company, 1757), 20ff. Also Samuel Webster, *The Winter Evening Conversation Vindicated* (New Haven: Edes and Gill, 1758), 100ff; and Charles Chauncy, *Five Dissertations on the Scripture Account of the Fall; and Its Consequences* (London: C. Dilly, 1785).
2. See Chapter III.
3. Webster, *Winter Evening's Conversation,* 12.

fundamental disagreement between the Arminians and most Calvinists concerned the total effect of Adam's sin.

The Old Calvinists rejected the position of the Arminians and viewed Adam as the legal representative of man; when he sinned, his guilt fell on his descendants. Though they did not take pains to defend the doctrine of the imputation of Adam's sin, the vigor of the New Divinity argument placed them in a position where they came to regard their position as orthodox. When Edwards, Sr. wrote his treatise, *Doctrine of Original Sin Defended,* primarily in opposition to the works of John Taylor, he undercut the doctrine of imputation. He insisted that it is a "most Evident and acknowledged *Fact,* with respect to the state of all mankind, without exception of one individual among all the natural descendents of Adam, . . . that God actually deals with Adam and his posterity as one."[4] In the face of this "metaphysical" innovation the uncreative Old Calvinist party reasserted historic tradition. Chauncey Whittelsey, in writing to Ezra Stiles, remarked,

> His Scheme, in proportion as it is admitted by any Mind, will, I think, unavoidably lessen the odiousness of Sin, in the view of that Mind. . . . If his Scheme is read for true Orthodoxy, some, I fear, will become Deists from yr dislike of what is said to be orthodox Christianity.[5]

At this point, the distinction between the Old Calvinist party and the other two groups seemed to rest only on the reassertion of traditional Calvinistic formulations, rather than on a specific interpretation of the doctrine of sin.

The New Divinity position stressed the personal identity between Adam and his posterity. As we have seen, Edwards, Sr. inaugurated the discussion. "The guilt a man has upon his soul at his first existence, is one and simple, viz., the guilt of the original apostasy, the guilt of the sin by which the species first rebelled against God."[6] The depravity of man

is not to be looked upon as sin belonging to them, *distinct* from their

---

4. Jonathan Edwards, Sr., "Doctrine of Original Sin," *The Works of President Edwards, in Four Volumes* (New York: Leavitt, Trow & Co., 1844), Vol. II, 484.

5. *Extracts from the Itineraries and Other Miscellanies of Ezra Stiles,* ed. Franklin B. Dexter (New Haven: Yale University Press, 1916), 591.

6. Edwards, Sr., "Doctrine of Original Sin," *Works,* Vol. II, 482.

participation in Adam's first sin: it is as it were the extended pollution of that Sin, through the whole tree, by virtue of the constituted union of the branches with the root.

The action of Adam, in which his posterity has participated, brought an "innate sinful depravity of the heart" to all men.[7] This view rests on Edwards' metaphysical assumptions, particularly his assumption that God is the immediate cause of what is.

Lacking his metaphysical genius, and even his point of view, Edwards' disciples were inclined to ignore his explanation of constitutional identity. They became preoccupied with the problems of human responsibility and divine permission of sin. Rejecting, though somewhat hesitantly, the doctrine of imputation, they stressed man's own rebellion. "This sin, which takes place in the posterity of Adam, is not properly distinguished into original and actual sin, because it is all really actual, and there is, strictly speaking, no other sin but actual sin."[8] Sin is not imputed to Adam's posterity, but men are guilty of Adam's sin because it is *their* sin.[9] "This evil bent of our hearts is not of his making, but is the spontaneous propensity of our own wills."[10] All sin stems from the nature and quality of the exercises which take place in a moral agent.[11] Later, Nathaniel Emmons (1745–1840), pastor of the

---

7. Edwards, Sr., "Doctrine of Original Sin," *Works,* Vol. II, 482, 309.
His discussions never minimized the total effect of sin. In 1734, during a revival at the Northampton Church, he wrote,

> ... if men were guilty of sin, but in one particular, that is sufficient ground of their eternal rejection and condemnation. ... Their guilt is like great mountains heaped one upon another, until the pile is grown up to heaven. They are totally corrupt, in every part, in all their faculties; and all the principles of their nature, their understandings, and wills; and in all their dispositions and affections, their heads, their hearts, are totally depraved; all the members of their bodies are only instruments of sin; and all their senses, seeing, hearing, tasting, etc., are only inlets and outlets of sin, channels of corruption. There is nothing but sin, no good at all. ... Now if one sinful word or thought has so much evil in it, as to deserve eternal destruction, how do they deserve to be eternally cast of[f] and destroyed, that are guilty of so much sin.

J. Edwards, Sr., *The Justice of God in the Damnation of Sinners* (Hartford: J. Babcock, 1799), 15–17.
8. Samuel Hopkins, *The Works of Samuel Hopkins* (Boston: Doctrinal Tract and Book Society, 1854), Vol. I, 224.
9. Hopkins, *Works,* Vol. I, 218.
10. Joseph Bellamy, *The Works of Joseph Bellamy, D.D.* (Boston: Doctrinal Tract & Book Society, 1853), Vol. I, 153.
11. Bellamy, *Works,* Vol. I, 231.

church in Franklin, Massachusetts, who is usually regarded as part of the New Divinity tradition, reasserted this same point. ". . . It is impossible to conceive of a corrupt and sinful nature prior to, and distinct from corrupt and sinful exercise."[12] John Smalley insisted that the "view that makes Adam's sin responsible for man's sin seems rather calculated to ease the conscience of man, by casting all real blame back upon the first sin only."[13] He, like the other New Divinity men, insisted that a "pinch" of sin corrupted man totally. In direct opposition to the Arminian tradition, the "consistent" Calvinists stressed the doctrine of total depravity, but a depravity which is constituted by man's actual sin, and which is not to be attributed to the imputation of Adam's guilt.

Perhaps because of the attacks of the Arminians, which were becoming louder and more frequent, the New Divinity men turned their attention to the justification of sin in a world created and governed by God. The senior Edwards had not focused on this issue; he was preoccupied with what he observed about man, not with a justification for what he found.

There were some incipient and unresolved problems which his opponents raised and with which his defenders, especially Samuel Hopkins, became preoccupied. Why is there sin? What happens to those dying in infancy? What purpose does sin serve? How can a benevolent God permit man's waywardness?

The "consistent" Calvinists' basic explanation for the theological problems raised by sin was that through sin God fully expresses His power and glory and promotes human happiness. One sermon in a well-known series by Hopkins was entitled "Sin Through Divine Interposition an Advantage to the Universe."[14] In Hopkins' view, a view which he supported by frequent scriptural references,

> the world, considered as fallen or sinful, and redeemed by Christ, is better and far more glorious than it was considered as without sin. . . .
> We are taught that God's greatest and more glorious work is to bring

---

12. Nathaniel Emmons, *The Works of Nathaniel Emmons*, ed. Jacob Ide (Boston: Congregational Board of Publication, 1860), Vol. II, 622–623.

13. John Smalley, *Sermons, On a Number of Connected Subjects* (Hartford: Printed for Oliver D. Cooke; Lincoln and Gleason, printers, 1803), 191ff. Smalley (1734–1820) was pastor of the Congregational Church in New Britain, Connecticut.

14. Hopkins, *Works*, Vol. II, 483ff.

good out of evil—to make sin in general, which is the greatest evil, the means of the greatest good.[15]

But though God uses sin to show His power and glory, that is no license for sin. "The Creature's aims and ends, in committing sin are wicked and vile; but God's aims and designs, in permitting the creature thus to act, are wise and holy."[16] This does not imply that there is something good in sin itself. It is only in using it that God makes sin an "advantage to the Universe." "God's permitting sin was as high an exercise of holiness as any we can think of."[17] Other New Divinity men affirm a similar position.

> ... Upon the whole, all things considered, He judged it best to permit the angels to sin and man to fall, and so let misery enter, into his dominions ... his design was to display all his perfections, and fill the whole earth with his glory.[18]

Stephen West stated,

> that it was the positive design and purpose of God, that moral evil should come into existence in his system and even rise to that astonishing height to which it hath risen here in our world, what can be more evident from the word of God?[19]

Clearly, there was a common effort by the New Divinity men to view sin as conducive to the happiness of man, and to the good of the universe.

An illustration of the technical rigidity into which the New Divinity position had developed is seen in the work of Jonathan Edwards the Younger. Edwards had a dilemma. He felt a tie to the doctrine of imputation, yet sought to follow his father's reasoning, but without his father's metaphysical presuppositions. In the course of his analysis he ignored the position of those against whom he was writing, and thus, it seems, found himself with no audience. In a sermon delivered before the General Association of Connecticut in

---

15. Hopkins, *Works,* 503. (Here is an illustration of "governmental" thinking. See Ch. VII.)

16. Hopkins, *Works,* Vol. II, 509.

17. Hopkins, *Works,* Vol. II, 527.

18. Bellamy, "True Religion Delineated," *Works,* Vol. I, 42, 45.

19. Stephen West, *An Essay on Moral Agency* (Salem: T. C. Cushing, 1794), 247.

1786, he directed his attention to the problem of the sense in which
the sin of Adam is imputed to all his posterity.

> The idea of imputation in this case has been more reprobated than in
> either of those just mentioned. That Adam's sin should be ours, and
> that we on account of it should be judges and condemned as sinners,
> or that we should be the same person as Adam, or that God should so
> consider or suppose us, has appeared to many to be absurd, impious
> and impossible. But if we conceive that our standing or falling was
> suspended on the standing or falling of Adam; that Adam having
> fallen, God permitted us all to fall also; and that he so ordered things
> that we are liable to the numberless calamities of life, and thus are
> treated as if we were sinners; on such a representation, no man, I
> conceive, can fasten an absurdity. Undoubtedly God who had a right
> to suffer Adam to fall and become a sinner, had the same right to have
> suffered all mankind to become sinners by their own personal acts,
> without any reference to the sin of Adam. And if so, what can be said
> to show that he had no right to permit them to fall in consequence of
> the fall of Adam? If he had a right to permit them to fall though
> Adam had not fallen, surely the fall of Adam did not deprive him of
> that right. But the right remaining, he might exercise it, if he saw
> fit, on occasion and in consequence of Adam's sin, as well as on any
> other occasion. To determine these things was the part of divine,
> sovereign wisdom only; so that whatever that should determine and
> establish, would be perfectly right.[20]

The implications of this were clear:

> One consequence of Adam's sin to himself was that he became
> habitually depraved; and the same is the consequence to all his pos-
> terity. Another consequence to him was that he became frail in body,
> and liable to pain, disease, casualty and death; and the same is the
> consequence to all his posterity. Another consequence to him was
> that the very earth was cursed for his sake, so that it was only in the
> sweat of his brow that he could eat bread; and there again the same is
> true of his posterity.[21]

It would be difficult to sway an Arminian with the argument that

20. Jonathan Edwards the Younger, "Christ Our Righteousness," *The Works of Jonathan Edwards, D.D., With a Memoir of his Life and Character by Tyron Edwards* (Andover: Allen, Morrill and Wardwell, 1842), Vol. II, 270–271.

21. Edwards the Younger, "Christ Our Righteousness," *Works*, Vol. II, 271.

"... in the dispensation of providence by which the posterity of Adam are born into the world in a fallen and calamitous state, God manifests his abhorrence of the sin of our common father."[22] Edwards the Younger thus turned the course of the debate sharply. His father had started with the observation that there is sin; Edwards the Younger began with the observation that there is punishment and discipline in creation and that thus something must have offended God's government of the universe.[23]

The changed perspective in Edwardsean theology is also seen vividly in the respective discussions by father and son concerning the end of creation. The senior Edwards said "the great and last end of God's works which is so variously expressed in Scripture, is indeed but *one;* and this *one* end is most properly and comprehensively called, *The Glory of God.*"[24] Edwards the Younger re-interpreted this "end of creation" to mean that "the happiness of mankind was the end of their creation."[25] He tried to tie it to his father's affirmation.

> The display of divine glory, is the display of infinite power, wisdom, and goodness. And to display these perfections, is to produce a system of intelligent creatures, to the highest possible degree excellent and happy.[26]

But this was a mere short step from the position of the Arminians. The concerns of the revolutionary era had even permeated the thought of this stalwart defender of Calvinism.

Another side of the debate developed concerning the problem of human responsibility and "free will." The relation of man's freedom to his moral responsibility has always been a fervently discussed issue in Reformed theology. It was Jonathan Edwards, Sr. who attempted to recall New England theology to a vigorous Reformed basis by showing logically, in his treatise on the will, that there is no such thing as freedom of the will; man, being sinful, will always act contrary to the will of God.[27] When his son reached the peak of his

---

22. Edwards the Younger, "Christ Our Righteousness," *Works,* Vol. II, 271.

23. See Ch. VII.

24. Edwards, Sr., "The Nature of True Virtue," *Works,* Vol. II, 254.

25. Edwards the Younger, "The Soul's Immortality, and Future Retribution," *Works,* Vol. II, 319.

26. Edwards the Younger, "The Soul's Immortality," *Works,* Vol. II, 318.

27. Edwards, Sr., *Freedom of the Will,* ed. Paul Ramsey. Vol. I of *The Works of Jonathan Edwards* (New Haven: Yale University Press, 1957). Ramsey's Introduction is helpful.

career a generation later, the issue was still a dominant one in theological circles.

The Arminian party made several efforts to answer Edwards, Sr. The earliest and fullest reply was *An Examination of the Late Rev. Edwards' "Enquiry on Freedom of the Will"* (1770) by James Dana (1735–1812). "Let a man look into his own breast, and he cannot but perceive inward freedom—*inward freedom*—For if freedom be not in the mind, it is no where and Liberty in the mind implies self-determination."[28] Dana's characteristically anthropocentric essay prompted Stephen West to reassert the Edwardsean argument in his *Essay on Moral Agency* (1772). However, neither Dana's work nor Stephen West's was of the calibre of the later controversy between Samuel West and Jonathan Edwards the Younger.

Much earlier in the century, Samuel West (1738–1808), pastor of the Hollis Street Church in Boston, had written his *Essays on Liberty and Necessity, in which the True Nature of Liberty is Stated and Defended; and the Principal Arguments used by Mr. Edwards and others, for Necessity are Considered,* though he was not prepared to publish the work until 1793.[29] West was more outspokenly Arminian than Dana; the latter would have preferred the label Old Calvinist. The controversy between Samuel West and Edwards the Younger was clearly drawn between an Arminian, and a man who thought himself a defender of the New Divinity. As their arguments indicated, both believed that there could be no middle ground between them.

West's treatise illustrated the Arminian position. "To act, to determine, to will, or to choose, is to be free."[30] How often those very words had been used by the opponents of the elder Jonathan Edwards. West argued that a man moved to act by something extrinsic to his own volition is only a machine, or a passive agent. Edwards, Sr. had often argued that man's sin is caused by a sinful disposition. To say this, in West's view, was to see man's actions as the effect of an extrinsic cause.[31] On the contrary, West insisted,

---

28. James Dana, *An Examination of the Late Reverend President Edwards's Enquiry on Freedom of Will* (Boston: Printed by Daniel Kneeland for Thomas Leverett, 1770), v.

29. Samuel West, *Essays on Liberty and Necessity* (Boston: Samuel Hall, 1793).

30. Samuel West, *Essays on Liberty and Necessity,* 16. Both Charles Chauncy's *The Mystery Hid . . . The Salvation of All Men* and Samuel West's essay had been written around the middle of the century but not published until late in the century. This indicates that changes leading to less hostility against more liberal interpretations of doctrine were taking place in New England theology.

31. Samuel West, *Essays on Liberty and Necessity,* 23.

man's volition is "the mind acting or operating" and nothing else.[32] He used the example of God's nature.

> If God's volitions are not the result of some cause but are considered as God's willing or causing, it will follow, that to assert, that volition is no effect, is not in itself an absurdity; for if it were, it could not be predicated of Deity.[33]

Is there a necessary connection between motive and action? Edwards argued yes; West argued no.[34] West's objection, like that of all Arminians, was his belief that making God responsible for all of man's actions removed the basis for man's responsibility. West did not thereby deny that God foreknows the actions of man.

> To assert, that the Deity may infallibly foreknow, that an agent will act in a certain particular manner, when, at the same time, he infallibly foreknows that the said agent will have a power of acting in a different manner, implies no contradiction; for there is nothing affirmed in one proposition, which is denied in the other.[35]

Though the volition of moral agents does not necessarily depend on God's decree, they "are much the objects of the Divine Knowledge, as though they were produced immediately by his positive efficiency."[36]

> Thus, the Divine Being knew, from all eternity, that Peter would deny and that Judas would betray, his master; But had the reverse taken place, and Peter had betrayed and Judas had only denied, his Master, this would not have made infallibility deceitful and fallible; because then this latter proposition would have been an eternal truth, viz., that Peter would betray, and that Judas would only deny, his Master: And Deity would, from all eternity have infallibly foreknown this proposition, as a certain and infallible truth.[37]

It appears that, regarding this issue, West was trying to preserve two doctrines which may seem to be mutually exclusive—divine foreknowledge and man's responsibility. It is clear that the major

---

32. Samuel West, *Essays on Liberty and Necessity,* 23.
33. Samuel West, *Essays on Liberty and Necessity,* 23.
34. Samuel West, *Essays on Liberty and Necessity, Second Part* (Boston, 1794), 4.
35. Samuel West, *Essays on Liberty and Necessity,* 47.
36. Samuel West, *Essays on Liberty and Necessity,* 52–53.
37. Samuel West, *Essays on Liberty and Necessity,* 53.

objection against Edwards, Sr.'s view of the will was that it appeared to be a denial of man's responsibility. According to the Arminian position, man's will must be self-determining.

> ... the principle of self determination is the only one that is consistent with true humility, and a sense of ill desert; for when a man considers that he is not moved by an extrinsic cause to do evil, but that his wickedness, has originated wholly from himself, he must feel himself exceedingly vile and unworthy of any Divine Saviour; but if he feels himself efficaciously moved by Deity to any wicked act, he cannot feel himself guilty of any ill desert . . . for he will think it very unjust, that he should be punished for being just what the Deity had made him to be.[38]

During his pastorate in New Haven, Edwards the Younger was working on his essay, *Dissertation Concerning Liberty and Necessity,* though the work was not published until 1797. The question of man's responsibility and its relation to God's government had long been an essential part of his theological reflections.

Edwards, like his father, argued that man's freedom lay in his action as an agent.

> Though we hold that our volitions are the effects of some extrinsic cause, and that we are passive, as we are the subjects of the influence of that cause; yet we hold, that we are not merely passive; but the volition is in its own nature an act or action, and in the exercise of it, we are active, though in the causation of it we are passive, so far as to be the subjects of the influence of the efficient cause.[39]

We have noted that one of the major Arminian objections to the Edwardsean view of the will was the thesis that no extrinsic cause determines the action of the mind. Edwards answered this objection by suggesting that choice is either determined and caused by the mind itself, which is to say that choice is an effect and has a cause, or that volition comes into existence without a cause, which would, in Edwards' view, lead to the worst kind of capriciousness.[40] As far as

---

38. Samuel West, *Essays on Liberty and Necessity, Second Part,* 23.
39. Edwards the Younger, "A Dissertation Concerning Liberty and Necessity," *Works,* Vol. I, 310.
40. Edwards the Younger, "A Dissertation Concerning Liberty and Necessity," *Works,* Vol. I, 320ff.

he was concerned the Arminian position allowed no more freedom than his own.

> As to liberty of self-determination, or the causation of volition, by ourselves, if this were possible, and were decreed by God, or by any means were rendered previously certain, there would be no more liberty in it than if we did not cause those particular volitions and no others.[41]

Working on the basis of his father's argument, Edwards argued that man's only freedom is exemption from natural necessity. The Arminian idea of liberty meant "an exemption from all previous certainty that an action will be performed," but, Edwards contended, "then no action of man or any other creature is free; for on this supposition every such action must come to pass without divine prescience; by mere chance, and consequently without cause."[42] Necessity which is inconsistent with moral agency, or praise and blame, is natural necessity.[43]

In Edwards' mind there was a clear connection between motive and volition.

> . . . Volition never takes place without some motive, reason or cause of its existence, either in the views of the mind of him, who is the subject of the volition, in the disposition, bias or appetite of his mind or body, or from the influence of some extrinsic agent.[44]

Any discussion of the problem of the will, without acknowledg-

---

41. Edwards the Younger, "Free Agency and Absolute Decree Reconciled," *Works*, Vol. II, 503.

42. Edwards the Younger, "Remarks on the Improvements Made in Theology by His Father, President Edwards," Ms. in Hartford Seminary Library, 8, 9. In further elaboration of this position he wrote:

> Self determination, therefore, is, in its very nature a determination without motive; and a determination without motive, is a determination without design; and a determination without design, is a determination in the dark, or a blind determination, a determination at hap-hazard and by mere chance. And such an action as this is neither virtuous nor vicious; and is worthy of neither praise or blame."

"God the Author of All Good Volitions and Actions," *Works*, Vol. II, 352.

43. Edwards the Younger, "A Dissertation Concerning Liberty and Necessity," *Works*, Vol. I, 308.

44. Edwards the Younger, "A Dissertation Concerning Liberty and Necessity," *Works*, Vol. I, 344. See also Edwards the Younger, "God the Author of All Good Volitions and Actions," *Works*, Vol. II, 350ff.

ment of the fact that volition has an effect and a cause, is certain to result in error.

> If volition be no effect and have no cause, it proceeds from no power or faculty in human nature as its cause; not from the power of will, nor even from any self-determining power, whether it consists in the will or in any part of human nature.[45]

The younger Edwards felt that only his father's analysis could reconcile divine foreknowledge with human responsibility. Man is the agent in willing, though his volition is determined by an external cause. ". . . We have a natural power to choose or refuse in any case; but we have no moral power, or power opposed to moral necessity."[46] Divine foreknowledge makes certain that man will act in a particular way, but it is not the immediate cause of the volition. "Divine prophecy is not the cause of the futurity of the event foretold, yet no man will say that it does not prove the certain futurity of the event."[47] Man, operating under moral necessity, is free only in relation to natural necessity. To say otherwise equates freedom with uncertainty, contingency, and fatalism.[48] God, therefore, determines man's volitions.

> We grant, that the Deity is primary efficient cause of all things and that he produces volition in the human mind by such second causes as motives, appetites, biases, etc., and the human mind, in being the subject of the divine agency whether mediate or immediate, is passive.[49]

In order to reconcile man's responsibility with this divinely determined moral necessity, Edwards concentrated on the action resulting from the volition. Therein lies man's freedom and his accountability.

---

45. Edwards the Younger, "A Dissertation Concerning Liberty and Necessity," *Works,* Vol. I, 394.

46. Edwards the Younger, "A Dissertation Concerning Liberty and Necessity," *Works,* Vol. I, 313.

47. Edwards the Younger, "A Dissertation Concerning Liberty and Necessity," *Works,* Vol. I, 408.

48. Edwards the Younger, "A Dissertation Concerning Liberty and Necessity," *Works,* Vol. I, 419.

49. Edwards the Younger, "A Dissertation Concerning Liberty and Necessity," *Works,* Vol. I, 426.

> The plain dictate of reason is, that we are accountable whenever we
> deserve praise or blame; and that we do deserve praise or blame,
> whenever we exercise tempers or have volition either good or evil,
> benevolent or malicious, kind or selfish; and this without any inquiry
> whether these volitions happened by pure contingence, or proceeded
> from some cause whether within or without the mind.[50]

Man is not condemned by the cause of the volition, but by the result
of the volition.[51] "The essence of the virtue and vice of benevolence
and malice lies in the nature of those affections and not in their
cause."[52]

To the Arminians, Edwards' position made God the author of
sin. But neither Edwards nor his fellow New Divinity men appeared
overly concerned with this charge.

> . . . If by author of sin is meant the permittor or not hinderer of sin,
> and at the same time, *a disposer of the state of events in such a manner,* for
> wise, holy and most excellent ends and purposes, *that sin,* if it be
> permitted and not hindered, *will most certainly follow,* I do not deny,
> that God is the author of sin; it is no reproach, for the Most High to
> be thus the author of sin.[53]

Edwards, absorbed with the conception of God as the moral governor of the universe, was, like Hopkins, willing to make such an
admission.

The way in which Edwards the Younger joined these two
themes—the nature and extent of sin, and the "freedom of the
will"—makes clear the harsh and legalistic flavor of late eighteenth
century New Divinity. In theological reasoning, as well as in personal relations, Edwards was never one to spare the word to save

---

50. Edwards the Younger, "All Divine Truth Profitable," *Works,* Vol. II, 116.

51. Edwards the Younger, "A Dissertation Concerning Liberty and Necessity,"
Works, Vol. I, 431.

52. Edwards the Younger, "Free Agency and Absolute Decree Reconciled," *Works,*
Vol. II, 505.

53. Edwards the Younger, "A Dissertation Concerning Liberty and Necessity,"
Works, Vol. I, 440. In his article on "Benevolence of God in Inflicting Punishment" he wrote,
It must be granted by all who believe the existence and perfection of God, that
whenever he sends on his creatures any calamity, sickness or death, he does it from the
purest goodness and benevolence, to the system of intelligence. On the same principles
we have a right to argue, that whenever he inflicts damnation on any creature, he is
actuated by the same goodness and benevolence.
Works, Vol. II, 468.

people's feelings. The question in the minds of many in his parish and literary audience was well put in his own words: "Where is the consistence between God's laying a man under a moral necessity of sinning, and then punishing him for that sin?" His answer was not equivocal.

> How can God consistently make a man sick, and then apply medicines or any remedy toward his restoration? Punishment is inflicted to prevent either the subject of the punishment, or others, from falling into the same practice. If there be no inconsistence in bringing sickness on a man, and then healing him by medicine; where is the inconsistence in bringing sin, which is moral sickness, on a man, and whereby both he and that system are so far morally diseased, and then by punishment healing him or the system? . . . For in laying a man under a moral necessity of *sinning,* as he is supposed still to *sin,* nothing is done to impair his moral agency or his desert of punishment. . . . God may as consistently punish a sinner, whom he himself has laid under a moral necessity of sinning, as he may punish him, provided he be laid under the same moral necessity by another being, or by mere chance. . . . A good master may strictly forbid his servant to steal; yet convinced that he does steal, the master may in a particular case, wish him to steal, and even leave money exposed to him that he may steal, and ultimately with a design that an advantage may be put into the master's hand, to convict, punish, and reform his servant. There is no inconsistence in the master's thus forbidding theft, and yet from the motive before mentioned wishing to have it committed.[54]

He would admit no difference between the "Great First Cause {who} is the efficient of the sensation of heat . . . and the same Great Agent {who} is the efficient cause of volition."[55] And at that point even Edwards' analytical skill and power of intellect could not protect him from the charge that he saw man as a puppet, controlled by God, moved this way and that by the "Great First Cause."

---

54. Edwards the Younger, "A Dissertation Concerning Liberty and Necessity," *Works,* Vol. I, 444–446.

55. Edwards the Younger, "A Dissertation Concerning Liberty and Necessity," *Works,* Vol. I, 381.

CHAPTER NINE

Dismissal

During the late 1780's and early 1790's friction arose between Edwards and his congregation. As its pastor's theological position became elaborately clear to the White Haven Congregation, the latent dissenting preferences of its lay leaders came into the open. Edwardsean theology had not become thoroughly ingrained in the thought of the church, and it was not difficult for those who were in conflict with their pastor's affirmations to find ways in which his ministry could be challenged.

One source of developing hostility between Edwards and the leaders of his congregation was his intransigent attitude toward the other churches of the town. In Edwards' mind, relationships with other churches depended on the theological allegiances of the respective ministers, and thus, from the very beginning of his ministry in New Haven, he was embroiled in ecclesiastical controversy. Controversy over the issue of public testimony of regeneration had caused a group to withdraw from the White Haven Church to form the Fair Haven Church. During the first decade of Edwards' ministry, several efforts were made to have this requirement rescinded. In 1784, the White Haven Church voted to permit transfer members to subscribe to the Confession of Faith in private, but the pastor did not always follow the dictates of his parishioners.[1] Ezra Stiles' obser-

---

1. *Records of the White Haven Church,* December 5, 1784. In November of 1787 Edwards refused to admit a member of the East Haven Church to his church until that member made a public testimony of his religious experience. Stiles remarked that the prospective member was treated as a "heathen & publican, and [that Edwards] required a new profession of Religion as he would of a newly converted Heathen." *The Literary Diary of Ezra Stiles,* ed. Franklin B. Dexter (New York: C. Scribner's Sons, 1901), Vol. III, 286.

vation of the New Haven ecclesiastical scene explained why the White Haven Church remained isolated. "The general idea for those dozen years (1770–1782) has been that Mr. Whttly & his Chh were Arminians; Mr. Edwds & his Chh New Divinity; Mr. Mather & hs Chh Old Divinity."[2] This division did not last, however. When the Fair Haven Church called Edwards' former pupil, Samuel Austin, as pastor in 1786, Edwards was quite willing to participate in the ordination service, and during the years immediately following there were frequent interchanges between the two churches.[3]

Throughout his New Haven ministry, Edwards' relationship with the First Congregational Church was less than cordial. There was pressure, however, from members of his own congregation to renew communion with the First Church. In January, 1789, this question was discussed by the congregation.

> . . . The Church took into consideration the question concerning communion with the First Church in this city; & after some discourse upon it, as it appeared, that the Brethren were not yet agreed or ripe to act upon it, the further consideration of it was referred to an adjourned meeting of this church to be holden on Monday the 23rd of February next, at 3 o'clock at the house of the pastor.[4]

During succeeding meetings in February, April, June, August, and September no agreement could be reached. The church minutes for November, 1789, read: "On the question whether anything should be done by this church respecting uniting in lectures with the first church in this town, resolved in the negative."[5] There had appeared to be growing support for the two churches to have simple communion together, but this was prevented in April, 1789, when the First Church called James Dana to become its minister. Dana, a graduate of Harvard, was an ardent "Old Light" minister and strongly opposed to New Divinity doctrine. His settlement in Wallingford in 1758 had caused a prolonged conflict between the opposing schools

---

2. *The Literary Diary of Ezra Stiles*, Vol. III, 8. Chauncey Whittelsey was pastor of the First Church and Mather was pastor of the Fair Haven Church.

3. Austin remained as pastor for only two years. His strong New Divinity position was not shared by his congregation. See *Records of the Fair Haven Church*, 1789—the exact month is not given.

4. *Records of the White Haven Church*, January 26, 1789.

5. *Records of the White Haven Church*, November 9, 1789.

within Connecticut Congregationalism.[6] When the church council met at New Haven to install him as pastor, Edwards came prepared with a list of theological questions which he wished to ask Mr. Dana, and the latter countered with a similar set of questions directed to Edwards. Despite the protests of the New Divinity men, Dana was installed as pastor of the First Church. Edwards continued to refuse communion with that church because he felt that their new pastor was "unsound as to the trinity, election, & univ salvation as well as opposed to New Divinity."[7]

The developing uneasiness in New Haven with Edwards' strong New Divinity sentiments was part of a broader and growing hostility to New Divinity doctrine among the churches of Connecticut. Ezra Stiles, commenting in his diary on the changing theological scene, insisted that the successors of Edwards, Sr., Bellamy, and Hopkins, were not of the same calibre as the original Edwardseans.

> Now the younger class [of New Divinity adherents] are disposed to become Oracles themselves & wish to write & have their own Books come into Vogue . . . particularly Dr. Edwards, Mr. Trumbull, Mr. Judson, Mr. Robinson, Mr. Smalley, Mr. Spring, Mr. Strong of Hartford, Mr. Dwight, Mr. Emmons, etc. They all want to be Luthers. But they will none of them be equal to those strong Reasoners President Edwards & Mr. Hopkins.[8]

As a matter of fact, the New Divinity men were losing the support of their churches. Edwards' incessant "Preaching of New Divy & Rigidity in chh administrations had disgusted [his parishioners]. Perhaps there is not one of his chh & congregation of his New Divy sentiments."[9]

Financial difficulties between Edwards and the White Haven Society arose from this continuing conflict. When he was called to the church his salary was to be one hundred pounds a year, plus additional benefits.

---

6. See Leonard Bacon, *Thirteen Historical Discourses, on the Completion of Two Hundred Years, from the Beginning of the First Church in New Haven* (New Haven: Durrie and Peck, 1839), Discourse XIII, "James Dana at Wallingford and New Haven."

7. *The Literary Diary of Ezra Stiles,* Vol. III, 365.

8. *The Literary Diary of Ezra Stiles,* Vol. III, 275.

9. *The Literary Diary of Ezra Stiles,* Vol. III, 344.

... This Society will Provide and allow him the use of a suitable house lot with a Convenient Dwelling House and other necessary Buildings on it and some other land for Pasture Commodiously situated for his Improvement and keep the land well furnish[ed] and buildings in good repair. And also Provide and Deliver to him Annually at the house for his use a sufficient quantity of fire wood, and also pay him an annual salary sufficient for ye comfortable and honourable support of himself and family so long as he continues the minister of this Society and according to his ability [to] perform the work of the gospel ministry herein.[10]

The Society was not always able to meet these obligations to its minister. In the 1782 minutes of the Society we find evidence that Edwards complained that the original compact was not being fulfilled. In December, 1782, the Society offered Edwards a new contract which provided that in compensation for the amount they owed him he would be permitted to buy the parsonage for 250 pounds, a sum under its actual value. The yearly salary of one hundred pounds was to remain in effect. Edwards considered the new offer and wrote his decision to the Society.

To the Society of White Haven
Gentlemen
I have considered the proposals of the New Contract which you have laid before me by your Committee and my only hesitation to accept them has arisen from a fear that I should not be able to support my family on a Salary limited to One Hundred pounds, especially [since] the necessities of life are now so very high and as I may probably have an increase of family and consequently of expenses. However as I take the true intent and spirit of all such Contracts, tho limited to particular terms, to be, to support the gospel ministry among the people with whom they are made; and as I doubt not but that this is the intention of this Society in particular; I am induced to accept the proposals and to relinquish all legal claim to any larger salary than is specified in the proposal; still relying on the justice and generosity of the Society, which I have often experienced, and for which I take this opportunity thus publickly to thank them; that if it shall be found by experience and shall be made to appear to the

---

10. *Records of the Society of White Haven,* November 28, 1768.

satisfaction of the Society that the hundred pounds is not a sufficient support for myself and family the society will make such addition to it as they shall be convinced are necessary. But as I am certain the hundred pounds will not be sufficient support, unless it is put in my power to use it to the best advantage, it is to be understood that the salary be paid punctually at the end of every year; and as a motive to punctual payment, that the interest of that not paid at the end of any year shall be allowed me until it shall be paid. As to the part of the proposals which respects my leaving the society I understand the society to mean 'if of my own accord without their consent they on their part fulfilling the Contract shall leave the work of the ministry in the Society,' as in the proposals—if this answer be acquiesced in by the Society I desire it may be recorded with the other proceeding of the Society on this subject.

I am gentlemen your very humble servant

Jonathan Edwards.[11]

New Haven, June 8, 1783.

Edwards' hope for a larger salary was not to be realized. The membership of the White Haven Church had decreased greatly during his pastorate. Ezra Stiles estimated that in 1772 it had 480 members, First Church, 500, and the Fair Haven Church, 200. But in 1789 Stiles wrote that Edwards' church consisted of only nineteen male members![12] "Dr. Edwds people are exceedingy alienated from him; so that at his sacramt lect. last Thursday, he had but 20 women or females & ten men to attend in the whole Assembly—only 5 from his ch."[13] Stiles explained that a majority of the church members objected to Edwards' position on church membership and to his strong New Divinity sentiments.[14] He went on to say that many of Edwards' parishioners wanted to rejoin the First Church, but Edwards refused to co-operate because "he looks upon Dr. Dana as a Heretick."[15] The reason that the Church and Society were unable to meet the financial obligations to their pastor is obvious.

Edwards was not without staunch, powerful defenders. Un-

11. Letter of June 8, 1783, from Jonathan Edwards to the White Haven Society in *Records of the Society of White Haven.* Edwards was by no means destitute. In 1795 he purchased land in New York state purportedly worth $52,590. (Deed in Yale University Library.)

12. *The Literary Diary of Ezra Stiles,* Vol. III, 344.

13. *The Literary Diary of Ezra Stiles,* Vol. III, 438.

14. *The Literary Diary of Ezra Stiles,* Vol. III, 344.

15. *The Literary Diary of Ezra Stiles,* Vol. III, 344.

doubtedly, the major reason that he was not dismissed in the late
1780's or early 1790's was the fact that he received strong support
from Roger Sherman, one of the outstanding figures in revolutionary
America, and a member of the White Haven Church. Sherman was
Judge of the Superior Court of Connecticut, a member of the First
Continental Congress, and he also served on the committee which
drafted the Declaration of Rights, and the Declaration of Independence. He was the only person to sign all four of the major documents of this formative period in American history—The Articles of
Association of 1774, the Declaration of Independence, The Articles
of Confederation, and the Constitution. Because of his contribution
to the government, Sherman was a revered figure in New Haven.[16]
Thus, his support of Jonathan Edwards carried considerable weight.

We obtain a contemporary account of Edwards' work in New
Haven, and of the difficulties that existed between the White Haven
Church and its pastor, from Sherman's correspondence with fellow
parishioners.

In February of 1790, for example, Sherman wrote to Simeon
Baldwin asking for information concerning the White Haven
Church.[17]

New York, Feb. 4th, 1790

Dear Sir,

I this day received a letter from my son John dated Jan. 14th,
enclosing one for his wife which I have forwarded to you—He writes
that he has recovered his health, that Issac is there & their prospects
are good—you wrote me some time ago that you were notified to
attend a meeting of some members of our society—I wish to be
informed whether there is any new difficulty arisen, & how the
members stand affected to Dr. Edwards—I esteem him one of the
best of preachers that I am acquainted with, sound in the faith, &
pious and diligent in his studies and attention to the duties of his
office. I should be very sorry to have anything done to grieve him or
weaken his hands in the great and important work committed to his
charge. If he should leave the Society I should expect they would be

---

16. An interesting biography of this colonial figure is Roger Sherman Boardman,
Roger Sherman, Signer and Statesman (Philadelphia: University of Pennsylvania Press, 1938).

17. Simeon Baldwin, a member of the White Haven Church, was also a figure of
political importance. He was both Judge of the Superior Court of Connecticut and member of
the Congress.

divided & broken up—I hope all the well wishers to pure religion will use their influence to preserve peace, and avoid calling Society meetings unnecessarily, as I think it would only promote dissention. Our saviour says "wo to the world because of offense; but wo to that man by whom the offence cometh." I am willing that anything I have written should be made known if it will do any good, not only to the friendly but to the disaffected if there be any such. . . .

The joining with the first Society in Lectures has been urged by some, but a majority of the chh did not think it expedient. I believe it has never been moved for on the part of Dr. Dana nor do I think he would wish to have it take place. It is a matter of no great importance, if there were no diversity of sentiment between the two pastors, but as there really is, and as some members of our church would be dissatisfied with it, I think it would be highly criminal to insist upon it, so as to break the unity of the chh. Let each preach his own lecture, & every one may attend *either,* or *both,* at pleasure. . . . It is the duty of everyone to use their influence to that end, & to strengthen the hands and encourage the heart of Dr. Edwards in this ministerial work.

> I am very respectfully yours
> Roger Sherman[18]

Sherman must have received a reply from Baldwin suggesting that the relations between Edwards and his congregation were quite strained.[19] Shortly thereafter Sherman wrote to David Austin, who, in turn, replied in lengthy detail about the entire situation. It was Austin's position that he had done all he could to heal the breach within the church. The only hope for reuniting the pastor and church was for Edwards to alter "his line of conduct." Austin himself was "worn out with the difficulties." In blunt language he wrote that if Sherman had not been spending so much time away from New Haven he would also feel the way the majority of parishioners did. The fact that theological disagreements were an essential part of the controversy is seen in one of Austin's remarks:

> I do not conceive there is any diversity of sentiments among the members of the Chh or Society respecting the Spiritual doctrines of

---

18. Ms. Letter of February 4, 1790, from Roger Sherman to Simeon Baldwin (Yale University Library).

19. David O. Austin, the moderator of the White Haven Church, was a leading merchant in New Haven.

Religion. I believe that the peculiarities in Sentiment are with Dr. Edwrds alone.

Austin went on to say that if Edwards had always preached as he was at that time then "I have been greatly deceived in former times respecting his preaching, and his conduct appears to me (for several years past) very different from what it was five years ago."

Then Austin made the interesting charge that the pastor had spent too much time in his study.

> But what has he been doing there? has he been employed in studying how he may win his people to the practice of virtue & religion? has he not been imployed a great proportion of his time there in business of a pecuniary nature? has he not imployed himself in transcribing a volume of his father's sermons & printing them at Hartford? in transcribing the History of Redemption & preparing a copy to be printed in Scotland? and lately a volume of 33 sermons of his father's study and preaching? and has he not likewise been imployed a great part of his time for two years past in writing against Dr. Chauncey, the last of which performance, I believe his people who are unacquainted with the dispute do not desire to spend their time in acquainting themselves with it, nor will they think him entitled to their thanks, or pay, for such imployment.

According to Austin, Edwards should have been spending his time saving

> the souls of his people, who have supported him & his family in expectation of his giving himself wholly to the service of themselves & families; in visiting his people, in order to find out the state of his flock, in counseling, & exhorting young & old to the practice of virtue, & persuading many of the most virtuous men among us to the duties of professing publickly their friendship to the saviour of mankind. . . .[20]

Reading between the lines, it becomes clear that several issues had been festering between Edwards and his congregation, and that the major one was theological. The controversy behind the correspondence carried on by Sherman, Baldwin, and Austin concerned Edwards' charge against a respected physician and member of the

---

20. Ms. letter of February 20, 1790, from David Austin to Roger Sherman (Yale University Library).

White Haven Church, a Mr. James Beardselee, who was accused of holding to the doctrine of universal salvation. Other points of disagreement were easy to find once the pastor had attacked a well-liked member of the congregation on a theological point about which other members also felt uneasy.

Sherman replied to Austin. He defended Edwards out of personal friendship, but his letter demonstrates an intelligent understanding of the theological issues involved.

New York March 1, 1790

Dear Sir

I received your favor of the 20th Feby & am much obliged by the free & friendly information respecting the affairs of our Society. I am of your opinion that we do not differ much respecting the essential doctrines of religion. I am also very sensible that you have in time past exerted yourself more for the support of Dr. Edwards & his family than any other member of the Society, and therefore I expressed an ardent wish that your former friendship might be revived, and though I have no doubt that you yet bear him good will, but I want to have that cordial complacency that once existed be again restored.

You observe that I have been much absent & so have not had an opportunity to attend & be acquainted with his preaching in general of late years. I know that this has been the case but I have frequently attended his ministry ' had conversation with him on religious subjects to my great satisfaction. When I have been absent I have heard many good preachers which I esteem orthodox & pious, but I have found none that in all respects suits me better than Dr. Edwards—As to what you mention respecting his copying his father's writings for the press. I think he has much served the Interest of religion in a way that must have tended to furnish his mind for serving his own people transcribing those works must fix them in his memory much better than merely reading them. and if they yield to him some pecuniary advantage I think it a favourable circumstance, for I believe what the Society give him would not be sufficient to support his family without some other income.

I dont know what advantages his answer to Dr. Chauncy may produce to his own people or to others, the merit of it can be better judged of when it is published. But I think Dr. Chauncey's sentiments on that subject very erronious, & if believed will tend to relax the restraints on vice arising from the threatenings of the divine law against impenitent sinners.

It is true I did declare it to be my opinion at first in the case of Dr. Beardseley that such an opinion ought not to exclude a person from communion, but on further consideration of the matter, & finding a former determination of our church in point against any opinion I have viewed it in different point of light from what I did at first. I think we are as much bound to believe the threatnings, as the promises of the gospel.

There are damnable heresies, as well as practices 2 Peter 2.1. A man that is an heretic after two admonitions is to be rejected, Titus 3.10, showing that he that is subverted, and sinneth, being condemned of himself—that is as Dr. Guyne observes the evidence of his heresy appears from his own profession of his erronious principles & cant be proved any other way.

The punishment threatened to sinners is not greater than in the view of divine wisdom was best to accomplish the purposes of divine goodness for advancing the glory of God & the greatest good & happiness of his intelligent creatures. And any principles that tend to diminish the influence of those sanctions must be of dangerous tendency. The apostle says knowing the [temper?] of the Lord we persuade men—Sin and misery was first introduced into our world—by persuading Eve to disbelieve the divine threatning. When the tempter said to her ye shall not surely die. I have always view[ed] Dr. Edwards conduct in the case of Dr. Beardselee when he was nominated for a delegate—not only as proper but as an indispensible duty & what Dr. Beardselee ought to have received in a kind & friendly light. It was well known that reports were propagated not only in New Haven but in other towns that Dr. Beardselee was a universalist the evidence of the truth or falsehood of this report must be known only to himself and its being mentioned on the occasion when he was present, gave him opportunities to declare his sentiments, and if he had either disavowed his having even embraced the opinion, or had then declared that he had renounced it his character would have stood fair & his election took place—but if he at that time held to the opinion or was doubtful respecting the truth of the contrary doctrine he was unfit for that office.

The rule in the 18th Matthew is good & of undeniable authority in the case to which it is applicable.—but I think it does not all respect such a case as that but only personal injuries or such private offences that might be settled without a publick confession.—I Tim 5.20 Them that sin rebuke before all, that others may fear Gal 2.12–14 When Peter was come to Antioch I withstood him to the face because he was to be blamed. When I saw that they walked not uprightly according to the truth of the gospel I said unto Peter before them all, & c. As to the matter respecting joining with the first Society in the Lecture I should not esteem it a matter of much importance if their was no diversity of sentiment—whether one or two lectures were kept up I believe most of the people in the city might redeem time to attend both—

The former coalition was but a half way practice, to join in lectures & not exchange on the Sabbath I was for having a full understanding of each others sentiments & join fully or not at all.

Roger Sherman[21]

Despite Sherman's ardent defense of Edwards, members of the Society were not contributing to the support of the church. Edwards certainly could not remain in his pastorate if his salary were not paid. The problem reached an impasse in 1795 when the Society admitted financial defeat.

This Society being convened to consider their situation and consult this interest seriously regarding this as a crisis at which a judicial conduct is essential to their continuance as a Christian community think proper to state the following facts.

That for a long course of years we continued respectable for number & property and in the flourishing state of this society, were able to afford an abundant support to our pastors, and at the time of settling the Rev. Doctor Edwards we had every rational prospect of supporting him so long as he should be able to exercise the duties of a gospel minister in this Society.—Since that time we have maintained our standing thro many embarrasments peculiar to our circumstances.

In a course of years our members are greatly diminished. A great portion of those who compose Fairhaven Society went out from the midst of us. Others have been gradually leaving us and joining the Episcopal Church—a great number of those who united in settling our present pastor have been called to sleep with their father, & their children have chose to attend at other houses of worship—and several who are legally with us either attend elsewhere or stay at home & such pay their proportion of taxes with reluctance which circumstances have for some years past, obliged the Society to lay taxes hard to be

21. Ms. minutes of a letter of March 1, 1790, from Roger Sherman to David Austin (Yale University Library). This was a first draft of the actual letter that Sherman sent. The Yale Library has other manuscript letters of Sherman, Austin, Baldwin, and others, dealing with the controversy.

borne to compel all to pay who could in any possible manner procure the money to pay them, and which circumstances prevented the Society from making such abatements as humanity seemed to demand.

From such a concurrence of circumstances, we find ourselves exceeding embarrassed, & have reason to fear that they will put an end to our union as a Society unless timely prudence is applied.

Till this time we have exerted ourselves & have not spared our temporals for the support of our pastor in his work but while we see our worshipping assemblies thinly attended, our Youths leaving us and no prospect, at present, of a better situation, we cannot resolve to struggle any longer against so many discouragements—On the facts thus stated we judge this to be an important crisis for us, and that no time ought to be lost. While our members are so reduced and while so many causes concur to threaten our dissolution we have no rational prospect of long continuing in a state even to make a respectable separation. And we doubt not that Doct. Edwards will be disposed for a separation of the Society [and] judge it best.

Therefore, voted that Samuel Bishop, David Austin, Abel Burritt, Ebeneser Townsend, and Simeon Baldwin be a Committee to consider on the above statement of Facts and to judge whether in view of them the Society is at present in danger of a dissolution. Also to confer with Doct. Edwards on the same and to communicate to him whatever they judge proper for his forming an opinion on the above subject. Also to discuss with him what in the present juncture to be his duty & ours, and to make report of the result of such deliberations & conference at our next meeting.[22]

When the Committee from the Society met with Edwards he immediately expressed his hope that he would not be blamed for the impending dissolution of the pastoral relationship. The Committee assured him that such was not the case, and the Society formally voted that Mr. Edwards was not to be held responsible.

On April 26, 1795, at a meeting of the Church of White Haven, "the question was put, whether it be the desire of this church, that the pastoral relation between them and their present pastor, the Revd. Dr. Edwards, be dissolved; & it passed in the affirmative."[23] They proceeded to call a council to effect this resolu-

22. *Records of the Society of White Haven,* April 5, 1795.
23. *Records of the White Haven Church,* April 26, 1795.

tion.[24] Efforts were made to assure the public that the Church continued to hold Edwards in esteem.

> At a meeting of the Church of Christ in White Haven Society in New Haven, on the 14th Day of May 1795, Voted that David Austin & Samuel Bishop Esquires, the committee to wait on the council be instructed to return the thanks of this church to the Revd. Doctor Jonathan Edwards for all the good they have experienced by his ministry among them, & to assure him of their brotherly love and respect. In whatever part of the vineyard his talents and future labours may be employed, their prayer is, that he may be a successful minister of the New Testament, & finally be rewarded among the faithful servants of the Great Head of the church. And they now bid him an affectionate farewell.
>
> The foregoing vote was passed unanimously.
David Austin, Moderator[25]

In what appears to have been rather great haste, the ecclesiastical council met within the week, on May 19, 1795, and gave their approval to the action of the church and society. There appears to be, in the action of the council, a rebuke to the White Haven Church and Society for the action which they had taken, and the council took particular care to absolve Edwards of any responsibility.

> . . . The Council having taken the matter into serious & deliberate consideration, voted:
>
> That it appears to them expedient, under present circumstances, that the pastoral relation between Doct. Edwards & the church & society in White Haven be dissolved. They therefore advise that the relation be dissolved & it is accordingly dissolved.
>
> While we find it necessary to form this result, we feel ourselves deeply affected, that a minister whose praise is in the churches, & of whose abilities, prudence & faithfulness we entertain so high an opinion, should be reduced to such circumstances, as render it needful for him to be dismissed from his labours in so important & distinguished part of the vineyard. At the same time we rejoice, that Doct. Edwards' character stands clear from every impeachment; the society having explicitly voted, that they do not incriminate him at all, respecting the cause, which, in their opinion, has rendered necessary a dissolution of his relation to them. . . . We therefore do cheer-

---

24. *Records of the White Haven Church,* April 26, 1795.
25. *Records of the White Haven Church,* May 14, 1795.

fully & cordially recommend him to the churches, whenever God in his providence may call him, as a honored, pious, & faithful minister. We lament, that this church, which for a long course of years continued respectable for numbers & property should be so far reduced, as to be unable, any longer to enjoy the labours of so worthy & distinguished a pastor. . . . And we earnestly wish & pray, that the means, which they have taken to prevent a dissolution of the church & society, may not produce this effect they were obligated to prevent; but that in the great goodness of God, they may be preserved & increased, & be permitted again, notwithstanding present difficulties to enjoy the great blessing of a faithful ministry, & a regular observation of the gospel. . . .

Benjamin Trumbull, Moderator.[26]

The dismissal was complete.

Since both the White Haven and Fair Haven Societies had decreased in numerical strength, it was logical to unite the two groups. Committees were working to form a joint confession of faith and a church covenant for an impending union.[27] By November, 1796, within a year after Edwards' dismissal, this union had been consummated, and the last entry in the minutes of the White Haven Church reads,

. . . This church will unite with the Church of Fair Haven into one Church, and that the Brethren & sisters of the Churches of White Haven and Fair Haven be hereafter Members of one Church to be known by Name of the Church of Christ in the United Society of White Haven and Fair Haven . . . and that the first meeting of said United Church be this evening at the Dwelling House of Deacon David Austin. . . . Voted that the Church meeting be adjourned.

Test. David Austin, Moderator.[28]

The division of 1769 had been healed, but only after the removal of the original cause of the separation—Jonathan Edwards the Younger.

---

26. *Records of the White Haven Church,* May 19, 1795.

27. See *Records of the White Haven Church,* August 12, 1796; *Records of the Fair Haven Church,* August 21, 1796.

28. *Records of the White Haven Church,* November 27, 1796. See also the *Records of the Church of Christ in the United Society of White Haven and Fair Haven,* November 27, 1796, in possession of the United Church, New Haven. The product of the "union" was what came to be known as the "North" Church, because of its location on the New Haven Green. Later, in 1826, The "Third" Church was formed by followers of Nathaniel William Taylor with the "North" and "First" (Center) Churches. Not until 1884 was a union consummated by the "North" and "Third" Churches to form the present "United" Church.

CHAPTER TEN

Exile and a New Career

The news of Edwards' dismissal from the White Haven Church spread rapidly throughout Connecticut, but the vacant churches of the state did not move quickly to acquire his services. During the process of his dismissal there had been repeated efforts to absolve him of any responsibility in the action, but suspicion must have lingered in many minds that both his personality and theological convictions had contributed to the decline of the White Haven Church and necessitated his removal. Quite naturally, other churches were hesitant to call him to their pastoral service.

The small church in Colebrook, Connecticut, however, invited Edwards to supply their pulpit during the month of June, 1795. Colebrook is situated in the Litchfield Hills, some twenty miles northwest of Hartford, and even today far off the main roads.

In 1732 the General Court of Connecticut granted the large tract known as the "western lands" to the towns of Windsor and Hartford. This tract included the area west of Hartford, south of the Massachusetts line, north of Waterbury, and west to the Housatonic River.[1] Through agreement between the leading citizens of Hartford and Windsor, this land was divided, and Colebrook came under the proprietorship of Windsor. In May, 1756, the land within Colebrook was laid out and divided, though no settlers had yet come to the village. In 1760 the Connecticut General Assembly ran the "Old

---

1. Irving Manchester, *The History of Colebrook* (Winstead, Conn.: The Citizen Printing Company, 1935), 10. See also Benjamin Trumbull, *A Complete History of Connecticut* (New Haven: Maltby, Goldsmith and Co., 1818), Vol. II, 95ff., and *History of Litchfield County, Connecticut* (Philadelphia: J.W. Lewes & Co., 1881), 274ff.

North Road" through Colebrook. This road was a main colonial thoroughfare in the direction of Albany until 1800, and brought the first settlers to the area.

Colebrook did not grow rapidly. The first settlers came in 1765, and it was not until 1779 that the village was incorporated. By 1783 Colebrook boasted a population of 270, and efforts were made to build a town church. Finding a site suitable even to Colebrook's limited population was not easy. Since the center of the town would be built near the meetinghouse, the land immediately surrounding it would be most valuable, but settlers had built homes two or three miles in all directions. A further difficulty was encountered as the settlers within Colebrook became conscious of a geographical division into "south" and "north" Colebrook. The two areas were divided by a small stream, and each group wanted the church built on its side. In 1784 a committee agreed on a site on the north side of the stream near the village's original homes. The "southerners" became more vocal in their objections. Work was stopped and a compromise was reached. It was suggested that each side choose a site near the stream and lots would be drawn to make the final decision. All agreed. A site south of the stream was duly chosen in this way. But as the "northerners" looked across the stream and saw the imposing edifice rising on the "enemy's" side, they decided that they could not support the church and would have no part in calling a minister. Another conference was called. It was decided to move the half finished structure across the stream to a site on the north side. In the middle of winter, February, 1794, oxen and men pulled it some thirty rods (less than one-tenth of a mile). The task proved to be too difficult for them, and for six months their church perched atop a small hill with only the bare outlines of its structure completed. In August the people of Colebrook tried to move the building again but with no more success. It was only after fourteen years of disagreement that a site was chosen near the hill where the church had been left, and both sides agreed to give it their full support.[2]

---

2. The story of this struggle is in Irving Manchester, *History of Colebrook*. The author had access to a manuscript left by Reuben Rockwell, one of the participants in the struggle, and he made extensive quotations from this record. See also, *History of Litchfield County*, 278–280.

When Jonathan Edwards came to supply its pulpit in June, 1795, the church had not yet had a minister. Edwards was undoubtedly on trial. The town of Colebrook was settled by people from Windsor, where his grandfather, Timothy Edwards, had held a long pastorate; the Edwards family must have been well known among these settlers. Edwards himself had a family connection with the Colebrook Church. His aunt, Mary Pierpont Russell, lived in New Haven, and was also an aunt by marriage of Nathaniel Russell, a leading figure in the Colebrook Church. Another Colebrook connection for Edwards was the Reverend Samuel J. Mills of Torringford, who had been influential in forming the church and settling the village; Mills had been associated with Edwards in the work of the Connecticut Missionary Society and would have found his company in the Litchfield Association very congenial.

Edwards was occasionally invited back to Colebrook throughout the summer of 1795. On October 5, the church voted to elect a committee to ask him if he would accept a call. After agreement had been reached on a salary of 90 pounds, plus firewood, the North Consociation of Litchfield was convened at Colebrook on December 30 and 31, 1795, to install Edwards as pastor. Samuel Mills and Benjamin Trumbull, Edwards' life-long intimate friend from North Haven, took part in the installation service.

From all indications, Edwards' ministry at Colebrook was uneventful. He enjoyed a freer schedule than previously, and devoted himself to literary tasks. His grandson wrote that

> at Colebrook his [Edwards] labours were less arduous, and his residence was rendered most pleasant by the uninterrupted harmony and affection that subsisted between himself and the people; and as a consequence of both, his health became more finely established than it had been for years.[3]

The church itself could not have taken much of his time, for in 1795 it had only twenty-two members, nine men and thirteen women. He had an opportunity to complete "Liberty and Necessity," which, though written many years before, had never been properly finished.

---

3. Tyron Edwards, "Memoir," The *Works of Jonathan Edwards, D.D., with a Memoir of his Life and Character by Tyron Edwards* (Andover: Allen, Morrill and Wardwell, 1842), Vol. I, xxi.

He continued to participate in the missionary work of the Connecticut Association and it was during his stay in Colebrook that he helped to write the constitution for the Connecticut Missionary Society.

In 1798 and 1799 many Connecticut churches were enjoying the fruits of a new "awakening." Revivals were particularly widespread in Litchfield County;[4] especially in the villages of East Haddam, Lyme, New Hartford and Farmington. The fact that Edwards admitted twenty-seven new members to the church in 1799 indicates that Colebrook shared in this wave of religious enthusiasm. This large addition, together with the members added during the previous years of his ministry, brought the total membership to over sixty by 1799.

The quiet, scholarly, pastoral life that Edwards enjoyed at Colebrook must have been a welcome change from the difficult years at New Haven.[5] He was free of controversy and won the respect and admiration of the parishioners. These years gave him ample time to work on some of his most important essays—writings which made firm his line of descent in the New Divinity tradition. His work, however, was interrupted by a new request for his services.

* * * * *

On May 2, 1799, the Board of Trustees of Union College in Schenectady, New York, voted, without unanimity, to call Jonathan Edwards the Younger as their second President.[6] The col-

---

4. Charles Roy Keller, *The Second Great Awakening in Connecticut* (New Haven: Yale University Press, 1942), 37ff. See also Bennet Tyler, ed., *New England Revivals, as they Existed at the Close of the Eighteenth, and Beginning of the Nineteenth Centuries* (Boston: Massachusetts Sabbath School Society, 1846).

5. The only misfortune which appears to have come to him in this period was a serious fall from his horse some time in October of 1797. This accident caused a rather long convalescence and Edwards referred to its seriousness in a letter to his son.

> After the repeated admonitions, which I have lately had & the repeated imminent dangers with which I have been threatened, I should be stupid indeed, if I had no sense of mortality & my liableness to duty and sudden death. . . .

Ms. Letter of March 20, 1798, from Jonathan Edwards to Jonathan Walter Edwards (Yale University Library).

6. The vote was 10 for and 6 against inviting Edwards to Union College. See *Minutes of the Board of Trustees, Union College*, May 2, 1799 (Union College Library, Schenectady, New York).

lege had been founded in 1795, after fourteen years of struggle to establish an institution of higher learning in upper New York state. Several ethnic and religious groups had combined their efforts to build the college.

In 1779 the first petition requesting a charter for a college in northern New York, signed by 975 inhabitants, was submitted to the state legislature. This petition represented the "first really popular demand for higher education in America."[7] The area around Albany was populated for the most part by three groups with generally similar theological interests: Congregationalists from New England, Presbyterians from the middle colonies, and Dutch-Reformed settlers from New York and New Jersey.[8] Dutch Reformed people had moved up the Hudson River valley all during the eighteenth century.[9] Many were prevented from moving southward or westward because of the large number of Scotch-Irish, German, and English who had settled in the richer lands, though some Dutch did move into Pennsylvania as their New York area became increasingly populated. The Hudson River valley offered a fertile district into which they could expand. From there, they could travel along the Mohawk Valley into the sparsely settled lands of the western reserve. The same avenue lay open for many New Jersey Presbyterians. Since New England offered little hope for more productive economic and social opportunities, and because the Presbyterians of New York and New Jersey did not mix easily with their Scotch-Irish brethren to the south and west, the Hudson and Mohawk River valleys became their route of adventure. The New England Congregationalists, as we have noted, also moved into the "western lands" and intermingled with people of other backgrounds. The Schenectady-Albany area thus became a "melting pot" of these different groups. It was these people who called for the formation of a college.

The "father" of Union University was Dirck Romeyn, born in

---

7. D.R. Fox, *Union College, an Unfinished History* (Schenectady: Graduate Council, Union College, 1945), 10.

8. Codman Hislop, *Albany: Dutch, English, and American* (Albany, N.Y.: The Argus Press, 1936).

9. M. L. Goodwin, *Dutch and English on the Hudson,* The Chronicles of America Series, Vol. VII, ed. Allan Johnson (New Haven: Yale University Press, 1919).

1744 in New Barbadoes (Hackensack, New Jersey). He graduated from the College of New Jersey in 1765, a classmate of Jonathan Edwards the Younger; in 1766 he was admitted to the ministry of the Reformed Protestant Dutch Church. After serving parishes in New Jersey and participating in his church's struggle to found its own seminary there, he was invited to assume the Presidency of Queens College (now Rutgers) in 1784; instead, in the same year, he accepted the invitation to become pastor of the Reformed Dutch Church in Schenectady. Soon after his arrival, with the support of the Consistory, he inaugurated efforts to form an Academy in Schenectady, and this was accomplished in 1785. He and others in Schenectady and the surrounding region organized the "Academy and Library Company" and sought to secure a Charter for a college. The legislature required a minimum financial backing of $35,000, which was quickly raised. It was another decade, however, before the Charter was approved, on March 2, 1795. Though nearly half of the original trustees had a direct relation to the Dutch Church, the Charter stated that it was to be a non-sectarian institution:

> Neither shall any of them [Trustees] extend to exclude any person of any religious denomination whatever from equal liberty and advantage of education or from any of the degrees, liberties, privileges, benefits or immunities of the said college on account of his particular tenets in religion.[10]

Apparently, the name "Union University" was chosen to signify the fact that the college had been established through the joint effort of many individuals in the region. Beyond this, however, even if unintentionally, the name described the fact that the three leading figures of the college's earliest days came from diverse religious traditions: Dirck Romeyn was a Reformed Dutch pastor, John Blair

---

10. The text is found in A. V. Raymond, *Union University, Its History, Influence, Characteristics and Equipment* (New York: Lewes Publishing Company, 1907), Vol. I, 37. As evidence of the strong support the college received from the Reformed Dutch Church it is interesting to note that the first four members of the graduating class in 1797 became ministers in that tradition. See Cornelius Van Santvoord, "Union College in its Relations to the Reformed Church," in Edward T. Corwin, *A Manual of the Reformed Church in America (Formerly Reformed Protestant Dutch Church) 1628–1933* (New York: Board of Publication and Bible-School Work of the Reformed Church in America, 1922–33). Also Harold W. Blodgett, "Union College and Dirck Romeyn," *New York History* (July, 1945).

Smith, its first President, was a Scotch-Irish Presbyterian,[11] and Jonathan Edwards, its second President, a Congregationalist.

> Union College had emerged as a non-sectarian institution from a welter of conflicting interests, a "union" in fact of Presbyterians, Congregationalists, the Dutch Reformed, Episcopalians, of Federalists and Republicans, of the Hudson River aristocracy, and the vigorous democracy of the western reaches of the Mohawk country.[12]

Under the leadership of its first President, John Blair Smith, Union College began to earn an important place in American higher education. During his administration the college built its first building and graduated its first class. President Smith, however, resigned early in 1799 because of ill health. After unsuccessful efforts to secure the services of William Linn of New York City, the trustees voted to call Jonathan Edwards as the college's second President.

There were several reasons why the trustees turned to Edwards. Andrew Raymond, the historian of Union College, has reported: "It is said that Dr. Edwards was chosen President of Union College at the suggestion of Dr. Romeyn."[13] The fact that the two had been classmates at the College of New Jersey makes this suggestion credible. Certainly, the testimony of John Blair Smith, the retiring President, must also have been favorable to Edwards; Edwards, Sr. had remained a distinguished and revered name in the history of the College of New Jersey, and Smith's intimate connection with that school would have impressed this fact upon him. So it was not unnatural for him to support the candidacy of a man who, through his father and through his own life work, had remained interested

---

11. John Blair Smith (1756–1799) was a son of Irish immigrants. He graduated from the College of New Jersey in 1775 and then taught at and became President of Hampden-Sydney College in Virginia. In 1791 he became pastor of the Pine Street Presbyterian Church in Philadelphia, to which he returned in 1799 after serving four years as President of Union College.

12. Codman Hislop, "Eliphalet Nott: The Formative Years, 1773–1804," Unpublished Ph.D. dissertation, Harvard University, February, 1953, 218. Nott was President of Union College from 1804–1866. See also Codman Hislop, *Eliphalet Nott* (Middletown, Conn.: Wesleyan University Press, 1971).

13. Raymond, *Union University*, 13. See also Andrew Yates' reminiscences of this period, written to the anonymous author of "Memoir of Jonathan Edwards," *American Quarterly Register*, Vol. VIII (1836), 293. Yates was a colleague of Edwards on the faculty of Union College.

and active in the affairs of the Presbyterian Church. Smith's endorsement of Edwards was not, however, shared by all the Trustees.

There is no indication, either in any of the histories of Union College, or in the minutes of the Board of Trustees, why the Trustees were divided concerning extending the call to Edwards. Undoubtedly, the association of the Edwards name with certain strict theological beliefs, and also with unfortunate ecclesiastical difficulties, influenced the dissenting members. Some may have felt that Jonathan Edwards' character would not promote harmony and stability in a precarious "union." Nonetheless, on May 2, 1799, a favorable vote was cast.

Tutor Andrew Yates conveyed the Trustees' invitation to Edwards at Colebrook.[14] After deliberations with his congregation and with a council from the Litchfield Association, Edwards accepted the call, though members of his church protested against his leaving. By the middle of July the Edwards family was packed and ready to move.

They arrived in Schenectady in late July, 1799. He recounted that the school "was lighted at night by the scholars, on account of my arrival."[15] It did not take Edwards long to become aware of the complex situation of the young college, and the difficulties with which it might present him, as we can see in a letter he wrote to his son in August of 1799.

> . . . Besides the danger of governing scholars, the greatest to which I am exposed, I conceive to be that which arises from the collisions of parties in religion. The Episcopaleans, the Presbyterians, & those of the Dutch Church, are very jealous of each other; & as the College is *Union College* & designed to embrace those several denominations; you may easily conceive that difficulties may arise from that source. But there has not yet been time for me to experience much of them. I doubt whether the college will ever have a large number of students, so long as they board with the inhabitants, as the inhabitants will fix their own price for board. The College at Williamstown is the rival &

---

14. Edwards did not receive the invitation in person, for he wrote in May of 1799, "On my return from Hartford, I found Mr. Yates had been here on his way to New Haven and had left me a call to the Presidency of Union College." Ms. letter of May 17, 1799, from Jonathan Edwards the Younger to Jonathan Walter Edwards (Yale University Library).

15. Ms. letter of July 31, 1799, from Jonathan Edwards the Younger to Jonathan W. Edwards (Yale University Library).

their Board is cheaper for the reason just mentioned. The trustees do not appear to me to be sensible of the disadvantage to which they are subjected by this means.[16]

He seemed to suspect that important difficulties would soon arise and wrote, "People are very kind to us.—But honey-moon is not yet over."[17]

On the whole, Edwards' tenure in office appears to have been undistinguished. One Union College historian merely says,

> Although the records of the College give little evidence of outward prosperity during his brief administration, it cannot be doubted that his strong personality made a profound impression, and his name certainly added greatly to the reputation of the college.[18]

Even the minutes of the Trustees offer little insight into the workings of his administration. His friend and colleague, Andrew Yates, wrote in praise of his work:

> In the management of college, his discipline was mild and affectionately parental, and his requirements reasonable. Such a character for government in president Edwards, was unexpected to some who professed to know his disposition, and had formed their opinions of him in this respect. It was therefore the more noticed. There was an apparent austerity and reserve in his manner, which, no doubt, arose from the retirement of study and from habits of close thought, and would leave such impression after the slight acquaintance; but in his domestic intercourse and with his intimate friends, while conscientiously strict and prompt in his duties, and while he acted with decision, he was mild and affectionate. The same spirit characterized his government of the college. It was probably conducted with greater mildness and affection than would have been exercised, had not the prevailing expectations of some intimated the danger of his erring on the side of severity. His pupils, like a well regulated family under faithful discipline, were respectfully attached to him.[19]

---

16. Ms. letter of August 17, 1799, from Jonathan Edwards the Younger to Jonathan W. Edwards (Yale University Library).

17. Ms. letter of August 30, 1799, from Jonathan Edwards the Younger to Jonathan W. Edwards (Yale University Library).

18. Raymond, *Union University*, Vol. I, 70.

19. "Memoir of Jonathan Edwards," *American Quarterly Register*, Vol. VIII, 294.

He missed his old friends in Connecticut and indicated his feeling of loss in a letter to Benjamin Trumbull.

Schenectady Feb 24, 1800

My dear Friend and Brother

Tho removed such a distance as to render communication difficult & rare, I shall never forget you, I reflect with a mournful pleasure, on the many agreeable hours & days wh we have spent together. May these be a prelude to endless [hours] of communion in bliss & glory!

I hope you and your family enjoy health peace & prosperity, temporal & spiritual. I have hitherto found this a healthy place & have reason to bless a kind providence for so much health granted to me & my family. May we be truly thankful.

Since I saw you I have received your generous present of your discourses; for wh please to accept my thanks. Without compliment, I think it very useful & seasonable publication, & hope it may do much good. I am especially pleased wh the discourse on the inspiration of the Scriptures, tho the rest are good. I hope you will go on to do good.

As to myself, the college goes on in the usual manner, without anything very peculiar good or bad; unless it be, that our general Assembly have lately voted to give the college 10,000 dollars.

There is a revival of religion in two places, within 20 miles of this town, as well as in some part of Genesee. I do not think of any other information, which would be worth relating.

Mrs. Edwards & my daughter join me in respects to yourself & Mrs. Trumbull & kind compliments to your daughters.

I am, Revd and Dear Sir,
your affectionate Brother,
Jonathan Edwards[20]

*   *   *   *   *

The significance of the last months of Edwards' life lay outside his specific relationship to Union College.

By the time Jonathan Edwards the Younger left the College of

---

20. Ms. letter of February 24, 1800, from Jonathan Edwards the Younger to Benjamin Trumbull (Yale University Library).

New Jersey, late in 1768, the Presbyterian Church was reaching far into the frontier of New York, Pennsylvania, and to the south. The immigration of new Scotch-Irish settlers in the years preceding the Revolution speeded this movement,[21] and new Presbyteries were formed as the geographical boundaries of the church expanded. The Pittsburgh area began to achieve what became a lasting reputation as a center of American Presbyterianism; New York, with its great expanse of unclaimed land, attracted many settlers, not only from New England, but also from the middle colonies.

Before the Scotch-Irish had achieved sufficient numbers to weight the church's balance of power in their own favor, John Witherspoon arrived in Princeton, in August, 1768, to become President of the College of New Jersey.[22] He came without firsthand knowledge of the deep Old Side-New Side cleavage within American Presbyterianism, and it was hoped that he might be a uniting force to bring the opposing groups together. In fact, he did just that. We have already noted the alliance of New Side Presbyterians (largely of English descent) with the Connecticut Congregationalists.[23] The influence of the leading figures of the Connecticut Churches— Edwards, Sr., Bellamy, Hopkins, and others—was felt strongly by New Side Presbyterians. Witherspoon, however, held no allegiance to Edwardsean theology and was suspicious of those who did. It is significant that the two tutors most closely associated with New Divinity doctrine, Jonathan Edwards the Younger and Joseph Periam, left the College of New Jersey in 1769, a year after Witherspoon arrived. "On the campus the advocates of the New Divinity developed a full grown persecution complex."[24] Bellamy's works,

---

21. The increasing number of Scotch-Irish who entered the Church in this period were, in later years, to assert their growing strength against the English strain within Presbyterianism.

22. The circumstances leading to this invitation are noted in Chapter III.

23. It is clear that if constructive denominational relations were to be carried on between Congregationalism and Presbyterianism in America it would be between the parties within each church that had common interests. The New Side Presbyterians and the Connecticut-western Massachusetts Congregationalists, because of geographical proximity and common theological concerns, were able to enjoy harmonious and fruitful relations throughout the first half of the eighteenth century. Both other groups, the Old Side Presbyterians and the Congregationalists, were forced to make their own path. There was little interchange between the Old Side Presbyterians and the Congregationalists, or between the liberal group within Congregationalism and the Presbyterian church at large.

24. L. Trinterud, *The Forming of an American Tradition, a Re-examination of Colonial Presbyterianism* (Philadelphia: Westminster Press, 1949), 224.

for example, were circulated among the students only after the title pages had been torn out. These two factors, the increasing number of Old Side Scotch-Irish who entered the church and slowly took over important positions which had belonged to the New Side group, and Witherspoon's subdued hostility to New Divinity doctrine, constituted a heavy loss in position and influence for the church's New England element.

For the most part, the New Side party was confined to the Presbyteries of New York, Suffolk, Dutchess, and New Brunswick—all in the New York-New Jersey area. This section retained its important voice in the church, even though it lost much of the influence it had held in 1758 at the union of the New York and Philadelphia synods. Its only room for expansion, however, lay either to the south, where it would be swallowed up by the Scotch-Irish group, or to the upper New York area, where there were churchmen from other denominations. As missionary needs grew, the New Side contributed to its own loss of prestige, for in serving the expanding frontiers it "aided in bringing into the church so large a part of the immigrating Scotch-Irish that the character of the Presbyterian Church was radically altered."[25]

This change in the church's character was gradual. The ties which had linked American Presbyterianism and Connecticut Congregationalism continued. The defense of Calvinism by the New Divinity party, while not shared in all particulars, was admired by the brethren to the south.

Though the two churches had always practiced a rather easy interchange of ministers, many New Side Presbyterians and Connecticut Congregationalists sharing common backgrounds, no concrete ties existed between them before 1766. In that year the Synod of New York and Philadelphia sent a letter to the General Association of Connecticut, requesting a meeting of delegates from both churches to confer on mutual problems.

> Rev and Dr Brethren
> The Synod of New York and Philadelphia at their annual meeting in May 1766 have among many other expedients to promote the interests of the Redeemer's Kingdom, concluded upon the most ma-

---

25. Trinterud, *The Forming of an American Tradition,* 227.

ture Deliberation, that a general meeting of Delegates both from your Chhs & our Presbyteries would answer this important purpose—our earnest Desire to accomplish so good an end has engaged us to embrace this opportunity of your next general association to propose the matter to your Serious Deliberation & to invite you to a general Consultation about such things as may have a hopeful tendency to promote & defend the Common Cause of Religion against the attacks of its various enemies. As we are all Brethren, embarked in the same Interest, perfectly agreed in Doctrine & Worship, Substantially pursuing the same method of Discipline & chh government, & we trust all animated with the Same Laudable Zeal to advance the Kingdom of our Common Lord, we cannot but hope for your ready concurrence with our invitation. Your Good Sense & general acquaintance with human nature must necessarily lead you to see that a more intimate acquaintance with each other's views & Designs will enable us with greater Harmony & Consistence & of consequence of greater Success, to support the Common Cause in which we are all equally engaged. A general agreement in any measure that may be adopted to preserve our Religious Liberties against all Encroachments, and to Bless the benighted Brethren on our Borders with the glorious light of the Gospel must promise desirable Success. . . .[26]

A delegation of commissioners was appointed; all but one were New Side adherents, having either been born and educated in New England or trained by and sympathetic with the Log College men. The Connecticut General Association approved the Synod's proposal immediately, and the first convention was held in May, 1766.[27] The Presbyterian character of Connecticut Congregationalism made these meetings possible. The Convention of 1766 was the natural outgrowth of the common concerns and character of both churches.

A basic cause underlying these annual meetings was the effort of American Episcopalians to secure an American bishop, a move feared by both Congregationalists and Presbyterians. The work of the Anglican church in America was greatly handicapped because it was completely dependent upon the Bishop of London and the Soci-

---

26. This letter is in the *Records of the General Association of ye Colony of Connecticut, Begun June 26, 1738; Ending June 19, 1799* (Hartford: 1888), 57–58.

27. Conventions were held in Guilford, Conn., in May, 1766; Elizabethtown, N.J., November, 1766; New Haven, September, 1767; Elizabethtown, October, 1770; Norwalk, Conn., September, 1771; Elizabethtown, September, 1772; Stamford, Conn., September, 1773; Elizabethtown, September, 1774; and Greenfield, Conn., September, 1775. Usually there were from 20 to 25 clergymen attending.

ety for the Propagation of the Gospel in Foreign Parts.[28] But there was strong opposition to the establishment of an American bishop because Presbyterians and Congregationalists feared encroachments on their political and religious freedom as had been the pattern in England. The Annual Conventions of Presbyterians and Congregationalists were designed primarily to bind the two churches together in a united front against the Anglican threat. Though it was not explicitly stated, this defensive posture was the basis for the Plan of Union formed by the Convention of 1766 in Elizabethtown, New Jersey.[29] A predominant theme of all the Annual Conventions was the call to unite forces against the formation of an Anglican bishopric in America. The Conventions, however, had more far-reaching effect on Presbyterian-Congregational relations than they did on developments within the Episcopal Church.

In the years immediately following the Revolution the Annual Conventions were not held. The major reason for this failure to renew communication was that the Presbyterian Church was undergoing a change in church government. The expansion of America's frontiers—temporarily halted by the Revolution—burst forth with new vigor as waves of settlers journeyed deeper into Pennsylvania, New York, Virginia, and the border states, and even beyond, into Ohio and Indiana.[30] The large, unwieldly Synod of New York and Philadelphia was not able to unify the church; it could exercise but little authority and discipline. Distant Presbyteries were frequently unrepresented in the annual meetings of the Synod; at the Synod of 1785 only thirty ministers and six elders were present.[31] The general proposal to reorganize the governing bodies of the church was

---

28. See Arthur L. Cross, *The Anglican Episcopate and the American Colonies* (New York: Longmans, Green, and Co., 1902). An excellent discussion of this problem is found in L. Trinterud, *The Forming of an American Tradition*, Chapter 13, "The Threat of Anglican Establishment."

29. *Minutes of the Convention of Delegates from the Synod of New York and Philadelphia, and from the Association of Connecticut: Held Annually From 1766–1775, Inclusive* (Hartford: Printed by E. Gleason, 1843), 10.

30. For a fully documented study of the directions in which Presbyterians expanded in Pennsylvania see Guy Klett, *Presbyterians in Colonial Pennsylvania* (Philadelphia: University of Pennsylvania Press, 1937).

31. Trinterud writes, "attendance from 1775–1783 inclusive had been, in order: 24, 18, 26, 11, 19, 15, 20, 30, 43 for the clergy; 5, 3, 4, 3, 7, 4, 4, 9, 10 for the elders." *The Forming of an American Tradition*, 281. This was not due to the war alone. In 1784 only 30 ministers were present out of a total of 123 on the rolls of the Synod. *Records of the Presbyterian Church in the United States of America* (Philadelphia: Presbyterian Board of Publication, 1841), 501, 502.

supported by all factions, but quite expectedly, differences over specific plans arose everywhere. Witherspoon's influence was important here, both for the steadying influence he exerted on the various factions of the church, and for the resulting plan of government, patterned after the Church of Scotland, which he helped to form. In 1788 the Synod of New York and Philadelphia agreed upon the final plan for the formation of the General Assembly, and John Witherspoon was elected to moderate the first meeting in 1789.

In 1790 an overture was put before the Presbyterian General Assembly to resume relations with the Connecticut General Association, relations which had been interrupted by the war.

> Whereas there existed, before the late Revolution, an annual convention of the clergy of the congregational churches, in New England, and of ministers belonging to the Synod of New York and Philadelphia, which was interrupted by the war;—this assembly, being peculiarly desirous to renew and strengthen every bond of union between brethren so nearly agreed in doctrine and forms of worship as the members of the congregational and presbyterian churches evidently are, and remembering with much satisfaction the mutual pleasure and advantage produced and received by their former intercourse,— did resolve,—that the ministers of the congregational churches in New England, be invited to renew their annual convention with the clergy of the Presbyterian church. . . .[32]

In the same year the General Association of Connecticut agreed that a "further degree of union between the churches of this State and their brethren of the Congregational and Presbyterian churches throughout the United States of America would be expedient and desirable."[33] It is clear from the minutes of their respective governing bodies that both churches desired closer ties. After 1790 the Annual Conventions resumed.

Jonathan Edwards was a delegate to the meeting of September, 1791. This was the first time that he had taken an active and official part in the efforts to form some concrete tie between the two churches. In the early 1770's when Edwards came to New Haven, the White Haven Church was not a member of the General Associa-

---

32. *Extracts from the Minutes of the General Assembly of the Presbyterian Church, in the United States of America, from A. D. 1789 to A. D. 1802* (Philadelphia: 1790), 5.

33. *Records of the General Association,* 153.

tion and thus Edwards did not take part in their deliberations. It was not until 1786 that the White Haven Church participated in the activities of the Association and sent its pastor to the annual meeting. Nonetheless, Edwards' whole ministry in New Haven had been spent in contact with both denominations. He was invited, in 1786, to become pastor of Jonathan Dickinson's former church in Elizabethtown, New Jersey, an offer he declined with great hesitation. In 1785 he had been awarded a D.D. degree by the College of New Jersey. The minutes of the White Haven Church carry numerous requests from Edwards to be absent on successive Sundays so that he might serve churches in New York and New Jersey. When he met with the delegates to the Annual Convention of 1791, Edwards understood the needs of both churches as well as anyone. From that meeting, to the time of his death, he took an active part in these annual discussions.

In 1794 the General Assembly of the Presbyterian Church proposed that the delegates appointed by each church to sit in the meetings of the other "shall have a right, not only to sit and deliberate, but also to vote, on all questions which shall be determined by either of them."[34] This proposal was accepted by the General Association.

Theological kinship and similar ecclesiastical structures facilitated these meetings in a way that had not been possible between Massachusetts Congregationalists and the Presbyterians. We have already noted that around the middle of the century the ties between the two groups had been strengthened by the respect in which Edwards, Sr., and the New Divinity men were held in the Presbyterian Church. After the coming of Witherspoon and the gradual shifting away from New Divinity sentiments, one might expect that ties between the churches would decrease. For a time, enthusiasm for close communion did wane, but the threat of an American Episcopal bishop drew the two parties back together. During the period from the entrance of John Witherspoon (1768) to the end of the century, the discussion of the pros and cons of closer ties between the two churches took place on a non-theological level. This may be partly attributed to the growing influence of Ezra Stiles in the

---

34. *Extracts from the Minutes of the General Assembly, A.D. 1794*, 8.

Congregational Church and John Witherspoon in the Presbyterian Church. Neither made any lasting mark as a theologian, but each was a master of diplomacy who strove to unify his church. Stiles disliked New Divinity doctrine throughout his life, but he never engaged in extensive theological debate, and as President of Yale he attempted to heal the rupture between Edwardseans and Old Calvinists. Witherspoon engaged himself in a similar task. He asserted his neutrality between Old Side and New Side and was thus able to begin to unite a church which had been disunited since much earlier in the century. So figures of theological moderation dominated both churches.[35] It appears that the unification efforts being made by the Presbyterians and Congregationalists were based on polity similarities and not on clearly stated theological agreement.

There also existed a movement for closer co-operation between the Reformed Dutch Church and the Presbyterians of the Synod of New York and Philadelphia. The Dutch Church was divided between those who wished to be more independent from the Classis of Amsterdam and those who sought to preserve strong Old World ties. The former group advocated the use of English, proposed the establishment of a college where clergy could be trained, and expressed sympathy for revivalistic measures. The conservative party resisted such innovations. A 1761 plan to support a Reformed Church Professorship at the College of New Jersey was quietly dropped; in 1793 a plan to unite Queen's College and the College of New Jersey was rejected by the Trustees of Queens.[36] In 1785 a committee concerning "Fraternal Correspondence," composed of delegates from the Presbyterian General Assembly and the Dutch Synod, proposed guidelines for co-operation, but no formal action was taken.[37] In 1798, at the invitation of the Synod of the Dutch Church, another effort, including the Associate Reformed Church, was made to enact a "plan of correspondence and intercourse" between the Dutch Church and the Presbyterian Church.[38] The report

---

35. Witherspoon and Stiles were not far apart theologically, perhaps because neither was very articulate in theological matters.

36. William H.S. Demarest, *A History of Rutgers College, 1766–1924* (New Brunswick, N.J.: Rutgers College, 1924), 173ff.

37. *The Acts and Proceedings of the General Synod of the Reformed Protestant Dutch Church in North America* (New York: 1859), Vol. I, 131–132.

38. The minutes from the joint committee are found in *The Acts and Proceedings of the General Synod,* 281ff. The plan provided for "The Communion of Particular Churches," "The

of the joint committee was unanimously approved by the General Assembly, but was not accepted by the Reformed Dutch Church or the Associate Reformed Church.[39] The plan was similar to the proposals simultaneously being considered by the Presbyterians and Congregationalists. Apparently, the Dutch were concerned that even this semi-formal co-operation could lead to dilution of doctrinal and ecclesiastical distinctiveness, and the majority preferred informal fraternal ties. Jonathan Edwards may have participated in these discussions.

When Edwards moved to Schenectady in the summer of 1799 he entered an ecclesiastical situation which was quite different from that in his Connecticut home. His new and close association with Presbyterians stimulated his desire to again become part of the Presbyterian Church structure, and by 1800 his name appeared on the rolls of the Presbytery of Albany. In that year, oddly enough, Edwards was sent by the General Assembly of the Presbyterian Church as a delegate to the General Association of Connecticut!

Edwards had always been interested in the missionary work of Connecticut Congregationalism. We have already noted that he was an organizer of the Connecticut Missionary Society, a group which sent many men to upper New York. The vigorous impetus to missionary endeavors brought by the Second Great Awakening turned his attention, and that of other Connecticut Congregationalists, to the areas now being settled. The records of the Presbyterian Church for this period are also full of notations concerning new missionaries to the "western reserve." In the general atmosphere of co-operation which existed between the two churches it was a natural step to begin efforts to unify this missionary work. The result was the Plan of Union of 1801.

It has often been asserted that the Plan of Union took shape after a chance meeting between John B. Smith of Union College and Eliphalet Nott, a young clergyman from Connecticut who was later

Friendly Interchange of Ministerial Services," and "A Correspondence of the several Judicatories of the conferring Churches." In brief, the conferees advocated inter-communion of members in "good standing," exchange of clergy, and the right of corresponding members to sit and vote in the judicatories of the other churches. They were not to vote on "constitutional" questions and were to be limited to three in number; nevertheless this was a significant proposal.

39. The approval of the General Assembly is noted in *A Digest from the Records of the General Assembly of the Presbyterian Church* (Philadelphia: 1820), 311.

to become President of Union (1804–1866). Nott wrote about this meeting some sixty-two years later:

> . . . I came from the State of Connecticut in the summer of 1795, on a mission to the "new settlements" in Western New York, which could hardly be said to extend beyond Rome. Almost all beyond Rome— much this side of it—was wilderness.
>
> My training had been in the Orthodox Congregational Church—my sympathies were with it; and so were my opinions in regard to Church government. And it was my purpose, and I deemed it to be my duty, to extend its influence, and to form churches to be in the same ecclesiastical connection, and under the same form of government.
>
> In passing through Schenectady, I stopped over night at a public house opposite the Academy building, then occupied by the College, and learned that there was to be a prayer meeting or lecture there that evening. I felt it my duty to attend it, and was solicited to preach by Dr. Smith, then President of Union College, who, after sermon, invited me to his house to spend the night. He inquired concerning my views, and objects, and theatre of action. Having told him, he said to me,—"The Orthodox Churches of New England hold substantially the same faith as the Presbyterian, of which the Shorter Catechism is the common symbol. How this being the case, is it wise, is it Christian, to divide the sparse population holding the same faith, already scattered, and to be hereafter scattered, over this vast new territory, into two distinct ecclesiastical organizations, and thus prevent each from enjoying those means of grace which both might much sooner enjoy but for such division? Would it not be better for the entire Church that these two divisions should make mutual concessions, and thus effect a common organization on an accommodation plan, with a view to meet the condition of communities so situated?"
>
> The arguments employed by Dr. Smith were deemed conclusive by me, gave a new direction to my efforts, and led, through the influence of other Congregationalists whom I induced to co-operate, to the formation of those numerous Presbyterian Churches on the "accommodation plan" of which, though the plan has been abandoned, the fruits remain to the present day.[40]

Nott makes no reference whatever to the long history of close

---

40. William B. Sprague, *Annals of the American Pulpit* (New York: R. Carter and Brothers, 1859), Vol. III, 403. Nott wrote about his recollections of John B. Smith.

Presbyterian-Congregational relations. E. H. Gillett, the Presbyterian historian, has perpetuated Nott's estimate of this meeting.

> This [Plan of Union] originated, therefore, with the ex-President of Hampton-Sydney College [John B. Smith] and was carried into effect largely through the influence of the younger clergyman [Eliphalet Nott] who had passed the night with him on his journey to his missionary field.[41]

In point of fact, the Plan of Union was not such a sudden action. The fact that the churches had been co-operating long before this meeting, and that the total missionary situation of both churches was so similar, suggests that the meeting between John B. Smith and Eliphalet Nott was only incidental to the formation of the Plan of Union.

Jonathan Edwards attended the meeting of the General Association of Connecticut in June, 1800, as a Presbyterian delegate, and it was there that discussion of a plan for missionary co-operation was begun. Williston Walker found "every reason to believe that the originator of the discussion and of the subject in the Connecticut Association was the younger Jonathan Edwards."[42] The Association passed a resolution calling for concrete discussions of such a plan of cooperation with the Presbyterians.

> The Revd Messrs John Smalley, Levi Hart and Samuel Blatchford are hereby appointed a Committee of this General Association, to confer with a committee to be appointed by the General Assembly of the Presbyterian Church, if they see cause to appoint such a committee, to consider the measures proper to be adopted both by this Association and said Assembly, to prevent alienation, to promote harmony and to establish, as far as possible an uniform system of Church government, between those inhabitants of the new settlements, who are attached to the Presbyterian form of Church Government, and those who are attached to the congregational form: and to make report to this Association. . . .[43]

This Committee of the Association was directed to meet with the

---

41. E. H. Gillet, *History of the Presbyterian Church in the United States of America* (Philadelphia: Presbyterian Board of Publication, 1864), Vol. I, 394.

42. Williston Walker, *The Creeds and Platforms of Congregationalism* (New York: Charles Scribner's Sons, 1893), 529.

43. *Records of the General Association,* 208–209.

General Assembly in May, 1801. Jonathan Edwards, who attended the General Assembly of 1801 as a delegate of the Presbytery of Albany, was appointed chairman of a committee of both churches to devise a working arrangement for the "new settlements." Edwards, therefore, had a major responsibility for the precise formulation of the Plan of Union.

> Regulations adopted by the General Assembly . . . and by the General Association of the State of Connecticut. . . . With a view to prevent alienation and promote union and harmony in those new settlements which are composed of inhabitants from these bodies.
>
> 1st. It is strictly enjoined on all their missionaries to the new settlements, to endeavour by all proper means, to promote mutual forbearance and accommodation, between those inhabitants of the new settlements who hold the presbyterian and those who hold the congregational form of church government.
>
> 2nd. If in the new settlements, any church of the congregational order shall settle a minister of the presbyterian order, that church may, if they choose, still conduct their discipline according to congregational principles, settling their difficulties among themselves or by a council mutually agreed upon for that purpose: But if any difficulty shall exist between the minister and the church or any member of it, it shall be referred to the Presbytery to which the minister shall belong, provided both parties agree to it, if not, to a council consisting of an equal number of presbyterians and congregationalists, agreed upon by both parties.
>
> 3rd. If a Presbyterian church shall settle a minister of congregational principles, excepting that if a difficulty arise between him and his church, or any member of it, the cause shall be tried by the Association, to which the said minister shall belong, provided that both parties agree to it, otherwise by a council, one half congregationalists and the other half presbyterians, mutually agreed on by the parties.
>
> 4th. If any congregation consist partly of those who hold the congregational form of discipline and partly of those who hold the presbyterian form; we recommend to both parties, that this be no obstruction, to their uniting in one church and settling a minister: and that in this case, the church choose a standing committee from the communicants of said church, whose business it shall be, to call to account every member of the church, who shall conduct himself inconsistently with the law of Christianity, and to give judgment on

such conduct; and if the person condemned by their judgment be a presbyterian, he shall have liberty, to appeal to the Presbytery, if a congregationalist, he shall have liberty to appeal to the body of the male communicants of the church; in the former case the determination of the Presbytery shall be final, unless the church consent to a further appeal to the Synod of the General Assembly; and in the latter case, if the party condemned shall wish for a trial by a mutual council, the cause shall be referred to such council. And provided the said standing committee of any church, shall depute one of themselves to attend the Presbytery, he may have the same right to sit and act in the Presbytery, as a ruling elder of the Presbyterian Church.

On motion resolved, that an attested copy of the above plan be made by the stated clerk, and put into the hands of the delegates of his Assembly to the General Association, to be by them laid before that body for their consideration, and that if it should be approved by them, it go into immediate operation.[44]

This statement was approved by the General Association in June, 1801.

It is true that no one can be called the "father" of the Plan of Union. Its seeds go back at least thirty-five years to the first convention of Presbyterians and Congregationalists. Yet, of all who promoted this union no one name stands out in the records of either church as does that of Jonathan Edwards. He had the unique opportunity to encourage the plan in the General Association of Connecticut, and to put it into practice when he participated in the Presbyterian General Assembly.

Six weeks after the approval of the Plan of Union, Edwards was dead. He was taken ill by what was then called "intermittent fever." It is difficult to be certain exactly what that meant. Within a week after the first indication of illness "nervous symptoms appeared, and indicated his approaching dissolution. The progress of the disease, from this date, was very rapid, and he experienced its debilitating effects so much, that within three days, he was almost entirely deprived of his speech, of the free use of his limbs, and at intervals of his reason."[45] His illness was short. Those who watched with him during this time recounted that he said, "From my uneasy feelings

---

44. *Extracts from the Minutes of the General Assembly, A. D. 1801,* 6–7.
45. "Memoir of Jonathan Edwards," *American Quarterly Register,* Volume VIII, 296.

in this burning fever, during the last night, my mind has been led to reflect on the miseries of those wretched souls who are doomed, forever, to devouring fire and everlasting burnings;—if I feel so restless under this malady of body, what must be their sufferings?"[46] One wonders if he was trying to comfort himself, or to warn those who heard him speak.

On August 1, 1801, at the age of 57, Jonathan Edwards died. His death was mourned by the whole town of Schenectady, as well as by his students and colleagues at the college. According to his wish, his body was buried in the cemetery behind the First Presbyterian Church of Schenectady. His funeral was held in the Dutch Reformed Church. The sermon preached at his funeral by Robert Smith was eloquent:

> Men and Brethren! What mean those tolling bells and sable signs? Why that melancholy gloom, which rests upon your countenances? alas! alas! a golden pillar in the temple of God is fallen—a radiant lamp in the seat of sciences extinguished—a star of the first magnitude is set—the Great Edwards is no more; *therefore we mourn.*[47]

The death of Jonathan Edwards the Younger marks the end of one era and the beginning of a new period in American history. His life began with the trials of the birth of the nation and ended with the beginning of the great westward expansion. Theologically, he spans the time from the First Great Awakening and the depth of theological insight brought by his father, to the Second Great Awakening and the beginning of new avenues of theological thought. His was truly an age of transition, and through his life and labor we have a vantage point to view both his own age and the immediate and pressing issues which lay ahead in the early years of the nineteenth century.

---

46. Tyron Edwards, "Memoir," *Works of Jonathan Edwards, D.D.*, Vol. I, xxiii.

47. Robert Smith, *A Discourse on the Occasion of the Death of the Rev. Jonathan Edwards, D.D., President of Union College* (Albany: C. & G. Webster, 1801), 1.

CHAPTER ELEVEN

Jonathan Edwards the Younger and the American Reformed Tradition

Some historical figures are more significant for helping one understand the context and course of human events than for their own unique contributions. Jonathan Edwards the Younger is such a man. He did important individual work, but beyond that he illumines our understanding of his age.

In this concluding chapter we shall review a century and a half of developments in the American Reformed tradition, both before and after the time of Edwards, and summarize his role in those developments.

The Congregational Church had nearly the entire seventeenth century to grow its roots in American soil. It faced problems of ecclesiastical adjustment during its early years. The Cambridge Platform of 1648, the enunciation of the Half Way Covenant in 1662, the Reforming Synod of Massachusetts in 1679–80, and the Saybrook Platform of 1708 were essentially efforts to establish the structure of Congregationalism. Even so, there never was simple unity in Congregationalism. The bifurcation of New England into eastern Massachusetts, and western Massachusetts and Connecticut, though largely caused by geographical and economic factors, created two ecclesiastical factions within Congregationalism. The "liberal" tendencies of eastern Massachusetts, illustrated by the work of Wise, Brattle, and Leverett, were resisted by the rest of New England. There was growing awareness of theological differences between these sections, and the ecclesiastical rift was illustrated by Connecticut's Saybrook Platform, as compared to Massachusetts' refusal to develop a similar structure.

By the latter years of the eighteenth century the theological break between Boston and Northampton or New Haven was clear. The ever present ecclesiastical differences between the Old Lights and New Lights persisted, but the overriding preoccupation of Congregationalism was doctrinal. The issues of English thought during this century helped considerably to determine the articles of debate. The theological effort of the elder Jonathan Edwards was directed against the thought of Clarke, Taylor, Shaftesbury, Collins and their like. He attempted to reinterpret Reformed doctrine to meet the challenge from these men. Around him and after him, a school of thought which became known as New Divinity or Consistent Calvinism developed. His disciples were not his equals, but their task was different than his. The inroads made by Arminianism presented to them a challenge which their mentor had not been forced to face in the same way. Edwards, Sr. had not played a defensive role; he was an interpreter. His successors, however, were challenged by strong and united Arminian adversaries; and by equally vocal "Old Calvinists," heirs to the theology of the Half Way Covenant who resisted both Arminianism and New Divinity doctrine. The theological struggles of their day were carried on in an age whose revolutionary political ethos was hostile to evangelical theology.

The Presbyterian task was different. It was a much younger American church—its first Presbytery formed as recently as 1706. During the eighteenth century, its problems of ecclesiastical adjustment were paramount, though unarticulated theological differences underlay divisions concerning polity. The church consisted of two major national groups—the Scotch-Irish and the English. During the twenty years after 1706, the English strain had undisputed control of the church. Many of their leaders were either descendants of, or trained by, the Congregationalists of Connecticut, and they looked to Yale College as their educational home. The revivalistic fervor of the New Light Congregationalists centered in western Massachusetts-Connecticut was congenial to the developing New Side party of Presbyterianism. The Log College in Neshaminy,

Pennsylvania, had been started by William Tennent, a Scotch-Irishman, who felt the need for a school to educate new Presbyterian ministers; but the Log College's revivalistic emphasis was not shared by the increasing number of Scotch-Irish who entered the middle colonies after 1720. These new immigrants were intimately tied to the Scottish Church, and did not easily accommodate themselves to the English strain within American Presbyterianism. Thus, a struggle developed between the Scotch-Irish and the English for control of the church. The Old Side opposition to the revivals, and its reluctance to adopt new means to strengthen the church in America, brought the small Scotch-Irish group emanating from the Log College into alliance with the English faction. Thus, the Presbyterians were divided, not only along national, but also along geographical lines. The close connection between Connecticut Congregationalism and the Presbyterians of New York and New Jersey, set those Presbyterians off from the Scotch-Irish settling in the areas further south.

During this period Presbyterianism could claim no figures of theological importance. The New Side party's close tie to the Connecticut Congregationalists made it natural that the major theologians of the New England church would exert great influence on the Presbyterians, who had no important theologians of their own. The work of Jonathan Edwards, Sr., Samuel Hopkins, and Joseph Bellamy was studied by the students at the College of New Jersey, and Edwards' election as President of Princeton in 1758 illustrates this close affiliation.

The rapid changes occurring in the middle colonies during this century influenced the development of American Presbyterianism. The balance of power between the Old Side and New Side began to shift as waves of Scotch-Irish entered the colonies. Thus, efforts to heal the division of 1741, which had been caused by basic disagreements between the two groups, culminated in the reunion of 1758. From that time on, the Scotch-Irish gained power. The arrival of John Witherspoon as President of Princeton in 1768 marked a turning point in the history of the church. The Edwardsean influence at the College of New Jersey was broken, and ties with Connecticut Congregationalism began to be questioned.

In this context the role of Jonathan Edwards the Younger

becomes clear. He arrived in Princeton in 1758. Excepting the years 1766–1767 when he studied with his father's two chief disciples, Samuel Hopkins and Joseph Bellamy, he spent the ten years from age thirteen to twenty-three at Princeton. He had stronger ties with Presbyterianism than any of the other major figures of New Divinity Calvinism. One year after John Witherspoon came to Princeton, Edwards left to become minister of the White Haven Church in New Haven. Though we know that he would not have found the atmosphere at Princeton congenial had he remained, he nevertheless belongs to the group within Congregationalism and Presbyterianism which continued to hold these two churches together, despite the efforts of a growing number of Presbyterians to create a thoroughly distinctive church.

His concern for unity was expressed concretely when he became President of Union College in Schenectady, New York. Upon his arrival there he joined the Synod of New York, and became intimately tied to the Presbyterian Church. Edwards played a major role in the efforts to combine the missionary work of these churches on the New York frontier. He was a member of the committee of the Presbyterian General Assembly which drafted the Plan of Union of 1801, and he helped to bring it to fulfillment in the General Association of Connecticut. The long history of close relations between the English strain within Presbyterianism and the Connecticut Congregationalists was more important to the Plan of Union than the efforts of one man, but Edwards played a significant role.

In American theology Edwards was an apologist for the New Divinity tradition. During his years, the theological efforts of the Arminian theologians (Charles Chauncy, Samuel West, and Jonathan Mayhew, for example) were becoming bolder and more outspoken. Their hesitation to publish their views diminished as the eighteenth century passed, and in its later years they found many supporters. Jonathan Edwards the Younger's theological labors were directed against their attacks on the theology of Edwards, Sr.

As a result of these efforts, and because he did not share the widespread humanized spirit of his age, Edwards brought a character to Calvinistic theology that contributed to its decline. He thought in terms of God as the King, the Governor of the Universe. Man had to fit the scheme which God had designed. Through the commands of Scripture, the sovereign ruler had made explicit what He expected of His creatures, and in order to preserve the happiness of man and creation, man must not deviate from the prescribed path. Unfortunately, man did so, and punishment must result, otherwise God's government would crumble. Edwards the Younger perceived a universe structured in terms of reward and punishment; his motive for the Christian life was no longer the "glory of God" or "benevolence to Being in General" about which his father wrote, but the stability of divine rule. And yet, God being sovereign and all powerful, man could not rebel against him unless it was permitted or ordained by God. Edwards' theology was rigid and legalistic and basically unacceptable to an age which was confident of its power, freedom, and self-determination. It was this interpretation of Calvinism, perpetrated by Edwards and other New Divinity men, which precipitated its demise; the next generation wrestled with his problems but interpreted them in a way which deviated from his premises, and adopted the perspectives which he had fought in his own age.

Nathaniel Emmons' comment about Edwards is insightful. ". . . The senior President [Edwards, Sr.] had more *reason* than his son; but the son was a better *reasoner* than his father."[1] Edwards the Younger lost almost completely the mystical Neo-Platonic strain of his father's thought, and, attempting to carry out its implications as faithfully as he could, he lost much of its genius.

From our perspective, the tragedy of his life seems to be his incapacity to see beyond his times. He failed to offer new life to Reformed Theology. By the end of his life it was clear that new theological directions were necessary if orthodox Calvinism was to remain theologically vital. The New Divinity tradition was dying; the successors of Edwards, Sr. had lost both the vitality and creativity of his thought. Such an analysis even applies to the younger Edwards' work to cement close relations between Presbyterians and Congregationalists. Unfortunately the Plan of Union was formulated without close attention to the theological issues involved in

---

1. Nathaniel Emmons, *The Works of Nathaniel Emmons*, ed. Jacob Ide (Boston: Congregational Board of Publication, 1860), Vol. I, 135. The reviewer of *The Works of Jonathan Edwards, D.D.* for the *Princeton Review* of 1843 also put this nicely when he wrote that Edwards the Younger deviated "from the temperate zone of Reformed and Puritan Theology into the arctic regions of Hopkinsianism." *The Biblical Repertory and Princeton Review for the year 1843*, 53.

the ecclesiastical union. The Union occurred without discussion of the basic conception of the church held by each denomination. Thus, when Presbyterians began to produce their own theological leaders, the issues left undiscussed in 1801 had to be faced.

* * * *

A brief examination of the early years of the nineteenth century gives a broader perspective in which to view the developments of the lifetime of Jonathan Edwards the Younger. The new century brought new issues to the American Reformed tradition, and some of them stemmed from the unresolved questions of the eighteenth century.

In 1795, the year that Edwards left New Haven for Colebrook, the Presidency of Yale College changed hands. Ezra Stiles died and Timothy Dwight, Edwards' nephew and pupil, was elected as his successor. Dwight, who is remembered as one of the leading figures of the Second Great Awakening, assumed his position at a time when religious life, both at Yale College and throughout New England, was at low ebb. The Second Great Awakening began in churches whose preferences were with the New Divinity tradition. Gradually, however, its scope broadened, and under the influence of Dwight, Nathaniel William Taylor, and Charles Finney it was transformed and then propagated across the nation.[2]

Theologically, Dwight was said to represent "no special school in New England Divinity."[3] But Sidney Mead has shown that, despite Edwardsean sympathies, Dwight's basic empathy was with the Old Calvinist school of New England theology.[4] His efforts to "awaken" the churches stressed the "means of regeneration."

> All the efficacy, which I have attributed to the Means of Grace, does not, I acknowledge, amount to regeneration, nor ensure it. But it amounts to what St. Paul terms *planting* and *watering*. The *increase*

---

2. See Charles Roy Keller, *The Second Great Awakening* (New Haven: Yale University Press, 1942), and Alice F. Tyler, *Freedom's Ferment* (Minneapolis: The University of Minnesota Press, 1944).

3. Frank Hugh Foster, *A Genetic History of the New England Theology* (Chicago: University of Chicago Press, 1907), 361–363.

4. Sidney Mead, *Nathaniel William Taylor, 1786–1858, A Connecticut Liberal* (Chicago: University of Chicago Press, 1942), Chapter VII, "Old Calvinist to Taylorite."

must be, and still is, given by God only. In the same manner, God must create the grain; or husbandman, after all his ploughing and sowing, after all the rain and the sunshine, will never find a crop. Still, these are indispensable means of his crop; so indispensable, that without them, the crop would never exist. As truly, in the ordinary course of providence, there will, without the use of the Means of Grace, be no spiritual harvest. There will be no Instructions given; no Impressions made; and no realizing convictions of guilt, danger, and dependence, produced: and without these, there will be no regeneration of the soul, and no title obtained to eternal life.[5]

Nathaniel Taylor, a student of Dwight, pastor of the First Congregational Church in New Haven, and later Professor of Didactic Theology at Yale College, discussed the corollary problem of the freedom of the will.[6] Taylor acknowledged that he departed from the thought of Jonathan Edwards, Sr. He felt that Edwards did not enter "fully into the nature of moral agency, showing wherein it consisted" but rather was satisfied only to "expose [the] absurdities of self-determination. . . ."[7] Mead has suggested that

> Taylor got around Edwards' conclusions respecting the freedom of the will not because he found a way to outlogic Edwards but because, unlike Edwards, he was willing to insist that the Divine Author "demands only a rational faith of rational beings" and even consents that "the book . . . shall be tried at the bar of human reason."[8]

In the face of Unitarian thought emanating from eastern Massachusetts, Taylor particularly desired to explain, in as palatable a way as possible, the Calvinistic view on sin and free will. To Taylor, moral depravity "is man's own act, consisting in a free choice of some object rather than God, as his chief good;—or a free preference of the worldly good, to the will and glory of God."[9] Taylor's phrase, "certainty with power to the contrary," became the key to New Haven theology. It is also important to note that Taylor was con-

5. Timothy Dwight, *Theology; Explained and Defended in a Series of Sermons* (New York: G. & C. & H. Carvill, 1830), Vol. IV, 59.

6. An excellent study of this period and of later developments in New England theology is John M. Giltner, "Moses Stuart, 1780–1852," Unpublished Ph.D. dissertation, Yale University, 1956.

7. Nathaniel Taylor, quoted in Mead, *Nathaniel William Taylor*, 102.

8. Mead, *Nathaniel William Taylor*, 108.

9. Nathaniel Taylor, *A Sermon Delivered in the Chapel of Yale College, September 10, 1828* (New Haven: A. H. Maltby, 1842), 8.

cerned about the democratic and optimistic ethos of the Jacksonian era.

In 1805, four years after the death of Jonathan Edwards the Younger, Unitarianism won control of Harvard when Henry Ware was installed as Hollis Professor of Divinity. The victory of the Unitarians brought the Old Calvinists and the Hopkinsians of Massachusetts together, and Andover Seminary was born from this union in 1808.[10] There was no longer time for "Calvinists" to be fighting among themselves; they must unite to combat the "heresy" of Harvard. In 1818, Jedidiah Morse, a former student of Edwards the Younger, helped to finance the publication of *American Unitarianism,* attempting to show a kinship between American and English anti-trinitarianism. A review of this volume in the *Panoplist* brought the rapid advances being made by Unitarianism to the attention of the orthodox.[11] William Ellery Channing's well-known

---

10. See James King Morse, *Jedidiah Morse, a Champion of New England Orthodoxy* (New York: Columbia University Press, 1939), Chapter VIII. The uneasy character of the orthodox alliance is illustrated by the following excerpt from a letter of Nathaniel Emmons. Though written 30 years after the event, it portrays Emmons as opposed to a Taylorite position, though sympathetic to its efforts and more akin to Bennet Tyler (see below, p. 180) yet refuting the New Divinity doctrine of total depravity which Tyler represented.

Franklin, August 7, 1838

Reverend Mr. Edward A. Park
Dear Sir
    [personal remarks to Park]
    . . . I rejoice to hear that you preach *doctrinally* and study the deep things of God which is fast growing out of practice. I would gladly attend to the serious & important questions which you propose for discussion if I were not conscious of my declining and declined mental and bodily infirmities. I am indeed sensible that old age has weakened my abilities to explain & defend the peculiar doctrines of the Gospel, yet I am not conscious, that it has in the least weakened my faith & confidence in their truth and importance. I have not given up any of my doctrinal opinions, am no nearer Taylorism than ever I was. I do indeed go about half way with Taylorites, and then stop and turn against them with all my might. And I go further with Tylerites, but stop at depravity. . . .

Natl Emmons.

Ms. letter of August 7, 1838, from Nathaniel Emmons to Edward A. Park (Yale University Library).

11. *The Panoplist* was a magazine founded in 1805 through the efforts of Jedidiah Morse. Its establishment reflects the effort of the "Hopkinsians" and Old Calvinists of Massachusetts to unite against the Unitarians. The magazine of the "liberal" group was the *Monthly Anthology.* The Hopkinsians had the *Massachusetts Missionary Magazine.* Morse felt that a magazine (*The Panoplist*) under the joint editorship of Leonard Woods and himself would afford a better platform for orthodox views. Thus the *Massachusetts Missionary Magazine* was combined with the new *Panoplist.* This periodical and other printed material served to disperse the debates of the day in which so many were involved. Moses Stuart wrote against W.E. Channing; Andrew Norton of Harvard countered with an attack on Stuart; Leonard Woods of Andover answered Norton; Henry Ware met the arguments of Woods, and so on.

Baltimore Sermon (1819) was a forthright appeal for "Unitarian Christianity," and confirmed the inroads the movement was making in other parts of the colonies.[12]

But even the clear challenge of the Unitarians could not cement the union of the Calvinists. By the early 1820's there were evident breaks in the orthodox front. Those influenced by the New Haven theology hesitated to send students to study under the Hopkinsian-flavored thought of Andover Seminary. There is no doubt that this was part of the reason for the establishment of the Theological Department of Yale College in 1822. Lyman Beecher and Charles Finney, the major revivalists of the day, were strongly influenced by New Haven Theology. When Finney began his revivalistic tours in the 1820's, the proponents of strict Calvinism found it easy to link his extreme measures with the theology stemming from New Haven.

The growing split among the orthodox was encouraged by the attempts of the Unitarians to show that New Haven theology differed quite clearly from Hopkinsianism, and from the theology of some of the leaders of the Presbyterian Church. "They began deliberately to drive wedges between New Haven and Princeton, between New Haven and Andover, defending themselves, as it were, by fostering division in the orthodox camp."[13]

Asahel Nettleton opened the attack on Nathaniel Taylor.

> You may speculate better than I can; but I know one thing better than you do. I know better what Christians will and what they will not receive; and I forewarn you, that, wherever you come out, our best Christians will revolt.[14]

Furthermore, Leonard Woods, Professor of Theology at Andover Seminary, who had spent much of his time attacking Henry Ware, the Hollis Professor of Divinity at Harvard and a Unitarian, also

---

12. The Dedham Case brought the issue between Unitarians and Congregationalists into the courts. In 1818, the same year that the Congregational Church in Connecticut was disestablished, the Congregational Church in Dedham, Massachusetts, split into Unitarian and orthodox factions. The Supreme Court of the state was faced with the question of which group owned the church property. Though the orthodox were the majority of church members, the more liberal faction controlled the Society. The Court ruled in favor of the latter.

13. Sidney Mead, *Nathaniel William Taylor*, 194.

14. Asahel Nettleton, quoted in Samuel Baird, *A History of the New School, and of the Questions Involved in the Disruption of the Presbyterian Church in 1838* (Philadelphia: Claxton, Remsen & Haffelfinger, 1868), 186–187.

began to concentrate his attack on Taylor, a fellow Calvinist. Other conservatives joined Nettleton and Woods, but no one engaged Taylor in debate more forcefully than Bennet Tyler, graduate of Yale, former President of Dartmouth College, and then pastor of the Second Church of Portland, Maine.

> His [Taylor's] views of native depravity, of means and regeneration are virtually Arminian; at least they will be so understood as to bring up a race of young preachers thoroughly anti-Calvinistic. The spirit besides, is like the he-goat of Daniel, bold and pushing—impatient of inquiry, or hesitation in other men. Now, what is to be done? Shall we sustain our Calvinism, or see it run down to the standard of Methodists, and laxer men? It is time that a note of remonstrance be struck up somewhere.[15]

When it came, the "remonstrance" led to the formation of the Theological Institute of Connecticut as a conservative seminary at East Windsor, Connecticut, to offset the "liberalism" of Yale, in 1833.[16]

During these years at the beginning of the nineteenth century, some Presbyterians were becoming aware of differences between the standards of their church and the conflicting interpretations of Calvinism emanating from New England. In 1811 Ezra Stiles Ely published his work, *A Contrast Between Calvinism and Hopkinsianism*, which stressed the difference between "true" Calvinism and the theology of the New Divinity men. During the same period the revivals led by Charles Finney and others in New England and New York further widened the breach between Old School Presbyterians, whose roots lay with the Old Side group of the eighteenth century, and the Congregational Church.

When the flavor of the developing New Haven theology began to seep into the Presbyterian Church, two groups within that church were involved. The Old School Presbyterians resisted the theological efforts of Nathaniel Taylor with vehemence; the New School, for the most part, accepted these new views and worked them into their theological systems.

The major figure of the New School party was Albert Barnes,

---

15. Bennet Tyler, *Letters on the Origin and Progress of the New Haven Theology* (New York: R. Carter and E. Collier, 1837), 24.

16. See C. M. Geer, *The Hartford Theological Seminary, 1834–1934* (Hartford: Lockwood & Brainard Co., 1934).

pastor of the Presbyterian Church in Morristown, New Jersey, and later pastor of the First Presbyterian Church of Philadelphia. In February of 1829 Barnes preached a sermon, *The Way of Salvation*, to his congregation at Morristown. That sermon was to become the focus for a theological battle within the church. Barnes insisted that man is not to be held "personally answerable for the transgressions of Adam, or of any other man; or that God has given a law which man has no power to obey."[17] Like Taylor, who clearly influenced him, Barnes said that man is not a sinner until he sins. He admitted that the language he used

> does not accord with that used on the same subject in the Westminster Confession of Faith and in other standards of doctrine. The main difference is that it is difficult to offer any clear and definite meaning to the expression "we sinned in him, and fell with him."[18]

Barnes suggested that reason is a guide for determining the evidence of revelation, "of the evidence of a divine revelation reason must be the absolute judge."[19] In 1830 Barnes was called as pastor of the First Presbyterian Church in Philadelphia. His settlement was challenged by a group within the Presbytery. During the course of the next eight years the Old School-New School groups became increasingly sharp, largely because of the influence of New Haven theology on the New School Presbyterians.

Old School men charged Barnes and his supporters with all manner of heresy. Concerning Barnes' view of man's sin, George Junkin, one of the ablest spokesmen for the Old School group, said:

> Mr. Moderator, I do honestly, and in the fear of God, and in love to brother Barnes, declare my belief, that this leads by a straight, forward, direct and short road to downright, desolating, damning Socinianism. . . . If this system is true, then I'll be a Unitarian.[20]

The Old School party recognized that the theological sentiments emanating from New Haven were involved.

17. Albert Barnes, *The Way of Salvation; A Sermon, Delivered at Morristown, New Jersey, February 8, 1829* (New York: Leavitt, Lord, 1836), 16.

18. Barnes, *The Way of Salvation,* 15.

19. Albert Barnes, *Inquiries and Suggestions in Regard to the Foundation of Faith in the Word of God* (Philadelphia: Parry and McMillan, 1859), 39.

20. George Junkin, *The Vindication, Containing a History of the Trial of the Rev. Albert Barnes* (Philadelphia: W.S. Martien, 1836), 141.

New Haven was the foster parent of these [New School] errors; and the *Quarterly* issued there. . . , was not only read extensively by Presbyterian ministers, but was the medium through which one of them [Barnes] published some of his more objectionable matters.[21]

In 1837, when the Presbyterian Church was divided into Old School and New School branches, other than strictly theological issues were involved. The two groups differed concerning the degree to which they should co-operate with interdenominational organizations; they disagreed on the constitutionality of the Plan of Union of 1801. The Old School Presbyterians declared the Plan of Union illegal because it did not provide for the proper functioning of the judicatories of the church. Legally, they were correct. But it was the failure of the Presbyterian and Congregational churches to discuss more carefully in 1801 the fundamental basis for their union which helped to foster this later schism. The issue of slavery was also a contributing factor to the division.[22] The early geographical division between Old Side and New Side carried over through this period: the strength of the New School was centered in the north, the Old School was predominant in the border states and in the south.

Though other issues were important, theological problems were central. "The real question on the subject of disorders now is, shall Congregationalism, in any shape, be tolerated in the Presbyterian Church?" stated Zebulon Crocker in 1839. The question he raised embraces pretty nearly the whole ground of complaint on the subject, and divided the church into two great parties.[23]

*   *   *   *   *

We have surveyed a century of developments within the American Reformed tradition and recounted the life and contributions of Jonathan Edwards the Younger. Edwards and his generation

21. James Wood, *Doctrinal Differences Which Have Agitated and divided the Presbyterian Church or Old and New Theology* (Philadelphia: 1853), 11–12.

22. See Edmund A. Moore, "Robert J. Breckenridge and the Slavery Aspect of the Presbyterian Schism of 1837," *Church History,* Vol. IV, December, 1935, 282–294, and Elwyn A. Smith, "The Role of the South in the Presbyterian Schism of 1837–38," *Church History,* Vol. XXIX (March, 1960), 44–63.

23. Zebulon Crocker, *The Catastrophe of the Presbyterian Church in 1837* (New Haven: B.&W. Noyes, 1838), 111–112.

are at the center of the story; in him and his age we see the factors which coalesced to bring new issues to American Christianity. In national affairs, church life, and theology, his was an age of transition. Edwards stands at the end of one period and the beginning of another in the American Reformed tradition.

Bibliography of the Manuscript Writings of Jonathan Edwards the Younger

The following abbreviations are used:

ANL—Andover Newton Seminary
CMS—Connecticut Missionary Society
HSL—Hartford Seminary Library
HSP—Library of Historical Society of Pennsylvania
HUL—Harvard University Library
PUL—Princeton University Library
YUL—Yale University Library, The Beinecke Rare Book and Manuscript Library
UCL—Union College Library

A. Manuscripts (Not Dated)

>   "Address to Graduates" (ANL)
>   "Church Covenant" (ANL)
>   "Corrigenda" (ANL)
>   "Deed to Lands in New York State" (YUL)
>   "Desiderata" (ANL)
>   "Improvements in Theology made by the late Jonathan Edwards, President of the College of New Jersey and by those who have pursued his line of thinking" (HSL)
>   "Lecture on Rhetoric" (ANL)
>   "Memoranda in Temporal Affairs" (ANL)
>   "Miscellaneous Observations on Preaching" (ANL)
>   "Notes on Communion Service" (YUL)
>   "Observations and Rules for Conduct in Private Life" (YUL)
>   "Order of Commencement" (ANL)
>   "Table of Doctrines and Subjects" (ANL)
>   "Three Confessions of Faith" (ANL)
>
>   Incomplete manuscript on the subject of baptism, 7–92 (HSL)
>   Incomplete manuscript on the subject of church discipline, 17–31 (HSL)

B. Manuscripts (Dated)

"Dedicatory Statement," September 17, 1763 (YUL)

"Logica Compendium," 1763 (ANL)

"Exempla Modorum in prima Figura," 1763 (ANL)

"Diary," May 25, 1764 to January 13, 1765 (YUL)

"Edwards' Will," September 8, 1785 (YUL)

"Statement Concerning Case of Discipline in North Haven Church, New Haven, October 2, 1786" (YUL)

"Order of Commencement at Union College, Schenectady, New York, May 6, 1801" (ANL)

C. Manuscripts (relating to Edwards)

"A Systematic Collection of Questions and Answers in Divinity" [prepared by Jonathan Edwards], January 22, 1794, copied by Maltby Gelston (YUL)

"The Theological Questions of Jonathan Edwards, D.D.," copied by Asabel Nettleton, September 27, 1809 (HSL)

D. Manuscript letters to Jonathan Edwards the Younger, from:

(YUL)

Jonathan Edwards, Sr., May 27, 1755

Mary Porter, September 23, 1770

Elisha Porter, August 14, 1772

Elisha Porter, February 24, 1778

Eleazer Porter, August 9, 1782

Timothy Edwards, July 23, 1782

Timothy Edwards, May 15, 1795

Joseph Bellamy, July 9, 1782

Stephen West, July 16, 1782

Isaiah Hochkiss, June 16, 1783

John Rippon, September 19, 1786

John Ryland, June 29, 1787

George Washington, August 28, 1788

Aaron Burr, May 30, 1789

Jerusha Edwards, 8 letters from May 29, 1790 to August 20, 1800

Andrew Law, March 28, 1791

Isaiah Thomas, April 28, 1792.
August 10, 1792

Calvin Chapin, 13 letters from February 20, 1796 to February 5, 1801

Mary Hoyt, January 9, 1796

Benjamin Trumbull, November 26, 1797

Chauncy Lee, January 5, 1800

B. DeWitt, April 2, 1800

Charles Williamson, April 14, 1800

William Wellers, no date
                February 27, 1801
Joel Benedict, July 8, 1800
John Henry, July 13, 1800
                March 19, 1801
Alpha Rockwell, November 4, 1800
Azel Backus, March 4, 1801
Edward Edwards, March 18, 1801
Jonathan Bird, March 21, 1801
Samuel Brooms, March 25, 1801
                March 28, 1801
John B. Johnson, March 31, 1801
Isaac Lewis, April 2, 1801
H. Kinney, April 4, 1801
Simon Hosack, April 25, 1801
Jeremiah Pratt, June 11, 1801
Robert Proudfit, June 6, 1801
John Erskine, June 24, 1801
Cyrus Comstock, July 4, 1801

(CMS)

David Riggins, September 29, 1794
Moses Welch, July, 1793
Ammi Robbins, 5 letters from June 22, 1783 to February 5, 1795
John Sergeant, June 27, 1799
Nathaniel Brown, January 6, 1799
Smith Cotton, July 15, 1794
William Robinson, August 27, 1794
Justus Mitchell, June 2, 1794
                August 29, 1796
Schiller Mansfield, May 14, 1794
Mr. Lyman, July 18, 1794
Samuel Mills, 6 letters from June 26, 1793 to August 7,
        1794
Cyprian Strong, June 20, 1794
                July 9, 1794
                August 1, 1794
Peter Starr, April 14, 1794
                November 8, 1794
John Shepard, October 5, 1793
                October 29, 1793
                November 29, 1794
Woodiah Russell, May 5, 1794

Aaron Kinne, 5 letters from August 12, 1793 to August 18, 1794
Andrew Eliot, June, 1794
Jeremiah Day, January 6, 1794
       July 7, 1794
       November 10, 1794
Asel Backus, July 7, 1794
Asabel Hooker, January 28, 1794
       August 11, 1794
       November 11, 1794
Theodore Hinsdale, June 27, 1793
       July 14, 1794
Samuel Nott, October 7, 1793
David Fuller, September 2, 1793
Moses Welch, July 1, 1793
Benjamin Wildman, July 15, 1793
N. Williams, October 7, 1793
David Huntington, December 18, 1793

E. Manuscript letters written by Jonathan Edwards the Younger to:

    (YUL)

Benjamin Trumbull, July 7, 1772
       February 24, 1800
Ebenezer Baldwin, January 17, 1774
Ezra Stiles, April 24, 1794
David Daggett, May 11, 1794
Committee of Connecticut Legislature, May 13, 1794
Stephen West, November 10, 1794
Jeremiah Atwater, October 30, 1795
Jonathan W. Edwards, 32 letters from August 5, 1795 to June 26, 1801
Prof. J. Meigs, July 10, 1799
Mary Porter, July 25, 1770
       August 28, 1770
Joseph Bellamy, June 4, 1770
Sarah Burr, March 17, 1770
       January 29, 1770
Samuel Hopkins, October 12, 1795
William Hillhouse, April 22, 1796
Samuel Hopkins, October 29, 1795
Lucy Edwards, June 1, 1764

    (ANL)

Timothy Dwight, April 18, 1772
       July 18, 1782

(HSL)

Joseph Bellamy, November 12, 1773
July 9, 1792
Benjamin Trumbull, February 24, 1800

(CMS)

Strong and Flint, August 24, 1799
Benjamin Trumbull, June 29, 1796
October 19, 1796
September 19, 1797

(HSP)

Levi Hart, July 27, 1786

F. Manuscript letters—family collections containing pertinent letters

(YUL)

Baldwin Family Papers
Roger Sherman Papers
Benjamin Trumbull Collection
John Trumbull Collection
Whittelsey Family Papers

G. Manuscript Sermons. The following sermons are listed by the date they were written. The numbers following the year date are those given by Edwards the Younger. (This list of manuscript sermons has been checked against that compiled by Wesley Evarts in his Th.D. dissertation on Edwards the Younger at Hartford Theological Seminary. I acknowledge my debt to his work.)

(ANL)

1772: 258
1774: 354
1776: 489
1778: 578
1781: 717
1783: 1 sermon not numbered
1786: 950
1787: 977, 981, 987
1788: 1045
1789: 1081, 1084, 1088, 1121
1790: 4 sermons not numbered
1791: 3 sermons not numbered
1792: 2 sermons not numbered
1793: 2 sermons not numbered
1794: 3 sermons not numbered

1795: 2 sermons not numbered
1796: 2 sermons not numbered
1798: 1 sermon not numbered
1799: 3 sermons not numbered
1800: 4 sermons not numbered
1801: 4 sermons not numbered

(HSL)

1766: III, IV
1767: VI
1768: XII, XVI, XVIII, XX, XXV, 30, 32, 34–36
1769: 39, 41–45, 76–79, 81–89, 91
1770: 92–93, 95–96, 98–100, 102–108, 110–123, 125–127, 129, 131–142
1771: 144–150, 154–156, 158–159, 161–164, 166–169, 171–176, 179–184, 188–190, 193–194, 196–201, 203
1772: 204–210, 213–217, 219–228, 230–238, 240–254, 256–257, 259, 261–263
1773: 264–275, 277–280, 282–285, 287, 289–290, 292–298, 300–304, 307–319, 321–330, 332–334, 336–339
1774: 340, 342–346, 348–350, 353, 355–370, 372–376, 378, 380–384, 386–387, 389–394, 396, 398, 400–407
1775: 408–417, 419–421, 423–425, 427–429, 432–434, 437–445, 447–455
1776: 456–460, 463–468, 470–474, 474–482, 484–488, 490–496, 498–499, 501, 503–505
1777: 508–510, 515–530, 532–537, 539–541
1778: 551, 553, 555–559, 562–563, 566–568, 570–577, 579–584, 586–589, 591–593
1779: 594–603, 605–606, 608–613, 615–616, 619, 622–627, 629–635, 639–647
1780: 644–670, 672–674, 676–678, 680–690, 694–695
1781: 696–704, 706–711, 713–716, 718–721, 723, 725–726, 728–732, 735, 737–741
1782: 743, 745–752, 754, 755, 756–767, 769–771, 773–774, 776, 778, 780–790
1783: 791–802, 804–807, 809, 811, 815, 817–823, 825–827, 829–834, 837–839
1784: 831, 832, 834, 836, 838, 839, 841–844, 846, 849, 850–860, 862–865, 867–869
1785: 884, 886, 888–890, 892, 894–896, 898, 900–904, 906–911, 913, 916, 919–924
1786: 926, 928, 929, 931–933, 935, 938, 941–945, 947–948, 952, 954, 956, 959, 960, 961, 962
1787: 978–980, 983, 986, 989–992, 994–1012, 1015–1018

1788: 1019–1021, 1023–1028, 1030–1031, 1033–1034, 1041, 1043–1053, 1058, 1060, 1063–1064, 1066–1070
1789: 1072–1073, 1076–1080, 1082–1083, 1085–1087, 1089–1090, 1092–1094, 1096–1098, 1100, 1102–1105, 1107–1112, 1115–1120
1790: 1122–1133, 1135–1137, 1139, 1141, 1143–1146, 1148, also 24 sermons not numbered
1791: 52 sermons not numbered
1792: 47 sermons not numbered
1793: 41 sermons not numbered
1794: 46 sermons not numbered
1795: 12 sermons not numbered
1796: 3 sermons not numbered
1797: 3 sermons not numbered
1798: 7 sermons not numbered
1799: 2 sermons not numbered
1800: 4 sermons not numbered

(PUL)

1767: X
1769: one sermon not numbered

(YUL)

1781: 727
1782: 772

Bibliography of the Published Works of Jonathan Edwards the Younger

1. *The Works of Jonathan Edwards, D.D., with a Memoir of his Life and Character by Tyron Edwards* (2 vols. Andover: Allen, Morrill and Wardwell, 1842). Some of the following writings were published separately; the date and place of publication are indicated in the parentheses. The remaining entries are, to the best of my knowledge, published only in the *Works*.

Volume I

(Theological treatises)

"The Salvation of All Men Strictly Examined; and the Endless Punishment of Those Who Die Impenitent, Argued and Defended Against the Objections and Reasoning of the Late Rev. Doctor Chauncy, of Boston, in His Book Entitled 'The Salvation of All Men, etc.,' with appendix Containing Remarks on Several Authors," 1–287 (New Haven: A. Morse, 1790).

"Brief Observations on the Doctrine of Universal Salvation, As Lately Promulgated at New Haven," 279–294 (New Haven: Meigs, Bowen and Dana, 1784).

"A Dissertation Concerning Liberty and Necessity; Containing Remarks on the Essays of Dr. Samuel West, And on the Writings of Several Other Authors on those Subjects," 295–468 (Worcester, 1797).

"Observations on the Language of the Muhhekaneew Indians; In Which the Extent of that Language in North America is Shown; Its Genius Grammatically Traced; and Some of its Peculiarities, and some Instances of Analogy Between that and the Hebrew are Pointed Out," 469–480 (New Haven: Josiah Meigs, 1788).

"Remarks on the Improvements Made in Theology by His Father, President Edwards," 481–492.

"Thoughts on the Atonement," 493–507 (*The Theological Magazine*, Vol. I, 51–64).

Jonathan Edwards the Younger

Volume II

(Sermons)

"Three Sermons on the Necessity of the Atonement, and Its Consistency with Free Grace in Forgiveness," 11–52 (New Haven: Meigs, Bowen and Dana, 1785).

"The Faithful Manifestation of the Truth, the End of Preaching," 53–74 (New Haven: Thomas and Samuel Green, 1783).

"The Injustice and Impolicy of the Slave Trade and of Slavery," 75–97 (New Haven: T. & S. Green, 1791).

"All Divine Truth Profitable," 98–123 (New Haven: A. Morse, 1792).

"The Marriage of a Wife's Sister Considered," 124–141 (New Haven: T. & S. Green, 1792).

"Faith and a Good Conscience Illustrated," 142–160 (New Haven: A. Morse, 1792).

"Human Depravity the Source of Infidelity," 161–172 (*The American Preacher* [4 vols., New Haven: Abel Morse, 1793], Vol. 4).

"God a Refuge and Help," 173–184 (New Haven, 1793).

"The Belief of Christianity Necessary to Political Prosperity," 185–209 (Hartford: Hudson and Goodwin, 1794).

"The Duty of Ministers to Preach the Truth," 210–223 (Hartford, 1795).

"The Minister's Parting Counsel," 224–237 (Suffield, Connecticut: Edward Gray, 1799).

"Submission to Rulers," 238–247.

"Mere Repentance No Ground of Pardon," 248–257.

"Christ Our Righteousness," 258–273.

"Christ Crucified," 274–290.

"Holding Fast Our Profession," 291–301.

"The Soul's Immortality, and Future Retribution," 302–322 (Hartford, 1797).

"False Refuges Unsafe," 323–339.

"The Parting Commendation," 340–347.

"God the Author of All Good Volitions and Actions," 348–360.

"The Law Not Made Void Through Faith," 361–377.

"The Acceptance and Safety of the Elect," 378–386.

"Grace Evidenced by Its Fruits," 387–400.

"The Glory of the Gospel," 401–411.

"The Broad Way," 412–427.

"Universal Salvation Inconsistent with Salvation by Christ," 428–446.

"Charity the Veil of Sins," 447–458.

(Articles) The following articles are reprinted in *The Works of Jonathan Edwards* from *The Theological Magazine* (3 vols. New York: 1796, 1797, 1799). In the parentheses are the references to *The Theological Magazine,* cited as T.M.

"Merit of Virtue and Demerit of Sin," 458–464 (*T.M.* I, 25–27).

"Modern Liberality," 464–465 (*T.M.* I, 193–194).

"The Divine Vengeance," 465 (*T.M.* I, 194).

"The Salvation of the Heathen," 465–466 (*T.M.* I, 195).
"Benevolence of God in Inflicting Punishment," 466–468 (*T.M.* I, 200–202).
"Promise of the Holy Spirit," 468–471 (*T.M.* I, 204–207).
"The Proof of the Moral Perfections of God, From the Light of Nature," 471–496 (*T.M.* I, 184–187; II, 55–59; III, 173–186).
"Immateriality of the Human Soul," 497–502 (*T.M.* I, 461–466).
"Free Agency and Absolute Decree Reconciled," 502–505 (*T.M.* II, 62–63).
"The Proof of God's Moral Perfections From Scripture," 505–508 (*T.M.* II, 199–203).
"The Doctrine of Election," 508–512 (*T.M.* II, 254–257).
"On Moral Agency," 512–517 (*T.M.* II, 275–280).
"Deistic Objections, with Answers," 518–526 (*T.M.* II, 422–424).
"Of Sinning not After the Similitude of Adam's Transgressions," 526–527 (*T.M.* II, 424–425).
"The Soul in the Intermediate State," 528–533 (*T.M.* III, 6–13).
"Short Comments on New Texts," 533–538 (*T.M.* III, 22–28).
"What is the Foundation of Moral Obligation?" 538–541 (*T.M.* III, 111–115).
"Concerning the Warrant of the Sinner to Believe in Christ," 541–543 (*T.M.* III, 222–224).
"Of Self-Love," 544–548 (*T.M.* III, 372–375).

2. Other Published Works

a. (Articles) The following articles were published in *The Theological Magazine*, though not reprinted in *The Works of Jonathan Edwards*. These articles were not signed by Edwards; however, his biographer, Tyron Edwards, indicated that Edwards wrote over the signature I, O. or Iota, Epsilon.

Volume I

"A Brief Essay on Striving to Enter in at the Strait Gate, Luke 13–24," 165–170.
"Of the Character of the God of Moses," 187–188.
"Sufficient Help," 196.
"Observations Concerning the Atonement," 246–248.
"On the Perseverance of the Saints," 403–411.

Volume II

"On the Innocent suffering for the Guilty," 37–38.
"Of Free Discussion," 170–171.
"Of the Return of the Jews to their own land in the Millennium," 176–180.
"Of the Happiness of the Universe," 426.
"The Authenticity of the Old Testament," 427.

Volume III

"On the Suffering of the Innocent," 130–131.
"On Practical Godliness," 132–133.

"On Hell Torments," 131–133.
"The Advantage of Christianty in this World," 425–429.
"On the Motives of Divine Conduct," 465.
"The Glory of God and the Happiness of Creatures," 465–466.
"The Damned Moral Agents," 466.

b. (Miscellany)

Jonathan Edwards, Sr., *Sermons on the Following Subjects* . . . (Hartford: Hudson and Goodwin, 1780). Preface by Jonathan Edwards the Younger.

Jonathan Edwards, Sr., *Twenty Sermons, on Various Subjects* . . . (Edinburgh: M. Gray, 1789). Preface by Jonathan Edwards the Younger.

The Theological Questions of President Edwards, senior, and Dr. Edwards, his son (Providence: Miller and Hutchens, 1822).

Edwards Amasa Park, editor, *The Atonement. Discourses by Edwards Jr., Smalley, Maxcy, Emmons, Griffin, Burge, and Weeks* (Boston: Congregational Board of Publication, 1859).

3. Biographies of Jonathan Edwards the Younger.

American Quarterly Register, Volume VIII, 1836, 289–298.

Christian Spectator, Volume V, 1823, 39–48.

Connecticut Evangelical Magazine, Volume II, 1802, 377–383.

Tyron Edwards, "Memoir," *The Works of Jonathan Edwards, D.D.*, Volume I, ix–xl.

Robert Smith, *A Discourse on the Occasion of the Death of the Rev. Jonathan Edwards, D.D., President of Union College. Delivered on Third Day of August, A.D. 1801, in the Reformed Dutch Church at Schenectady* (Albany: C. and G. Webster, 1801).

Chapter Bibliographies

The purpose of this bibliography is to aid others who wish to explore further some of the topics covered in this study. Some standard and some more recent essays have been omitted and space given to the less well known and often obscure but important sources.

CHAPTER ONE

The Early Years

An Account of the College of New Jersey. Woodbridge, N.J.: Published for the Trustees of the College of New Jersey by James Parker, 1764.

Alexander, Samuel Davies. *Princeton College During the Eighteenth Century.* New York: A. D. F. Randolph & Co., 1872.

Bellamy, Joseph. *The Works of Joseph Bellamy, D.D.* 2 Vols. Boston: Doctrinal Tract and Book Society, 1853.

Broderick, Francis J. "Pulpit, Physics, and Politics: The Curriculum of the College of New Jersey: 1746–1794." *William and Mary Quarterly,* Vol. VI (1949).

Burr, Nelson R. *Education in New Jersey, 1630–1871.* Princeton, N. J.: Princeton University Press, 1942.

A Catalogue of Books in the Library of the College of New Jersey, January 29, 1760. Woodbridge, N.J.: 1760.

Gambrell, Mary L. *Ministerial Training in Eighteenth-Century New England.* New York: Columbia University Press, 1937.

Gillett, Ezra Hall. "Men and Times of the Reunion of 1758," *American Presbyterian Quarterly Review* (1868).

Goen, Clarence C. *Revivalism and Separatism in New England, 1740–1800; Strict Congregationalists and Separate Baptists in the Great Awakening.* New Haven: Yale University Press, 1962.

History of the College of New Jersey from its Commencement, A. D., 1746 to 1783. Princeton: 1884.

Jones, Electa F. *Stockbridge, Past and Present; or, Records of an Old Mission Station.* Springfield, Mass.: Samuel Bowles and Co., 1854.

Paterson, William. *Glimpses of Colonial Society and the Life at Princeton College, 1766–1773.* Ed. W. Jay Mills. Philadelphia: J. B. Lippincott Company, 1903.

Patten, William. *Reminiscences of the Late Rev. Samuel Hopkins, D. D. of Newport, R. I.* Providence: I. H. Cady, 1843.

Sedgwick, Sarah Cabot, and Christina Sedgwick Marquand. *Stockbridge, 1739–1939; A Chronicle.* Great Barrington, Mass.: Berkshire Courier, 1939.

Wertenbaker, Thomas Jefferson. *Princeton, 1746–1896.* Princeton: Princeton University Press, 1946.

CHAPTER TWO

The Ecclesiastical Heritage of Jonathan Edwards the Younger

Alexander, Archibald. *Biographical Sketches of the Founder and Principal Alumni of the Log College.* Philadelphia: Presbyterian Board of Publication, 1851.

Allen, Joseph H. "The Ecclesiastical Situation in New England Prior to the Revolution." *Papers of the American Society of Church History,* Vol. III (1897), 67ff.

Andrews, Charles M. *The River Towns of Connecticut.* Johns Hopkins University Studies in Historical and Political Science. Baltimore: Publication Agency of Johns Hopkins University, 1889.

Bailyn, Bernard. *The New England Merchants in the Seventeenth Century.* Cambridge: Harvard University Press, 1955.

Benson, L. F. "The Scotch-Irish in America." *Journal of the Presbyterian Historical Society,* Vol. IX, 21ff.

Blaikie, Alexander. *A History of Presbyterianism in New England.* Boston: Alexander Moore, 1882.

Blake, Silas Leroy. *The Separates; or, Strict Congregationalists of New England.* Boston: The Pilgrim Press, 1902.

Bridenbaugh, Carl. *Cities in the Wilderness.* New York: Ronald Press, 1938.

————. *Mitre and Sceptre; Transatlantic Faiths, Ideas, Personalities, and Politics, 1689–1775.* New York: Oxford University Press, 1962.

Chauncy, Charles. *The New Creature Describ'd and Consider'd as the Sure Characteristick of a Man's Being in Christ.* Boston: Printed by G. Rogers for J. Edwards and S. Eliot, 1741.

————. *The Out-pouring of the Holy Spirit.* Boston: Printed by T. Fleet for D. Henchman and S. Eliot, 1742.

————. *Seasonable Thoughts on the State of Religion in New England.* Boston: Printed by Rogers and Fowle, for Samuel Eliot, 1743.

Contributions to the Ecclesiastical History of Connecticut. New Haven: 1861.

Dickinson, Jonathan. *Remarks Upon a Discourse Intituled an Overture. Presented to the Reverend Synod of Dissenting Ministers Sitting in Philadelphia, in the Month of September, 1728.* New York: Printed by J. Peter Zenger, 1729.

Dunaway, Wayland Fuller. *The Scotch-Irish of Colonial Pennsylvania.* Chapel Hill: University of North Carolina Press, 1944.

Edwards, Jonathan, Sr. *The Works of President Edwards, in Four Volumes.* New York: Leavitt, Trow and Co., 1844.

Finley, Samuel. *Clear Light Put Out in Obscure Darkness.* Philadelphia: Printed by B. Franklin, 1743.

Ford, Henry J. *The Scotch-Irish in America.* Princeton: Princeton University Press, 1915.

Gaustad, Edwin. *The Great Awakening in New England.* New York: Harper, 1957.

_____. "Theological Effects of the Great Awakening in New England." *Mississippi Valley Historical Review,* Vol. XL (March, 1954), 681–706.

Gillett, Ezra Hall. *History of the Presbyterian Church in the United States of America.* 2 Vols. Philadelphia: Presbyterian Board of Publication and Sabbath School Work, 1864.

Goen, Clarence C. *Revivalism and Separatism in New England, 1740–1800; Strict Congregationalists and Separate Baptists in the Great Awakening.* New Haven: Yale University Press, 1962.

Henderson, Henry F. *The Religious Controversies of Scotland.* Edinburgh: T. & T. Clark, 1905.

Hodge, Charles. *The Constitutional History of the Presbyterian Church in the United States of America.* Philadelphia: Presbyterian Board of Publication, 1851.

Klett, Guy Soulliard. *Presbyterians in Colonial Pennsylvania.* Philadelphia: University of Pennsylvania Press, 1937.

Lothrop, Samuel Kirkland. *A History of the Church in Brattle Street.* Boston: W. Crosby and H.P. Nichols, 1851.

Maxson, Charles Hartshorn. *The Great Awakening in the Middle Colonies.* Chicago: The University of Chicago Press, 1920.

Mather, Increase. *The Order of the Gospel, Professed and Preach'd by the Churches of Christ in New England.* Boston: 1708.

Mathews, Lois K. *The Expansion of New England.* Boston: Houghton Mifflin Company, 1909.

Miller, Perry. *Errand Into the Wilderness.* Cambridge: Harvard University Press, 1956.

_____. "The Half Way Covenant." *New England Quarterly,* Vol. VI (1933).

_____. "Jonathan Edwards' Sociology of the Great Awakening." *New England Quarterly,* Vol. XXI (March, 1948), 50–77.

_____. "The Marrow of Puritan Divinity." *Publications of the Colonial Society of Massachusetts,* Vol. XXXII (1933–1937).

_____. *The New England Mind: From Colony to Province.* Cambridge: Harvard University Press, 1953.

_____. *The New England Mind: The Seventeenth Century.* Cambridge: Harvard University Press, 1954.

_____. "Preparation for Salvation in Seventeenth-Century New England." *Journal of the History of Ideas,* Vol. IV (June, 1943).

Nichols, Robert Hastings. "The First Synod of New York, 1745–1758, and its Permanent Effects." *Church History,* Vol. XIV (Dec., 1945), 239–255.

Parkes, H. B. "New England in the Seventeen-Thirties." *New England Quarterly,* Vol. III (July, 1930).

Records of the Presbyterian Church in the United States of America. Philadelphia: Presbyterian Board of Publication, 1841.

Schaff, Philip. *The Creeds of Christendom.* New York: Harper and Brothers, 1905.

Shipton, Charles H. "Immigrants to New England, 1680–1740." *Journal of Political Economy,* Vol. XLIV (1936).

Stoddard, Solomon. *The Doctrine of Instituted Churches Explained and Proved from the Word of God.* London: 1700.

––––––. *The Safety of Appearing at the Day of Judgment.* Boston: D. Henchman, 1729.

Sutherland, Stella H. *Population Distribution in Colonial America.* New York: Columbia University Press, 1936.

Tanis, James R. *Dutch Calvinistic Pietism in the Middle Colonies. A Study in the Life and Theology of Theodorus Jacobus Frelinghuysen.* The Hague: Martinus Nijhoff, 1967.

Tracy, Joseph. *The Great Awakening. A History of the Revival of Religion in the Time of Edwards and Whitefield.* Boston: Tappan and Dennet, 1842.

Trinterud, Leonard J. *The Forming of an American Tradition. A Re-examination of Colonial Presbyterianism.* Philadelphia: Westminster Press, 1949.

––––––. "The New England Contribution to Colonial American Presbyterianism." *Church History,* Vol. XVII (March, 1948), 32–43.

Walker, George Leon. *Some Aspects of Religious Life of New England.* New York: Silver, Burdett and Co., 1897.

Walker, Williston. *Creeds and Platforms of Congregationalism.* New York: Charles Scribner, 1893.

––––––. "Why Did not Massachusetts Have a Saybrook Platform?" *The Yale Review* (May, 1892).

Webster, Richard. *A History of the Presbyterian Church in America, from its Origin Until the Year 1760, with Biographical Sketches of its Early Ministers.* Philadelphia: Presbyterian Historical Society, 1858.

Weis, Frederick Lewis. *The Colonial Churches and the Colonial Clergy of the Middle and Southern Colonies, 1607–1776.* Lancaster, Mass.: Society of the Descendants of the Colonial Clergy, 1938.

Wertenbaker, Thomas Jefferson. *The Founding of American Civilization; The Middle Colonies.* New York: Charles Scribner's Sons, 1949.

––––––. *Princeton, 1746–1896.* Princeton: Princeton University Press, 1946.

White, Eugene S. "Decline of the Great Awakening in New England, 1741–1746." *New England Quarterly,* Vol. XXIV (March, 1951).

Wise, John. *The Churches Quarrel Espoused.* Boston: John Boyles, 1715.

––––––. *A Vindication of the Government of New-England Churches.* Boston: John Boyles, 1772.

Wright, Conrad. *The Beginnings of Unitarianism in America*. Boston: Starr King Press, 1955.

Zeichner, Oscar. *Connecticut's Years of Controversy 1750–1776*. Chapel Hill: University of North Carolina Press, 1949.

CHAPTER THREE

The Theological Heritage of Jonathan Edwards the Younger

Aaron, Richard Ithamar. *John Locke*. London: Oxford University Press, 1937.

_____. "Limits of Locke's Rationalism," in H. J. C. Grierson, *Seventeenth Century Studies Presented to Sir Herbert Grierson*. Oxford: The Clarendon Press, 1938.

Ahlstrom, Sydney E. "The Saybrook Platform: A 250th Anniversary Retrospect." *Bulletin of the Congregational Library* (Oct., 1959).

Bangs, Carl Oliver. *Arminius; A Study in the Dutch Reformation*. Nashville: Abingdon Press, 1971.

Bellamy, Joseph. *An Essay on the Nature and Glory of the Gospel of Jesus Christ*. Washington: John Colerick, 1798.

Bushman, Richard L. *From Puritan to Yankee; Character and the Social Order in Connecticut, 1690–1765*. Cambridge, Mass.: Harvard University Press, 1967.

Butterfield, Lyman Henry, ed. *John Witherspoon Comes to America; A Documentary Account Based Largely on New Materials*. Princeton: Princeton University Library, 1953.

Cassirer, Ernst. *The Philosophy of the Enlightenment*. Trans. Fritz C. A. Koelln and James P. Pettegrove. Boston: Beacon Press, 1955.

Chauncy, Charles. *The New Creature Describ'd and Consider'd as the Sure Characteristick of a Man's Being in Christ*. Boston: Printed by G. Rogers for J. Edwards and S. Eliot, 1741.

_____. *Seasonable Thoughts on the State of Religion in New England*. Boston: Printed by Rogers and Fowle, for Samuel Eliot, 1743.

Clarke, Samuel. *A Discourse Concerning the Unchangeable Obligations of Natural Religion, and the Truth and Certainty of the Christian Revelation*. 5th ed., corrected. London: Printed by W. Botham for J. Knapton, 1719.

_____. *The Scripture-Doctrine of the Trinity. In Three Parts*. London: James Knapton, 1712.

Colie, Rosalie Littell. *Light and Enlightenment; A Study of the Cambridge Platonists and the Dutch Arminians*. Cambridge, Eng.: Cambridge University Press, 1957.

Colligan, J. Hay. *The Arian Movement in England*. Manchester: The University Press, 1913.

Cragg, Gerald Robertson. *From Puritanism to the Age of Reason*. Cambridge, Eng.: Cambridge University Press, 1950.

Edwards, Jonathan. "The Nature of True Virtue." *The Works of President Edwards, in Four Volumes*. Vol. II. New York: Leavitt, Trow and Co., 1844.

Foster, Frank Hugh. *A Genetic History of the New England Theology*. New York: H. Holt and Company, 1932.

Haroutunian, Joseph. *Piety Versus Moralism; The Passing of the New England Theology.* New York: H. Holt and Company, 1932.

Harrison, A. H. W. *Arminianism.* London: Gerald Duckworth & Co., 1937.

————. *The Beginnings of Arminianism to the Synod of Dort.* London: University Press, 1926.

Hazard, Paul. *European Thought in the Eighteenth Century, from Montesquieu to Lessing.* New Haven: Yale University Press, 1954.

Hopkins, Samuel. *The Works of Samuel Hopkins D. D.* Ed. Edward A. Park. Boston: Doctrinal Tract and Book Society, 1854.

Locke, John. *An Essay Concerning Human Understanding.* Ed. Alexander Campbell Fraser. Oxford: Clarendon Press, 1894.

Lowrie, Ernest Benson. *The Shape of the Puritan Mind: The Thought of Samuel Willard.* New Haven: Yale University Press, 1974.

McCosh, James. *The Scottish Philosophy.* New York: R. Carter and Brothers, 1880.

Mather, Increase. *An Appeal of Some of the Unlearned, Both to the Learned and Unlearned.* Boston: 1709.

————. *A Dissertation, Wherein the Strange Doctrine Lately Published in a Sermon, the Tendency of Which, is, to Encourage Unsanctified Persons (While Such) to Approach the Holy Table of the Lord, is Examined and Confuted.* Boston: Printed by B. Green for Benj. Eliot, 1708.

Mead, Sidney Earl. *Nathaniel William Taylor 1786–1858, a Connecticut Liberal.* Chicago: The University of Chicago Press, 1942.

Miller, Perry. "The Half Way Covenant." *New England Quarterly,* Vol. VI (1933).

————. "Solomon Stoddard 1643–1729." *Harvard Theological Review,* Vol. XXXIV (Oct., 1941), 278–320.

Morgan, Edmund Sears. *The Birth of the Republic, 1763–1789.* Chicago: University of Chicago Press, 1956.

————. *Visible Saints; The History of a Puritan Idea.* New York: New York University Press, 1963.

Pettit, Norman. *The Heart Prepared; Grace and Conversion in Puritan Spiritual Life.* New Haven: Yale University Press, 1966.

Pope, Robert G. *The Half-Way Covenant; Church Membership in Puritan New England.* Princeton: Princeton University Press, 1969.

Smith, Hilrie Shelton. *Changing Conceptions of Original Sin; A Study in American Theology Since 1750.* New York: Scribner, 1955.

Stephen, Leslie. *History of English Thought in the Eighteenth Century.* 2 Vols. New York: G. P. Putnam's Sons, 1876.

Stoddard, Solomon. *An Appeal to the Learned, Being a Vindication of the Right of Visible Saints to the Lord's Supper.* Boston: 1709.

————. *The Inexcusableness of Neglecting the Worship of God, Under a Pretense of Being in an Unconverted Condition.* Boston: 1708.

————. *The Safety of Appearing at the Day of Judgement, in the Righteousness of Christ, Opened and Applied.* Northampton: Printed by Thomas M. Pomroy for S. & E. Butler, 1804.

Stromberg, Roland N. *Religious Liberalism in Eighteenth-Century England.* London: Oxford University Press, 1954.

Taylor, John. *The Scripture Doctrine of Original Sin.* London: 1738.

———. *A Supplement to the Scripture Doctrine of Original Sin.* London: J. Waugh, 1767.

Toland, John. *Christianity Not Mysterious: or, A Treatise Shewing That There is Nothing in the Gospel Contrary to Reason, nor Above it: and that No Christian Doctrine Can Be Properly Called a Mystery.* London: 1696.

Trumbull, Benjamin. *A Complete History of Connecticut, Civil and Ecclesiastical, From the Emigration of its First Planters, from England, in MDCXXX, to MDCCXIII.* Vol. II. Hartford: Hudson & Goodwin, 1797.

Wallace, Robert. *Anti-Trinitarian Biography.* 3 Vols. London: E. T. Whitfield, 1850.

Waterland, Daniel. *A Vindication of Christ's Divinity: Being a Defense of Some Queries, Relating to Dr. Clarke's Scheme of the Holy Trinity.* Cambridge: Printed for C. Crownfield, 1719.

Westfall, Richard S. *Science and Religion in Seventeenth-Century England.* New Haven: Yale University Press, 1958.

Whitefield, George. *Eighteen Sermons.* Springfield, Mass.: Thomas Dickman, 1808.

Willey, Basil. *The Seventeenth Century Background.* London: Chatto & Windus, 1934.

Wise, John. *A Vindication of the Government of New-England Churches.* Boston: John Boyles, 1772.

Wright, Conrad. *The Beginnings of Unitarianism in America.* Boston: Starr King Press, 1955.

CHAPTER FOUR

The White Haven Church

CHAPTER FIVE

Pastoral Labors

Andrews, Charles McLean. *Connecticut's Place in Colonial History.* New Haven: Yale University Press, 1924.

Atwater, Edward E., ed. *History of the City of New Haven to the Present Time.* New York: W. W. Munsell & Co., 1887.

Bacon, Leonard. *Thirteen Historical Discourses, on the Completion of Two Hundred Years, From the Beginning of the First Church in New Haven.* New Haven: Durrie & Peck, 1839.

Baldwin, Alice M. *The New England Clergy and the American Revolution.* Durham, N.C.: Duke University Press, 1928.

Bidwell, Percy Wells. *Rural Economy in New England at the Beginning of the Nineteenth Century.* Transactions of the Connecticut Academy of Arts and Sciences, Vol. XX. New Haven: 1916.

Blake, Henry T. *Chronicles of New Haven Green from 1638 to 1862.* New Haven: The Tuttle, Morehouse & Taylor Press, 1898.

Clark, Joseph B. *Leavening the Nation; The Story of American Home Missions.* New York: The Baker & Taylor Co., 1903.

Connecticut Journal and New Haven Post-Boy (Friday, June 2, 1769).

Dexter, Franklin Bowditch, ed. *Extracts From the Itineraries and Other Miscellanies of Ezra Stiles, D. D., LL. D., 1755–1794.* New Haven: Yale University Press, 1916.

————, ed. *The Literary Diary of Ezra Stiles.* 3 Vols. New York: C. Scribner's Sons, 1901.

————. "New Haven in 1784," in *A Selection from the Miscellaneous Historical Papers of Fifty Years.* New Haven: Tuttle, Morehouse & Taylor Company, 1918.

Dutton, Samuel W. S. *History of the North Church in New Haven.* New Haven: A. H. Maltby, 1842.

Elsbree, Oliver Wendell. *The Rise of the Missionary Spirit in America, 1790–1815.* Williamsport, Penna.: The Williamsport Printing and Binding Co., 1928.

Gabriel, Ralph Henry. *Religion and Learning at Yale: The Church of Christ in the College and University, 1757–1957.* New Haven: Yale University Press, 1958.

Gambrell, Mary Latimer. *Ministerial Training in Eighteenth-Century New England.* New York: Columbia University Press, 1937.

Goodrich, Chauncy. "Invasion of New Haven by the British Troops." *Papers of the New Haven Historical Society,* Vol. II (July 5, 1779).

Greene, Lorenzo. *The Negro in Colonial New England, 1620–1776.* New York: Columbia University Press, 1942.

Holbrook, Stewart H. *The Yankee Exodus, an Account of Migration from New England.* New York: Macmillan Co., 1950.

Hopkins, Samuel. *The Works of Samuel Hopkins.* 3 Vols. Boston: Doctrinal Tract and Book Society, 1854.

Keller, Charles Roy. *The Second Great Awakening in Connecticut.* New Haven: Yale University Press, 1942.

Locke, Mary Stoughton. *Anti-Slavery in America from the Introduction of African Slaves to the Prohibition of the Slave Trade (1619–1808).* Boston: Ginn & Company, 1901.

Ludlum, David M. *Social Ferment in Vermont, 1791–1850.* Columbia Studies in American Culture, No. 5. New York: Columbia University Press, 1939.

Mathews, Lois K. *The Expansion of New England.* Boston: Houghton Mifflin Company, 1909.

Mitchell, Mary Hewitt. *History of the United Church of New Haven.* New Haven: The United Church, 1942.

————. "Slavery in Connecticut and Especially in New Haven." *Papers of the New Haven Colony Historical Society,* Vol. X. New Haven: 1951.

Osterweis, Rollin Gustav. *Three Centuries of New Haven, 1638–1938.* New Haven: Yale University Press, 1953.

Parker, Edwin P. *Historical Discourse in Commemoration of the One Hundredth Anniversary of the Missionary Society of Connecticut.* Hartford: 1898.

Purcell, Richard. *Connecticut in Transition, 1775–1818.* Washington: American Historical Association, 1918.

Records of the General Association of ye Colony of Connecticut, 1738–1799. Hartford: Case, Lockwood and Brainerd Company, 1888.

Robinson, William A. *Jeffersonian Democracy in New England.* New Haven: Yale University Press, 1916.

Simpson, Samuel. "Early Ministerial Training in America." *Papers of the American Church History Society,* Second Series, II (1910), 117–129.

Senior, R. C. "New England Congregationalism and the Anti-Slavery Movement 1830–1860." Unpublished Ph.D. dissertation, Yale University, 1954.

Sprague, William B. *Annals of the American Pulpit.* Vol. I. New York: R. Carter and Brothers, 1859.

Steiner, B. C. "History of Slavery in Connecticut," in *Labor, Slavery and Self Government.* Ed. H. B. Adams. Johns Hopkins Studies in History and Political Science, Vol. XI. Baltimore: Johns Hopkins Press, 1893.

Tracy, Joseph. *The Great Awakening.* Boston: Tappan & Dennet, 1842.

Trumbull, Benjamin. *A Complete History of Connecticut, Civil and Ecclesiastical, from the Emigration of its First Planters, from England, in the Year 1630, to the Year 1764; and to the Close of the Indian Wars.* 2 Vols. New Haven: Maltby, Goldsmith and Co., 1818.

Van Halsema, Dick. "Samuel Hopkins 1721–1803 New England Calvinist." Unpublished Th.D. thesis, Union Theological Seminary.

Weis, Frederick Lewis. *The Colonial Clergy and Colonial Churches of New England.* Lancaster, Mass.: 1936.

Weld, F. R. "Slavery in Connecticut." *Publications of the Tercentenary Commission of the State of Connecticut.* Vol. 35. New Haven: 1935.

Zeichner, Oscar. *Connecticut's Years of Controversy, 1750–1776.* Chapel Hill: University of North Carolina Press, 1949.

CHAPTER SIX

The Means of Regeneration

CHAPTER SEVEN

Universal Salvation

CHAPTER EIGHT

The Nature and Extent of Sin

(The Bibliography in Joseph Haroutunian, *Piety Versus Moralism; The Passing of the New England Theology,* New York: H. Holt and Company, 1932, is comprehensive. The works listed below have been of particular importance for this study and are under the headings: *New Divinity, Old Calvinist,* and *Arminian.*)

NEW DIVINITY

Adams, Hannah. *A View of Religions, in Two Parts. Pt. I Containing an Alphabetical Compendium of the Various Religious Denominations, Which Have Appeared in the World, from the Beginning of the Christian Era to the Present Day. Pt. II Containing a Brief Account of the Different Schemes of Religion now Being Embraced Among Mankind.* (Containing an article by Nathaniel Emmons on Hopkinsianism.) Boston: Manning & Loring, 1801.

Bellamy, Joseph. *The Works of Joseph Bellamy, D.D.* 2 Vols. Boston: Doctrinal Tract and Book Society, 1853.

Clark, Peter. *The Scripture-Doctrine of Original Sin, Stated and Defended. In a Summer-Morning's Conversation, Between a Minister and a Neighbour.* Boston: S. Kneeland, 1758.

Eckley, Joseph. *Divine Glory, Brought to View, in the Condemnation of the Ungodly.* Boston: Robert Hodge, 1782.

Edwards, Jonathan. *The Works of President Edwards, in Four Volumes.* New York: Leavitt, Trow & Co., 1844.

Emmons, Nathaniel. *The Works of Nathaniel Emmons.* 6 Vols. Ed. Jacob Ide. Boston: Congregational Board of Publication, 1860.

Hopkins, Samuel. *His Book.* Ms. in Huntington Library, San Marino, California.

———. *The Works of Samuel Hopkins.* 3 Vols. Boston: Doctrinal Tract and Book Society, 1854.

Sermons, Essays, and Extracts, by Various Authors, Selected with Special Respect to the Doctrine of Atonement. New York: George Forman, 1811.

Smalley, John. *The Consistency of the Sinner's Inability to Comply with the Gospel; With his Inexcusable Guilt in Not Complying with it.* Hartford: Green & Watson, 1769.

———. *Eternal Salvation on no Account a Matter of Just Debt; On Full Redemption Not Interfering with Free Grace.* Hartford: 1785.

———. *The Inability of the Sinner to Comply with the Gospel, His Inexcusable Guilt in Not Complying with it, and the Consistency of these with Each Other.* Boston: 1772.

———. *The Law in all Respects Satisfied by Our Saviour, in Regard to those Only Who Belong to Him.* Hartford: 1786.

———. *Sermons, On a Number of Connected Subjects.* Hartford: Printed for Oliver D. Cooke; Lincoln and Gleason, printers, 1803.

Smith, John E. "Introduction" to Jonathan Edwards, Senior's *Religious Affections.* New Haven: Yale University Press, 1959.

Strong, Nathan. *The Doctrine of Eternal Misery Reconcilable with the Infinite Benevolence of God, and a Truth Plainly Asserted in the Christian Scripture.* Hartford: 1796.

Trumbull, Benjamin. *Illustrations on the Nature and Importance of an Immediate Choice of God.* New London: Timothy Green and son, 1791.

West, Stephen. *An Essay on Moral Agency.* Salem: T. C. Cushing, 1794.

———. *Evidence of the Divinity of the Lord Jesus Christ.* Stockbridge: 1816.

———. *The Scripture Doctrine of Atonement, Proposed to Careful Examination.* Stockbridge: Printed at the Herald Office, 1809.

———. *Sketches of the Life of the Late Rev. Samuel Hopkins.* Hartford: 1805.

OLD CALVINIST

Dana, James. *An Examination of the Late Reverend President Edwards's "Enquiry on Freedom of Will."* Boston: Printed by Daniel Kneeland for Thomas Leverett, 1770.

Dexter, Franklin Bowditch, ed. *Extracts from the Itineraries and Other Miscellanies of Ezra Stiles, D. D., LL. D., 1755–1794.* New Haven: Yale University Press, 1916.

Hart, William. *Brief Remarks on a Number of False Propositions, and Dangerous Errors, which Are Spreading in the Country; Collected out of Sundry Discourses Lately Published, Wrote by Dr. Whitaker and Mr. Hopkins.* New London: T. Green, 1769.

———. *A Discourse Concerning the Nature of Regeneration and, the Way Wherein it is Wrought.* New London: T. Green, 1742.

———. *A Letter to the Rev. Samuel Hopkins, Occasioned by His Animadversions on Mr. Hart's Late Dialogue, In Which Some of His Misrepresentations of Facts, and of Other Things, are Corrected.* New London: T. Green, 1770.

———. *Remarks on President Edwards' Dissertations Concerning the Nature of True Virtue.* New Haven: T. and S. Green, 1771.

———. *A Scriptural Answer to this Question, viz. What are the Necessary Qualifications for a Lawful and Approved Attendance on the Sacraments of the New Covenant?* New London: T. Green, 1772.

———. *A Sermon, of a New Kind, Never Preached, nor Ever Will Be; Containing a Collection of Doctrines, Belonging to the Hopkintonian Scheme of Orthodoxy; or the Marrow of the Most Modern Divinity.* New Haven: T. and L. Green, 1769.

Hemmenway, Moses. *Seven Sermons, on the Obligation and Encouragement of the Unregenerate, to Labour for the Meat which Endureth to Everlasting Life.* Boston: Kneeland and Adams, 1767.

———. *A Vindication of the Power, Obligation and Encouragement to Attend the Means of Grace.* Boston: J. Kneeland, 1772.

Mills, Jedidiah. *Inquiry Concerning the State of the Unregenerate Under the Gospel.* New Haven: 1767.

Moody, Samuel. *An Attempt to Point Out the Fatal and Pernicious Consequences of the Rev. Mr. Joseph Bellamy's Doctrines, Respecting Moral Evil.* Boston: 1759. Boston: 1759.

ARMINIAN

Chauncy, Charles. *Five Dissertations on the Scripture Account of the Fall; and its Consequences.* London: C. Dilly, 1785.

———. *The Mystery Hid From Ages and Generations, Made Manifest by the Gospel-Revelation: Or, the Salvation of All Men.* London: C. Dilly, 1784.

———. *Twelve Sermons.* Boston: Printed by D. and J. Kneeland, for T. Leverett, 1765.

Mayhew, Jonathan. *Striving to Enter in at the Strait Gate Explain'd and Inculcated; and the Connexion of Salvation Therewith, Proved from the Holy Scriptures*. Boston: R. Draper, Edes & Gill and T. & J. Fleet, 1761.

Murray, John. *The Life of Rev. John Murray, Preacher of Universal Salvation. Written by Himself*. Boston: Universalist Publishing House, 1869.

Webster, Samuel. *A Winter Evening's Conversation Upon the Doctrine of Original Sin*. New Haven: James Parker, and Company, 1757.

————. *The Winter Evening Conversation Vindicated*. New Haven: Edes and Gill, 1758.

West, Samuel. *Essays on Liberty and Necessity*. Boston: Samuel Hall, 1793.

————. *Essays on Liberty and Necessity, Second Part*. Boston: 1794.

Wright, Conrad. *The Beginnings of Unitarianism in America*. Boston: Starr King Press, 1955.

CHAPTER NINE

Dismissal

Bacon, Leonard. *Thirteen Historical Discourses, on the Completion of Two Hundred Years, from the Beginning of the First Church in New Haven*. New Haven: Durrie and Peck, 1839.

Boardman, Roger Sherman. *Roger Sherman, Signer and Statesman*. Philadelphia: University of Pennsylvania Press, 1938.

Dexter, Franklin Bowditch, ed. *The Literary Diary of Ezra Stiles*. 3 Vols. New York: C. Scribner's Sons, 1901.

Records of the Church of Christ in the United Society of White Haven and Fair Haven.

Records of the Fair Haven Church.

Records of the Society of White Haven.

Records of the White Haven Church.

CHAPTER TEN

Exile and a New Career

The Acts and Proceedings of the General Synod of the Reformed Protestant Dutch Church in North America. New York: 1859.

Adams, John Quincy, ed. "The Records of the Middle Association of Congregational Churches of the State of New York 1806–1810." *Journal of the Presbyterian Historical Society*, Vols. X–XI (1923–24).

Alexander, Samuel Davies. *The Presbytery of New York, 1738 to 1888*. New York: A. D. F. Randolph and Company, 1887.

Barber, John Warner. *Connecticut Historical Collections, Containing a General Collection of Interesting Facts, Traditions, Biographical Sketches, Anecdotes, Etc., Relating to the History and Antiquities of Every Town in Connecticut, with Geographical Descriptions*. New York: Durrie & Peck and J. W. Barber, 1838.

Blodgett, Harold W. "Union College and Dirck Romeyn." *New York History* (July, 1945).

The Celebration of the Fiftieth Anniversary of Dr. Nott's Presidency of Union College. Schenectady: 1854.

Corwin, Charles E. *A Manual of the Reformed Church in America (Formerly Reformed Protestant Dutch Church) 1628–1933.* New York: Board of Publication and Bible-School Work of the Reformed Church in America, 1922–33.

Corwin, Edward T. *History of the Reformed Church, Dutch.* New York: 1895.

Cross, Arthur Lyon. *The Anglican Episcopate and the American Colonies.* New York: Longmans, Green, and Co., 1902.

Demarest, David D. *The Reformed Church in America. Its Origin, Development and Characteristics.* New York: Board of Publication of the Reformed Church in America, 1889.

Demarest, William H. S. *A History of Rutgers College, 1766–1924.* New Brunswick, N. J.: Rutgers College, 1924.

A Digest from the Records of the General Assembly of the Presbyterian Church. Philadelphia: 1820.

Extracts from the Minutes of the General Assembly of the Presbyterian Church, in the United States of America, from A.D. 1789 to A.D. 1802. Philadelphia: 1803.

Ferm, Robert L. "The Plan of Union of 1801." *Journal of Presbyterian History* (December, 1964).

Fox, Dixon Ryan. *Union College, an Unfinished History.* Schenectady: Graduate Council, Union College, 1945.

Gillett, Ezra Hall. *History of the Presbyterian Church in the United States of America.* 2 Vols. Philadelphia: Presbyterian Board of Publication, 1864.

Goodwin, Maude Wilder. *Dutch and English on the Hudson.* The Chronicles of America Series, Vol. VII, ed. Allan Johnson. New Haven: Yale University Press, 1919.

Harlow, Henry A. *A History of the Presbytery of Hudson. 1681–1888.* Middletown, N. Y.: Stivers, Slauson & Boyd, 1888.

Higgins, Ruth L. *Expansion in New York with Especial Reference to the Eighteenth Century.* Columbus: Ohio State University, 1931.

Hislop, Codman. *Albany: Dutch, English, and American.* Albany, N.Y.: The Argus Press, 1936.

———. *Eliphalet Nott.* Middleton, Conn.: Wesleyan University Press, 1971.

———. "Eliphalet Nott: The Formative Years, 1773–1804." Unpublished Ph. D. dissertation, Harvard University, February, 1953.

Historical Sketch of Union College. Washington: Gov't. Print. Off., 1876.

History of Litchfield County, Connecticut, with Illustrations and Biographical Sketches of its Prominent Men and Pioneers. Philadelphia: J. W. Lewis & Co., 1881.

Hotchkin, James H. *A History of the Purchase and Settlement of Western New York, and of the Rise, Progress, and Present State of the Presbyterian Church in that Section.* New York: M. W. Dodd, 1848.

Keller, Charles Roy. *The Second Great Awakening in Connecticut.* New Haven: Yale University Press, 1942.

Kennedy, William Sloane. *The Plan of Union; or a History of the Presbyterian and Congregational Churches of the Western Reserve, with Biographical Sketches of the Early Missionaries.* Hudson, Ohio: Pentagon Steam Press, 1856.

Kilbourne, Payne Kenyon. *A Biographical History of the County of Litchfield, Connecticut: Comprising Biographical Sketches of Distinguished Natives and Residents of the County.* New York: Clarke, Austin & Co., 1851.

Klett, Guy Soulliard. *Presbyterians in Colonial Pennsylvania.* Philadelphia: University of Pennsylvania Press, 1937.

Kromminga, John Henry. *The Christian Reformed Church, a Study in Orthodoxy.* Grand Rapids, Mich.: Baker Book House, 1949.

Lucas, Henry Stephen. *Netherlanders in America: Dutch Immigration to the United States and Canada, 1789–1850.* Ann Arbor: University of Michigan Press, 1955.

Manchester, Irving E. *The History of Colebrook.* Winsted, Conn.: The Citizen Printing Company, 1935.

"Memoir of Jonathan Edwards." *American Quarterly Register,* Vol. VIII (1836).

Minutes of the Board of Trustees, Union College, May 2, 1799. Union College Library, Schenectady, New York.

Minutes of the Convention of Delegates from the Synod of New York and Philadelphia, and from the Associations of Connecticut: Held Annually from 1766–1775, Inclusive. Hartford: Printed by E. Gleason, 1843.

Nichols, Robert Hastings. "The Plan of Union in New York." *Church History,* Vol. V (March, 1936), 29–51.

Raymond, Andrew Van Vranken. *Union University, Its History, Influence, Characteristics and Equipment.* 3 Vols. New York: Lewis Publishing Company, 1907.

A Record of the Commemoration of the One Hundredth Anniversary of the Founding of Union College Including a Sketch of its History. New York: 1897.

Records of the General Association of ye Colony of Connecticut Begun June 20, 1738; Ending June 19, 1799. Hartford: 1888.

Records of the Presbyterian Church in the United States of America: Embracing the Minutes of the Presbyterian . . . Synod of Philadelphia and New York, from A.D. 1758 to 1788. Philadelphia: Presbyterian Board of Publication, 1841.

Sprague, William B. *Annals of the American Pulpit.* Vol. III. New York: R. Carter and Brothers, 1859.

Smith, Robert. *A Discourse on the Occasion of the Death of the Rev. Jonathan Edwards, D.D., President of Union College.* Albany: C. & G. Webster, 1801.

Sweet, William Warren. *The Presbyterians 1738–1840.* New York: Harper and Brothers, 1936.

Trinterud, Leonard J. *The Forming of an American Tradition, a Re-examination of Colonial Presbyterianism.* Philadelphia: Westminster Press, 1949.

Trumbull, Benjamin. *A Complete History of Connecticut, Civil and Ecclesiastical, from the Emigration of its First Planters, from England, in the Year 1630, to the Year 1764; and to the Close of the Indian Wars.* 2 Vols. New Haven: Maltby, Goldsmith and Co., 1818.

Tyler, Bennet, comp. *New England Revivals, as they Existed at the Close of the Eighteenth, and Beginning of the Nineteenth Centuries. Compiled Principally from Narratives.* Boston: Massachusetts Sabbath School Society, 1846.

Walker, Williston. *The Creeds and Platforms of Congregationalism.* New York: Charles Scribner's Sons, 1893.

Westover, Myron F., ed. *Schenectady, Past and Present.* Strasburg, Va.: Shenandoah Publishing House, Inc., 1931.

CHAPTER ELEVEN

Jonathan Edwards the Younger and the American Reformed Tradition

Adams, John Quincy. *A History of Auburn Theological Seminary, 1818–1918.* Auburn, N.Y.: Auburn Seminary Press, 1918.

Baird, Samuel. *A History of the New School, and of the Questions Involved in the Disruption of the Presbyterian Church in 1838.* Philadelphia: Claxton, Remsen & Haffelfinger, 1868.

Barnes, Albert. *Inquiries and Suggestions in Regard to the Foundation of Faith in the Word of God.* Philadelphia: Parry and McMillan, 1859.

_____. *The Way of Salvation; A Sermon, Delivered at Morristown, New Jersey, February 8, 1829.* New York: Leavitt, Lord, 1836.

Berk, Stephen. *Calvinism versus Democracy: Timothy Dwight and the Origins of American Evangelical Orthodoxy.* Hamden, Conn.: 1974.

Brackett, W. O. "The Rise and Development of the New School in the Presbyterian Church in the U. S. A." *Journal of the Presbyterian Historical Society,* Vol. XIII (1928–1929).

Channing, William Ellery. *A Sermon Delivered at the Ordination of the Rev. Jared Sparks, to the Pastoral Care of the First Independent Church in Baltimore, May 5, 1819.* Baltimore: J. Robinson, 1819.

Crocker, Zebulon. *The Catastrophe of the Presbyterian Church, in 1837.* New Haven: B. & W. Noyes, 1838.

Dwight, Timothy. *Theology: Explained and Defended in a Series of Sermons.* 4 Vols. New York: G. & C. & H. Carvill, 1830.

Emmons, Nathaniel. *The Works of Nathaniel Emmons.* 6 Vols. Ed. Jacob Ide. Boston: Congregational Board of Publication, 1860.

Foster, Frank Hugh. *A Genetic History of the New England Theology.* Chicago: University of Chicago Press, 1907.

Geer, Curtis Manning. *The Hartford Theological Seminary, 1834–1934.* Hartford: Lockwood & Brainard Co., 1934.

Giltner, John M. "Moses Stuart, 1780–1852." Unpublished Ph.D. dissertation, Yale University, 1956.

Judd, G. N. *History of the Division of the Presbyterian Church in the U. S. A.* New York: 1852.

Junkin, George. *The Vindication, Containing a History of the Trial of the Rev. Albert Barnes.* Philadelphia: W. S. Martien, 1836.

Keller, Charles Roy. *The Second Great Awakening.* New Haven: Yale University Press, 1942.

Marsden, George. *The Evangelical Mind and the New School Experience.* New Haven: Yale University Press, 1970.

Mead, Sidney E. "Lyman Beecher and Connecticut Orthodoxy's Campaign Against the Unitarians, 1819–1826." *Church History,* Vol. IX (1940).

————. *Nathaniel William Taylor, 1786–1858, a Connecticut Liberal.* Chicago: University of Chicago Press, 1942.

Moore, Edmund A. "Robert J. Breckenridge and the Slavery Aspect of the Presbyterian Schism of 1837." *Church History,* Vol. IV (December, 1935), 282–294.

Morse, James King. *Jedidiah Morse, a Champion of New England Orthodoxy.* New York: Columbia University Press, 1939.

Norton, Andrews. *A Statement of Reasons for Not Believing the Doctrines of Trinitarians Concerning the Nature of God and the Person of Christ, Occasioned by Professor Stuart's Letters to Mr. Channing.* Boston: American Unitarian Association, 1880.

Rice, A. L. *The Old and New Schools.* Cincinnati: 1853.

Smith, Elwyn A. "The Role of the South in the Presbyterian Schism of 1837–38." *Church History,* Vol. XXIX (March, 1960), 44–63.

Stansbury, A. J. *Trial of the Rev. Albert Barnes Before the Synod of Philadelphia.* New York: 1836.

Stuart, Moses. *Letters to the Rev. Wm. E. Channing, Containing Remarks on his Sermon, Recently Preached and Published at Baltimore.* Andover: Flagg and Gould, 1819.

Taylor, Nathaniel W. *A Sermon Delivered in the Chapel of Yale College, September 10, 1828* (New Haven: A. N. Maltby, 1842).

Tyler, Alice F. *Freedom's Ferment: Phases of American Social History to 1860.* Minneapolis: The University of Minnesota Press, 1944.

Tyler, Bennet. *Letters on the Origin and Progress of the New Haven Theology.* New York: R. Carter and E. Collier, 1837.

Ware, Henry. *Letters Addressed to Trinitarians and Calvinists, Occasioned by Dr. Woods' Letters to Unitarians.* Cambridge: 1820.

Wood, James. *Doctrinal Differences Which Have Agitated and Divided the Presbyterian Church or Old and New Theology.* Philadelphia: 1853.

Woods, Leonard. *Letters to Unitarians Occasioned by the Sermon of the Reverend William E. Channing.* Andover: Flagg and Gould, 1820.

Wright, Conrad. *The Beginnings of Unitarianism in America.* Boston: Starr King, 1955.

Index